D0007193

# Adventures
*in* Evangelical Civility

# Adventures
## *in* Evangelical Civility

A Lifelong Quest *for* Common Ground

# RICHARD J. MOUW

**Brazos**Press
*a division of Baker Publishing Group*
Grand Rapids, Michigan

Published by Brazos Press
a division of Baker Publishing Group
P.O. Box 6287, Grand Rapids, MI 49516-6287
www.brazospress.com

Printed in the United States of America

Library of Congress Cataloging-in-Publication Data is on file at the Library of Congress, Washington, DC.

ISBN 978-1-58743-391-7

Unless otherwise indicated, Scripture quotations are from the New Revised Standard Version of the Bible, copyright © 1989, by the Division of Christian Education of the National Council of the Churches of Christ in the United States of America. Used by permission. All rights reserved.

Scripture quotations labeled KJV are from the King James Version of the Bible.

Scripture quotations labeled NIV are from the Holy Bible, New International Version®. NIV®. Copyright © 1973, 1978, 1984, 2011 by Biblica, Inc.™ Used by permission of Zondervan. All rights reserved worldwide. www.zondervan.com

Scripture quotations labeled RSV are from the Revised Standard Version of the Bible, copyright 1952 [2nd edition, 1971] by the Division of Christian Education of the National Council of the Churches of Christ in the United States of America. Used by permission. All rights reserved.

In keeping with biblical principles of creation stewardship, Baker Publishing Group advocates the responsible use of our natural resources. As a member of the Green Press Initiative, our company uses recycled paper when possible. The text paper of this book is composed in part of post-consumer waste.

16   17   18   19   20   21   22       7   6   5   4   3   2   1

To Phyllis,
loving and wise companion in the quest

# Contents

# Preface

S HORTLY AFTER I RETIRED AS PRESIDENT OF FULLER THEOLOGICAL
Seminary, I met a local businessperson in the aisle of a grocery story. He asked me the typical "How are you enjoying retirement?" questions, and then he said: "I hope you are writing your
autobiography! I'm sure there are some great stories to tell about
your twenty-year presidency at Fuller!" My response was that,
no, there was no autobiography in the works. But, I added, I was
beginning to write a memoir. "How is that different?" he asked.

I forget exactly how I answered his question, but I know it was
a quick response, meant to get me back to grocery shopping. His
question did motivate me, however, to do a Google search about
the meaning of "memoir." I discovered that a number of academic
conference sessions have been devoted to lengthy discussions about
what constitutes a memoir and that many a book reviewer has
complained that something an author claims is in the memoir
genre fails to meet the standards for inclusion.

I'll leave the details of that for literary critics to discuss. For my
part here, I only want to take note of a contrast that often shows
up in those discussions. There is a general consensus that a memoir

must be characterized by a "sustained narrative," and that when this is absent the result is frequently described as a "collage."

Autobiographies, as well as memoirs, are certainly meant to be "sustained narratives," but this book is certainly not an autobiography. There are no reports here about growing up in New Jersey, or being a pastor's son, or playing tuba in the high school band. The only reference to an early romance, for example, focuses on my teenage arguments with Mary Jane, a devout Catholic, about Marian dogma. If I were to discuss the most important of my human relationships—the life "adventures" (to use the word from my title) for which I am most grateful to God—I would focus on my life with Phyllis (to whom I dedicate this book). I would also say much about our son, Dirk; our daughter-in-law, Christine; and our two grandsons, Willem and Peter—but there is nothing about them in these pages. And the man from the grocery store will definitely not be offered here the kind of "great stories" about Fuller that he hoped I would narrate.

Nor is this book a detailed report of my intellectual pilgrimage as such. Someone once asked me to list the ten most influential books in my life, and I began with—and this was only half jokingly—*The Boy Scout Handbook* and the Sugar Creek Gang adventure stories, written for preteen evangelical boys. Most of us don't really mention in such contexts the subclass of the writings that have actually shaped our views of life. But I do not even discuss in these pages several of the books that have profoundly shaped my theological and philosophical perspectives. Given the theme that is my organizing principle here, there is no occasion to describe what an illuminating experience it was for me to read Father (later Cardinal) Avery Dulles's *Models of the Church* or works by and about Edith Stein, a Jewish convert who became a Carmelite nun and was killed by the Nazis. And those are only two prominent examples of many influences that are not treated in what follows.

Recently I read a comment by a writer, much younger than myself, who talked about having produced her third memoir. While she could easily be running the risk of telling us more about herself than most of us care to know, she is not violating the nature of the genre. A person can write multiple memoirs, but there can really only be a single autobiography. If one writes a second version of the latter, it is because there was more to add, or there were important revisions to make. A memoir, though, has a more limited scope. It typically has an explicit angle, a specific area of one's life that one wants to reflect upon.

My angle in this book has to do with the idea of *human commonness*. As I look back over my academic career—I write this now at age seventy-five—I see commonness as a theme that has been informing the main intellectual endeavors that have engaged me from the start of my academic career. More often than not, the theme has been an explicit topic that I have wanted to address. At other times, I can now discern, it was there just below the surface of what I was wrestling with. But it has been a consistent theme for me, whether in thinking about the implications of my Calvinist view of election, or my philosophical investigations of action theory and body/soul dualism, or my efforts to learn what I could from Mennonites, or my interfaith dialogues, and so on.

I make no effort here to bring all of this under a chronological scheme. I jump around a bit from one stage to another, and then back again, in my intellectual journey. This may give a "collage" impression at times. But my intention is to reflect on my intellectual travels in the form of what I have consciously intended throughout the writing as the development of a "sustained narrative."

In a casual conversation with a prominent theologian a few years ago, we engaged in a little bit of "What have you been reading lately?" chatter. We discovered that we had each recently read the same two memoirs, by authors whom we both knew personally. We agreed that the two books were good reading, but we also agreed that each contained elements of bitterness that detracted from the overall value of the narratives. "There's nothing worse than reading old academics trying to get even with people in their past, Richard," the theologian remarked as we took leave. "So let's agree that neither of us will make an attempt to settle some scores when we write about our own careers."

He and I made the vow together, and I think I keep it in this book. Truth be told, at no point in writing this book was I even tempted to settle any scores.

Well, with one exception—I do have a score (more than one, actually!) that I want to try to settle with myself. In fact, an awareness of the need to deal with that score has been one of my motivations for writing this set of reflections on my journey. The score is the worry that I have about the possible undesirable consequences of some of the approaches and viewpoints that I have argued for thus far in my career. Not that I am ready to back off on any major position that I will be reflecting upon in this book. But I still worry about unintended consequences of what I have advocated for over the past several decades, and the worry nags me as I reflect back. While I am convinced that each aspect of my quest for commonness was meant to achieve something worthwhile, the net effect of all those efforts could very well encourage some bad tendencies. So I find it necessary to spell that worry out and to explain what I have done in my own heart and mind to try to hold the dangerous tendencies in check. I will explain all of that in a final "confessional" chapter.

# 1

## Calvinists in an Edinburgh Pub

D URING THE 1770s, A GROUP OF SCOTTISH PRESBYTERIAN
pastors and elders met together regularly in an Edinburgh
tavern for dinner discussions about topics of common concern.
The conveners of this group were six members of the clergy, leaders in what the historian Richard Sher has labeled, in his major
study of the movement,[1] the "moderate literati" of that period in
Scottish history.

I wish I could go back and listen in on those tavern conversations as a fly on the wall. What I find intriguing is the fact that the
participants were, for the most part, fairly strict Calvinists who
were interested in promoting a more positive engagement with
things that were happening in Scottish culture. Many of their
discussions focused on the literary arts. Indeed, one of the leaders, the pastor John Home, had himself written a play that was
intended for stage production—a project that did not sit well with
the Presbyterian establishment, who saw theater as a significant
force for promoting social decay.

The majority of orthodox Presbyterians of the day were quite negative about the very cultural trends that were being celebrated in those dinner conversations. Shakespeare's writings, for example, were regularly condemned from Presbyterian pulpits, along with other cultural expressions that were seen as contributing to the erosion of the spiritual foundations of Scottish life.

The alarm that many church leaders exhibited regarding societal trends in general was also directed specifically to the group holding its dinner meetings in the taverns. The moderate literati among Presbyterian clergy were seen as serving the devil's cause. And this perception was only reinforced by the knowledge that the philosopher David Hume regularly joined the dinner discussions. Hume was widely viewed (with considerable justification) as a declared enemy of the faith, but he was reported to be drawn to what he saw as the high quality of cultural discourse that took place in those tavern conversations.[2]

In their efforts to promote a broad cultural dialogue, the leaders of these moderate literati, themselves strong Calvinists, made every effort to ground their positive outreach in their orthodox Reformed theology. While they, like their more negative Presbyterian colleagues, saw much that was happening around them as displeasing to God, they were convinced that the solution was not simply to condemn the trends but rather to promote a wide-reaching program for the cultivation of public virtue and societal well-being. And this project required, as Sher describes their vision, "a religiously inspired commitment to morality that would follow a proper understanding of the ways of Providence."[3] For these Calvinists this meant encouraging the cultivation of aesthetic sensitivities, a tolerance toward persons of other religious perspectives, and—more generally—a spirit of public "politeness."[4]

While aware of the perils posed by these efforts, these Calvinists were convinced, as Sher depicts their concerns, that the project of charting the path to becoming "a fully civilized individual" was worth the effort, as long as they could do so within a carefully articulated Calvinist perspective. Thus their diligence in attempting to clear the way, theologically and spiritually, for a Presbyterianism characterized by "genteel manners, religious moderation and tolerance, and high esteem for scientific and literary accomplishments."[5]

I said earlier that I wish I could have heard those conversations. But my interest in what the group had to say is not simply a matter of intellectual curiosity: I personally identify with both their Calvinist convictions and their cultural efforts. My enthusiasm for what they were attempting is held in check, however, by my realization that they basically failed in what they hoped to accomplish. Looking back, we can see that they did not in fact stem the tide of the more God-dishonoring aspects of the Scottish Enlightenment. Indeed, it can be argued that they actually helped that tide along by what they were advocating. The overt unbeliever David Hume may have been a decidedly minority voice in their dinner gatherings, but in the long run the religious skepticism that he stood for has now become the status quo in "high" cultural circles.

So I ask myself: What went wrong? Was there some inadequacy in the manner in which they went about their explorations? These questions are urgent ones for me. The moderate literati were engaged in searching for a basis for common cause between Christian believers and representatives of other perspectives in the larger human community. They certainly seemed firm in their basic convictions. They were Calvinists who were sensing a rather strong disagreement with many of their fellow Calvinists about the very legitimacy of their search for commonalities. Like those eighteenth-century literati, I am a Calvinist who has expended much energy on a similar journey for understanding how my Reformed theological perspective can allow for the kinds of commonalities those Scottish clergy were looking for. For me, the search has taken place in several contexts. As a teacher of philosophical and theological topics, I have always seen my pedagogical task as including the need to urge my students to look for ways to learn

from non-Christian systems of thought. In the early days of the
"evangelical social action" movement that emerged in the 1970s,
I sensed a special obligation—as a Dutch Calvinist who was expected, in the words of the Belgic Confession, to "detest" the
Anabaptists—to engage in a more positive manner the perspective of present-day Mennonite thinkers. In my years as president
of Fuller Seminary, I initiated programs of dialogue with Jews,
Muslims, and Mormons. And I have devoted considerable time
to friendly give-and-take with Catholics and liberal Protestants.
In my own attempts to find "proper bounds" for all of this, I have
concentrated on what I have called "convicted civility"—a concept
I borrow from Martin Marty, who once remarked that people these
days who have strong convictions are often not very civil, and civil
people often don't have very strong convictions.[6] My own overall
quest has been guided by a conscious desire to cultivate a civility
that is compatible with Calvinist convictions. So, while I admire
and take encouragement from those eighteenth-century Scottish
Calvinists, their example does give me pause about all of this.

I am theologically content, on the whole, with the kinds of
theological boundaries that I have attempted to respect throughout
my pilgrimage thus far. But I have also been reminded regularly,
especially in recent years, that there could be unintended consequences for my project—negative ones that encourage the wrong
kind of thing in the long run. For all my good intentions and proper
Calvinist motives, I have asked myself on occasion whether I am
unwittingly giving aid and comfort to the increasing relativism of
our own day, encouraging the widespread assumption that being
clear about borders is not a matter of great importance. It's not
that I see an alternative to keeping at it. Nor do I wish that the
eighteenth-century dinner discussants had simply chosen to stick
with the purely negative Calvinism that characterized the Presbyterian establishment of their day. I am convinced that there can
be no turning back from a sustained and continuing quest for
commonalities. But neither can I give up on paying attention to

my qualms. I have to keep reminding myself about the full scope of the theological tradition to which I claim allegiance, staying attuned to warning signals as well as to words of encouragement.

I'm glad that those eighteenth-century moderate literati saw the need to explore territories beyond the strict boundaries of their confessional identity. And I'm glad that they chose to include David Hume in their pub conversations. In my own way, I also have had my conversations with Hume and others like him—by sustained interaction with their thought—and have received much from those conversations. Indeed, I consider those intellectual encounters to be gifts from God. But I have also made a point of listening carefully to the theological concerns of the kinds of Calvinists who were quite critical of the patterns associated with the moderate literati of Edinburgh. And while I have not been willing simply to heed the critics' warnings, I have intentionally refused to drown out their accusing voices as I have looked for, and have regularly stood upon, the common ground that they saw as enemy territory.

# 2

## A Tale of Two Authors

I HAD TWO FAVORITE AUTHORS DURING MY FINAL TWO YEARS AS
an undergraduate: Ralph Waldo Emerson and Cornelius Van
Til. To those familiar with the thinking of each of them they will
certainly seem like an odd pair to have as favorites: Emerson, the
free-spirit shaper of New England transcendentalism, and Van
Til, the traditional Calvinist theologian at Westminster Seminary
who found even Karl Barth to be a dangerous threat to Reformed
orthodoxy. But my admiration for both of them at that stage in
my life set the agenda for many of my theological journeys for the
next half century, journeys that have been in large part motivated
by a search for commonalities among people with whom I have
serious disagreements.

### A "Quickening Effect"

I still occasionally go back to read Emerson, but his writings no
longer loom large on my reading list. My experience with Emerson
is much like what his contemporary Matthew Arnold reported. Early

on in his intellectual pilgrimage, Arnold testified, he found Emerson to be "the friend and aider of those who would live in the spirit," and he admired his "hopeful, serene, beautiful temper." But eventually, Arnold reported, he grew weary of Emerson's writings, even dismissing him at one point as one of the dislikable "moral desperadoes" in the world of letters. Nonetheless, he later sent a copy of one of his books to Emerson, accompanied by a note in which he told the American writer, "I can never forget the refreshing and quickening effect your writings had upon me at a critical time of my life."[1]

"Refreshing and quickening" captures my own early encounter with Emerson. I read his essays as a student at an evangelical college situated in a rural setting, and I regularly went for long walks. I am not normally given to nature-loving instincts. I seldom find myself longing for a lost Eden; my spiritual reveries are more likely to be anticipations of a Holy City. In my college days, my long walks were typically occasions for thinking about ideas or relationships, or for conversations with a good friend. But for a brief time it was different; reading Emerson made it possible for me to focus directly on nature in memorable—albeit, regrettably, not lasting—ways.

The one Emersonian experience that stands out in my memory was not unlike one that Martin Buber describes in his *Between Man and Man*. Buber tells about a time when, as an eleven-year-old, he experienced a "deeply stirring happening" while taking care of a horse on his grandparents' estate. Stroking the horse's mane and feeling its "life beneath my hand, it was as though the element of vitality itself bordered on my skin, something that was not I, was certainly not akin to me, palpably the other, not just another, really the Other itself; and yet it let me approach, confided itself to me, placed itself elementally in the relation of *Thou* and *Thou* with me." But in another, equally mysterious moment, Buber suddenly became aware of his own hand—and "something had changed; it was no longer the same thing." He never recovered the "I-Thou-ness" of the earlier moment.[2]

That was what happened to me once on a long walk during
that time in my late teens when I was reading Emerson—it is a
vivid memory of a kind of "Thou to Thou" experience with nature. I remember it, but have never been able to recapture it. I do
have moments in my life—quite regularly, actually—that I would
describe as "mystical." But these typically come to me in worship
settings, or during times of private devotion; they happen when my
focus is on God or matters relating to how God relates to human
beings. My Emersonian experience was different. It came from
an intense attention to nature itself—more specifically, to grassy
hillsides, flowers, trees, leaves lying on a woodland path. Not only
have I not had that kind of experience since; I do not even know
how to prepare the way for its retrieval. The fact that it occurred
at one time in my life I see as a gift. And while Emerson was not
himself the Giver, taking him seriously was certainly the occasion
for receiving the gift.

## Reading Van Til

It has been different for me with Van Til. His writings—their
actual substance—have been a more permanent gift than what I
received from Emerson. When I went off to the Houghton College campus for my junior year of undergraduate study, a friend
of mine, a pastor with strong Calvinist convictions, gave me a
ninety-four-page booklet titled *Common Grace*,[3] authored by Van
Til, a longtime professor of apologetics at Westminster Theological Seminary in Philadelphia. I had recently become a Calvinist
enthusiast by reading Charles Spurgeon's sermons, and I enjoyed
my long conversations with my pastor friend about the riches
of Reformed theology. My friend was convinced that I was now
ready for meatier stuff, so he introduced me to Van Til's thought.

*Common Grace* was the first serious piece of theological writing
that I ever read, and it had a profound impact on me. Here I discovered an ongoing theological conversation about topics pointed to by

the booklet's title: the theme of commonness. Given the realities of sin and grace, what can we assume that believers and nonbelievers have in common in their quest for truth? Can we expect to gain important insights into the nature of reality from the deliverances of the unregenerate mind? Is there an attitude of divine favor—one that can even be labeled as "grace"—that is directed toward all human beings, regardless of their final salvific status?

In my youthful enthusiasm I wrote to Van Til, asking him for clarification about his views on these matters. He not only responded graciously to my amateurish inquiries, but he sent me copies of several of his books and course syllabi—all of which I eagerly read. In reading Van Til, I also became interested in the writings of several of his conversation partners: the theologians of the "Old Princeton" school, especially Charles Hodge and Benjamin Warfield, as well as nineteenth- and early twentieth-century representatives of Dutch Calvinist orthodoxy—particularly Abraham Kuyper, Herman Bavinck, Klaas Schilder, and Herman Hoeksema. These thinkers, especially the Dutch theologians, came to loom large in my own continuing focus on issues of commonness. My first philosophy teacher at Houghton College was Ronald Nash, whose approach to philosophical questions was shaped by interests similar to Van Til's. But the actual substance of Nash's philosophical perspective was heavily influenced by the views of Edward John Carnell, then the president of Fuller Theological Seminary. Nash encouraged me to read Carnell's apologetics writings. Carnell had come under the influence of Van Til during his studies at Westminster but had later modified his views on issues of commonness, while pursuing a pair of doctorates at Harvard and Boston University. Van Til did not take kindly toward the changes in his former student's thinking on the subject, with the result that Van Til regularly singled out Carnell's views for special criticism. This made for interesting exchanges between Nash and myself. In a major paper I wrote for one of Nash's courses, I supported Van Til's critique of Carnell.

Not that I was totally negative about Carnell's approach. For one thing, Van Til himself did not see Carnell as having gone completely in a wrong direction. He conceded that Carnell "frequently argues as we would expect a Reformed apologist to argue."[4] What disturbed Van Til, however, was Carnell's willingness to engage in dialogue with unbelievers about the claims of Christianity prior to any direct appeal to Scripture. In one of his discussions of Carnell's approach, Van Til pointed to the line of argument that Carnell had set forth in the magazine *Moody Monthly*, in which Carnell gave advice to Christians about how they can defend the faith to unbelievers. When witnessing to someone who happens to be of "a philosophic turn," Carnell wrote, "you can point to the remarkable way in which Christianity fits in with the moral sense inherent in every human being, or the influence of Christ on our ethics, customs, literature, art and music." From there, Carnell went on, the believer can begin to speak personally about an experience with Christ; then, if the person continues to show an interest, the believer can discuss biblical passages in a way that will "permit the Spirit to work on the inner recesses of the heart."[5]

For Van Til, this was the wrong way to go. The only way to start engaging the unbeliever is with a direct appeal to the Bible. To be sure, he observed, unbelievers will see this as "circular reasoning," a Christian attempt to "prove that the Bible is true by an appeal to the Bible itself." But so be it. What they refuse to see is that they too inevitably engage in circular reasoning. Suppose a person insists, Van Til observed, that we can accept the Bible's authority only if that authority is first shown to be logically defensible. In that case, what is the basis for the appeal to logic? Is the appeal to logic itself logically demonstrable?[6]

This insistence on the need to begin with the Bible was correlated closely, in Van Til's approach, with his understanding of common grace. All human beings, Christian and non-Christian alike, live in God's world, where they are presented with God's revelation of his being and power in the created order, as well as in the internal witness of their own God-created consciences. This accounts for the commonalities that we all exhibit in the areas of thought and action. At the same time, though, since believers and unbelievers operate from two fundamentally different life directions—a desire to be in covenant-keeping relationship to God versus one of a rebellious covenant-breaking spirit—Christians are guided by presuppositions that are antithetical to those of our non-Christian neighbors. This means that we do not even operate with the same "facts" to which they claim access; for the believer, a tree is created by the Triune God of the Scriptures, while unbelievers, as those who "hold the truth in unrighteousness" (Rom. 1:18 KJV), see that tree from their God-denying point of view. Thus, while there is a common grace by which God keeps the unbelieving world from being as bad as it should be, given its rebellious presuppositions, the seeming agreement between Christian and non-Christian is "proximate." It does not go deep.[7]

At the time I found Van Til convincing on such matters on a theological level. But on a practical level my admiration for Emerson and other unbelieving thinkers made me uneasy with Van Til's perspective. When I went on to seminary and then to graduate studies in philosophy, I shifted decidedly in Carnell's general direction. Especially in my years of studying and teaching alongside unbelievers at secular universities, I found myself quite naturally drawn into the very kinds of discussions that Van Til had condemned: considering arguments for and against basic tenets of a theistic worldview, affirming a common moral sense with those who professed no belief in a divine lawgiver, exploring the ways in which the Christian faith had influenced culture in positive and negative ways, and so on. In engaging in those "commonness" explorations, though, I have never seen Van Til's warnings against such things as simply wrongheaded. As serious warnings, they are legitimate. Even as I deliberately act against them, I still feel their force.

What pulled me in the other direction, though, was that the Carnell-type approach has helped me to account for the fact that I have actually *learned* from non-Christian thinkers—thus my aforementioned sense of gratitude for the benefits I gained early on from reading the likes of Ralph Waldo Emerson. And on such matters I also came to take my inspiration from John Calvin himself. Before he gained his reputation as a great Protestant Reformer, Calvin had engaged in legal studies, and he learned much from some ancient Roman writers, particularly Seneca. Nor did Calvin repent of his earlier appreciation for such thinkers when he began to develop a theological perspective that placed much emphasis on the depravity of the fallen human mind. In spite of sin's pervasive influence in human affairs, Calvin argued, we can still witness in rebellious humanity an "admirable light of truth," so that the human mind, "though fallen and perverted from its wholeness, is nevertheless clothed and ornamented with God's excellent gifts." This means, he says, that when we reject something simply because it comes from a non-Christian source, we "dishonor the Spirit of God."[8]

Again, that kind of encouragement from Calvin himself has inspired me actively to learn from folks with whom I disagree on important issues, both in studying non-Christian writers and in engaging in direct dialogue with persons representing other theological and religious systems. In doing so, however, I have continued to struggle with the questions about "commonness"—questions about how, particularly from a Reformed theological perspective, we are to understand what it is that we share with people whose views of reality are different from our own. The Reformed tradition does point us to a number of resources upon which we can draw. Calvin himself talked about both a *semen religionis* and a *sensus divinitatis*—a "seed of religion" and a "sense of divinity"— that reside in the deep places of every human heart. In addition, Reformed thinkers (and others) have also on occasion drawn on the ideas of natural law, natural theology, general revelation, the shared *imago Dei*, and common grace. My own explorations have drawn heavily on the last of these conceptions, common grace. Here too I take my lead from Calvin, who describes the continuing capacity in every human being for a rational grasp of God's truth—even when the source goes unacknowledged—as resulting from a "peculiar grace of God."[9]

To be sure, Calvin could also speak very negatively about the products of the unregenerate mind. When Calvin credits the unredeemed with some grasp of the principles of civic fairness, for example, he quickly adds that even when the fallen human mind follows after truth, "it limps and staggers" in doing so.[10] In the lives of unbelievers, he says, the civic "virtues are so sullied that before God they lose all favor," so that anything in them "that appears praiseworthy must be considered worthless."[11] And while he acknowledges that "some sparks still gleam" in the unredeemed mind, that light is nonetheless "choked with dense ignorance, so that it cannot come forth effectively."[12]

In my early struggles with the issues of commonness, I clearly heard both of those voices: those who followed Calvin in praising the "natural mind" for being "ornamented" with wonderful gifts, as well as those who followed the Calvin who pointed to the ways in which the unregenerate thinker "limps and staggers."

### Reconciling the "Two Calvins"?

This seeming ambivalence in Calvin is what led one of the Reformer's mostly sympathetic biographers, William Bouwsma, to posit a tension deep within Calvin's own psyche—so deep in fact that Bouwsma resorts to positing "two Calvins, coexisting uncomfortably within the same historical personage." Bouwsma labels one of those Calvins "the philosophical Calvin," who, "as a rationalist and a schoolman of the high Scholastic tradition," favored a "static orthodoxy" and "craved desperately for intelligibility, order, certainty. Distrusting freedom, he struggled to control both himself and the world." The second John Calvin,

though, "was a rhetorician and a humanist" who "was flexible to
the point of opportunism, and a revolutionary in spite of himself."
This was a Calvin who "was inclined to celebrate the paradoxes
and mystery at the heart of existence."[13]

While I was attracted early on to both Calvins, I was never
content simply to listen to both of his voices without finding some
way to bring the two together theologically. This is where I found
much help from Abraham Kuyper, who went beyond Calvin to
see the two seemingly diverse strands in the light of a larger theological framework. Kuyper's doctrine of the antithesis recognized
that unredeemed cultural activity is directed by a spirit of rebellion, which stands in contrast to those God-honoring patterns
to which the redeemed are called. But his doctrine of common
grace spelled out the ways in which the rebellious motives of the
unredeemed are curbed, and even on occasion guided in a direction that serves God's cultural goals. Thus he can acknowledge
the Spirit's workings in the broad human community "wherever
civic virtue, a sense of domesticity, natural love, the practice of
human virtue, the improvement of the public conscience, integrity,
mutual loyalty among people, and a feeling for piety leaven life."[14]

In endorsing Bouwsma's "two Calvins" portrayal while imply-
ing that there was only one Kuyper, am I giving too little credit
to Calvin and too much to Kuyper? Perhaps. Calvin was highly
intelligent and seemed to be quite self-aware. It is likely that he
thought more than meets the eye about integrating what seem
like conflicting tendencies in his writings. And Kuyper did seem
in his practice to be a little less clear than he was in his theological
pronouncements about how to hold to the antithesis and common
grace in a coherent manner. For all of that, however, I do think that
what Kuyper did was an improvement on Calvin. For one thing,
Kuyper made a point of explicitly acknowledging the tension that
needs to be faced by a healthy Calvinism. The only way to give
honest recognition to the positive contributions of unbelievers to
our shared human life, he argued, is to acknowledge that there are

"internal" gracious dealings with all human beings. These dealings are not salvific in nature, but they are clearly on display where, as Kuyper rightly observes, we see such things as integrity, loyalty, and commitment to the common good. These phenomena are so obvious, Kuyper argues, that Calvinists must choose between two options: we must "either surrender our confession of the deadly character of sin, or hold on to that confession with all our might, but then also confess along with it that there is a common grace at work that in many cases restrains the full, deadly effect of sin."[15]

By acknowledging the "deadly character of sin"—the reality of the antithesis—while also acknowledging the genuine gifts that we receive from non-Christian thought and practice, Kuyper was giving us some handles to better wrestle with the theological issues that Calvin only pointed to. Specifically, Kuyper not only gave us two helpful theological labels—antithesis and common grace—but he went on to discuss in considerable detail the related theological issues associated with the handles. My good friend David Tiede, a gifted Lutheran theologian, once made a memorable observation in a devotional he gave to a group of theological administrators. The crude and even blasphemous language of the streets, Tiede said, often contains theological meanings that the speakers are oblivious to. His two examples were "What *in the hell* is going on?!" and "What *in heaven's name* is happening?!" These two expressions, Tiede said, get at important spiritual realities—namely, that there is a lot of hellish stuff going on in the world but that we can also on occasion discern things that draw, even if unwittingly, upon heavenly resources. Tiede was giving a practical and insightful expression of Kuyper's distinction between antithesis and common grace. And, like Kuyper, he was not providing clear and unimpeachable criteria for deciding between the heavenly and the hellish. Common grace and antithesis are theological tools of discernment. The antithesis idea helps us to see that the differences between belief and unbelief are real and pervasive. But the common grace idea tells us that the God whom Calvinists worship

and serve has not abandoned the unbelieving world. We know
that both the hellish and the heavenly are realities in the world.
We know that we can fully expect to catch glimpses—sometimes
even glorious ones—of truth, goodness, and beauty in the lives of
those who do not profess Christ, even while we must be on guard
not to be taken in by hellish deceptions. Both ideas encourage us
to keep our spiritual eyes open—always with an awareness that
we need to work hard at cultivating a God-honoring discernment.

## Clarifying Mysteries

The Catholic theologian Thomas Weinandy has observed that
we should not see the doing of theology primarily as a "problem
solving" activity. Rather, it functions at its best as "a mystery
discerning enterprise." To solve a problem, Weinandy notes, is to
make our puzzles go away, and that is not the kind of resolution
that we ought to expect as a matter of course in theological exploration. But we can hope to succeed in knowing "more precisely
and clearly what the mystery is."[16]

One key element in my own attempts to clarify theological mysteries is the need to see how antithesis and common grace stand in
relation to each other, and to find the proper tension point between
the two, so that each is properly acknowledged in both theology
and practice. In my estimation, Kuyper did well in this regard.
He serves as a fine example of a Calvinist who was eager to find
commonalities while being clearly aware of the deep differences.

In following Kuyper's example, I have been inspired by a term
that loomed large in Edward John Carnell's thought: "common
ground." As I reported earlier, I started off as a college student
endorsing Van Til's refusal to concede to Edward John Carnell
the legitimacy of looking for areas of agreement with non-
Christians in our apologetic efforts. My attraction to Van Til's
perspective would soon give way to much sympathy for Carnell's
side of the argument. And it wasn't just because I came to see

the attractiveness of Carnell's approach as a plausible apologetic methodology—although it certainly was that. More importantly, his way of viewing things gripped me experientially. I kept sensing, in various encounters with people beyond the boundaries of evangelical Calvinism, that my theological feet were actually finding real *patches* of common ground. I wasn't always sure how exactly I came upon those patches—thus the ongoing effort to develop appropriate tools for discerning the mysteries. Common ground has been for me an experiential reality. I have regularly experienced a profound sense—in reading a non-Christian philosopher, in engaging in debates on questions of public policy, in debating theological topics with persons of other Christian traditions—that I am standing together on a patch of common ground with someone whose views on serious matters are quite different from my own. The historian David Cannadine recently published an insightful apologia for the importance of holding on to the idea of human solidarity in spite of the attention given these days to human differences—religious, national, racial, ethnic, gender, lifestyle, and the like.[17] I especially like the subtitle chosen for his book: *Humanity beyond Our Differences*. It is that "beyond" or "beneath" that I often experience.

It is important, though, to assess that experience in the light of careful theological exploration. What *explains* the experience of standing on a patch of common ground? How do we tell that the experience is not deceptive? Fortunately, multiple theological resources are available to help in the search for explanatory insight. I have called upon several of them at various points in my journey, finding that one or another best addresses a specific experience of commonness. Among these, the notion that all human beings, redeemed or unredeemed, bear the marks of being created in the image of God is certainly a primary resource. I turn now to a report on my journey with this theological concept.

# 3

## A Many-Faceted "Imaging"

WHEN ONE OF MY SEMINARY PROFESSORS ASSIGNED G. C. Berkouwer's *Man: The Image of God* as required reading in a theology course, several of my fellow students complained that it was tedious reading. But I read it and reread it then, and have returned to it many times since. It has been an ongoing resource for reminders of some of the important questions and answers that are crucial for a theological—and philosophical—understanding of human nature. I have often urged my own advanced students to wrestle with Berkouwer's detailed discussion.

Berkouwer's book offers little comfort to anyone who is hoping for a straightforward account of what it means for a human being to be created in God's image. Right off, for example, Berkouwer introduces various treatments by theologians of a distinction between a broader and a narrower sense of the *imago*. Further distinctions and nuances soon follow: the formal versus the material aspects of the image; arguments about whether being created in God's "image" and being fashioned in God's "likeness" point to different realities; the original created image and the remnants of

18

the image in human fallenness; the image as relational and the image as ontological; the image by itself and the image linked to a *donum superadditum* (a supernatural gift that God adds on to the natural); the image as it is on display in the individual human person and the image as it is manifested in collective humanity; the image as partially restored in redemption and the image as it will be manifested when, as believers, "we will be like [Christ], for we will see him as he is" (1 John 3:2); and much more.

Much of that was considerable theological overload for what I encountered in the Anglo-American "philosophy of mind" discussions. But one particular stimulus for reaching for Berkouwer's book on my shelf during graduate school happened when I was working my way through P. F. Strawson's 1959 study, *Individuals*. Strawson made the case that "the concept of a pure individual consciousness . . . could not exist as a primary concept to be used in the explanation of the concept of a person." While this meant for him that the traditional mind-body problem was based on a confusion, Strawson did allow for at least the sheer possibility that a disembodied consciousness "might have a logically secondary existence," since it is not difficult for a person "quite intelligibly [to] conceive of his or her individual survival of bodily death."[1] But this notion of a disembodied consciousness makes sense, Strawson observed, only as "disembodied," as the continuing consciousness of "a former person"[2]—in the robust sense of a person as an entity to which "both predicates ascribing states of consciousness and predicates ascribing corporeal characteristics" are applicable.[3] Strawson went on to note, however, that there is a practical problem with this notion of disembodied existence. It is not clear, he observed, how we could think of this state of being as in any sense a situation in which we could be *doing* anything. At best it would be a matter of dwelling on memories of one's previous embodiment, or of a person's "taking a certain kind of interest in the human affairs of which he is a mute and invisible witness," which means that for all practical purposes there is "no difference between the continuance of experience and its cessation." This led Strawson to conclude his discussion of that topic with this observation, one that I found both refreshing and fascinating: "Disembodied survival, on such terms as these, may well seem unattractive. No doubt it is for this reason that the orthodox have wisely insisted on the resurrection of the body."[4]

Strawson obviously meant this allusion to resurrection as a kind of throwaway line. In spite of his actual intention, however, he was on to something important. And I continue to think that his basic point is well taken, both philosophically and theologically. But before pursuing the significance of this matter for philosophical anthropology, I want to do a little more sorting-out of the questions about human nature that have engaged theologians as they have reflected on the meaning of the image of God.

## A Shifting Focus

The anthropological topics that have loomed very large in past theological and philosophical discussions have often had to do with the questions of human composition to which I have already referred. In response to the basic metaphysical question about what it is that, in the most basic sense, accounts for the composition of a human person, the obvious options are dualism and monism. Either we are composed of two basic stuffs, the mental or spiritual and the physical, or we are made up of only one of these. The views of Bishop Berkeley and Mary Baker Eddy notwithstanding, a monism that sees reality in general and human beings in particular as nothing but mind or spirit has not been a serious option in the Christian tradition. Some form of metaphysical physicalism, in contrast, has often been proposed, and that as a way of rejecting the dualistic compositional perspective that has long dominated theological anthropology.

Does the biblical reference to human beings as created in God's image in any way address this issue? In one sense it does not. To be sure, there is a long-standing insistence in the Christian tradition that the biblical *imago* reference does provide a fairly straight-forward answer to the question of composition. Those who have argued thus have gotten to their conclusion by two moves. First, they have assumed that the reference to the image in Genesis is implicitly responding to what we might label, as a shorthand, the "differentiating feature" question. They ask, what is a significant property that is characteristic of both God and human beings and is not possessed by any other creature? And then they single out a compositional property. They will talk, for example, about the fact that God is Spirit. Then they will observe that human beings are like God in that they also are at least in part spirits, and that no other creatures (except the angels, whose creation predated the activity described in the Genesis creation account) are spiritual in this sense. Therefore, they conclude, being at least in part spiritual is what it means to be created in God's image.

This kind of understanding of what is meant by the *imago* has not fared well in more recent theological accounts, where the shift has been away from seeing the Bible as offering straightforward metaphysical teachings. Instead, the assumption is that the biblical writers focus primarily on the more functional-relational dimen-sions of the human person. Karl Barth's treatment of the *imago Dei* is one of the best-known examples of this approach. Barth dismisses past efforts to identify the image with spirituality or rationality as "arbitrarily invented interpretations" set forth by people who simply have "ignored the definitive explanation given by the text itself." As the right way of going about the investiga-tion, Barth points to the "divine plural" in the Genesis account of the creation of humankind: "Let *us* make man in *our* image, after *our* likeness" (Gen. 1:26 KJV). He does not see this as an intentional reference to God's triune nature, but he does insist that it rules out the notion of the biblical deity as a solitary sovereign. And it is significant, he observes, that this reference to a divine "us" is immediately followed by the reference to the creation of "male and female." This clearly suggests, he says, that there is a "simple correspondence . . . between this mark of the divine, namely that it includes an I and a Thou, and the being of man, male and female."[5] On this view, then, the image of God consists in human sociality, our being created for "I-Thou" relationships.

There are at least two problems with this as the "definitive" account of the *imago*, however. One is that male-and-femaleness as such is not a distinguishing mark of humanness—it is shared by many others in the animal kingdom. The second is that Barth himself seems to be reading more recent philosophical notions into the text with his use of the Buberian "I-Thou" construction. A more interesting difficulty, however, lies in the fact that a look at the text itself for the answer to the meaning of the image raises another significant candidate. Having created humans as male and female, God immediately gives them an *assignment*: they are to "have dominion" over the rest of the creation.[6] This feature—the exercising of dominion—has the advantage of applying uniquely to human beings among the creatures, as well as being a divine delegation of something that is central to God's character as the sovereign Ruler over all things. Thus being "imagers" of God is something that is on display when human beings *act*, when they exercise the authority that God has delegated to them.

Actually, there are also some problems with this "dominion" view as an account of what the biblical writer had in mind in referring to our being created in God's image.[7] But I continue to think that the functional-relational kind of account is the correct one, and that some combination of the sociality and the dominion characteristics is close to the truth about the image. The Dutch theologian Harry Kuitert has it about right in this comment:

> To look like God, to be His image, is not something we can do simply by being rational creatures or by having a good will. We cannot see God in man while man stands still. To look like God has to do with the purpose God has for man. The question, then, is what is man for, what is his calling? What is he here for? He is

here to reflect God, to reflect God the Covenant Partner. To be God's image means simply that we as men are to live as covenant partners with God and with our fellows on earth.[8]

Kuitert's notion of covenant partnership seems to integrate nicely what is important about both the sociality and the dominion emphases: "covenant" captures the importance of relationships, and "partner" points to the mandate to engage in a shared *doing*.

## Thinking about Composition

But let's return now to the composition question. As a typical expression of what I have called the functional-relational understanding of the biblical contribution to theological topics, Berkouwer boldly asserts that "the Scriptural anthropological concepts which vary so extremely never occur in a context which is concerned with the composition of man as such, in himself."[9] There is no dualistic picture of the human person in the Bible, he says. Rather, "in all of [Scripture's] varied expressions the whole man comes to the fore, in all his guilt and sin, his need and oppression, his longings and his nostalgia."[10]

Again, this strikes me as a helpful way of viewing the Bible's direct contribution to discussions of human nature. But there is still room to look for at least some biblical guidance on the composition topic. Berkouwer himself admits as much. He notes that any attempt to single out specific biblical terms for human "parts" ("spirit," "flesh," "body," "heart") in exploring compositional issues will inevitably run into much messiness. Such terms are used "in very concrete and extremely varied ways," as divine "revelation directs our glance toward man in his totality, in his relation to God." But Berkouwer does allow for the fact that while the Bible's intent is not "to reveal to us something of the composition of man," it can be thought of as pointing to the composition of the human person "as an anthropological given," even if it does so "only incidentally, in order to speak of man as a whole."[11]

Here is what I think we ought to do with what Berkouwer is trying to get at in this observation of what the Bible says "only incidentally" about composition. We cannot look to the Bible for a systematic presentation of the metaphysical "parts" of the human person. The biblical witness points us, rather, to our integral wholeness, and it reveals our guilt and loneliness, illuminating our deepest hopes and fears. Even more basically, we can learn from revelation that we are created for covenant partnership. And we could add some other things that fall within the scope of the functional-relational.

But in all of this, the Bible does "incidentally" say some things that have implications for our understanding of human composition. So we can legitimately ask questions of this sort: What kind of metaphysical entity must a human person *be* in order to be capable of covenant partnership? As we attempt to understand ourselves in our wholeness, what reductionist understandings of human nature should we be on guard against? While we cannot get a lot of metaphysical mileage from the Bible's unsystematic references to "spirit" or "heart" or "soul," we can certainly ask what kinds of beings we must be, in metaphysical terms, in order for the Bible to say what it means to say about us when it uses these terms.

An obvious topic that the Bible speaks about in this regard is the question of postmortem survival. This has been a much-debated topic in recent Christian discussions, with many philosophers and theologians, including some of my respected colleagues at Fuller Seminary, expressing discontent with any version of "dualism." I agree with these folks in their charges regarding how a Platonistic kind of dualism has often gone against the Bible's clear affirmation of the integrity and value of created physical reality. But none of that has convinced me that all versions of compositional dualism are wrongheaded. I have found most helpful in this regard the biblical-theological explorations of this subject by the Swiss theologian Oscar Cullmann in his fine essay "Immortality of the Soul or Resurrection of the Dead? The Witness of the New Testament"—a piece whose philosophical significance was rightly recognized by the philosopher Terence Penelhum when he included it in his short reader on the idea of the immortality of the soul.[12]

Cullmann illustrates what he sees as the clear difference between the Greek view of immortality and the Christian view of resurrected bodily life by presenting a stark contrast between the deaths of Socrates and Jesus. After a calm philosophical discussion with his friends, Socrates takes the hemlock in a seemingly cheerful anticipation of the separation of his soul from his body. Jesus, in contrast, sweats drops of blood in Gethsemane as he pleads with the Father to allow the cup of suffering to pass from him. And then on the cross he cries out in agony over his experience of abandonment.[13] The underlying issue here, says Cullmann, has to do with radically differing conceptions of the meaning of death. For Socrates, death is the welcome release of the spiritual from the physical. For Jesus, death is an enemy that threatens the destruction of the whole person.

As Cullmann reads the anthropological data of the New Testament, there is a compositional duality of sorts attributed to human beings there, but it is not that of a radically separable soul and body. While the words "soul" and "body" do appear on pages of Holy Writ, the real contrast for Paul and others is between "the inner" and "the outer" person. Our inner and outer lives need each other, says Cullmann. "Both belong together, both are created by God." Our inner lives require a home in a body. While this inner life "can, to be sure, somehow lead a shady existence without the body, like the dead in Sheol according to the Old Testament," this shadowy existence is not really "a genuine life."[14]

This leads Cullmann, like many other commentators associated with the post–World War II "biblical theology" movement, to celebrate the doctrine of the resurrection of the body as the central teaching with regard to postmortem survival. But Cullmann does not shirk from a fairly nuanced address to the nature of "the intermediate state," that is, the mode of existence that the believer can anticipate between the time of a person's death and the future resurrection of the body. He points out that in 2 Corinthians 5:1–10 the apostle Paul expresses anxiety over the "nakedness" of an interim condition when he is no longer in the body but not yet resurrected. But in this same passage, having expressed his "natural anxiety" over the very real threat posed by the destruction of the body, Paul also voices much confidence that he will experience "Christ's proximity, even in this interim state." The inner person is not abandoned by the Holy Spirit when the outer person disappears.[15]

The important philosophical question, of course, is what this means for the composition issue. It has been characteristic of the twentieth-century advocates of the functional-relational expositions of biblical anthropology—who typically draw a stark contrast between Platonic dualism and the "Hebraic view" set forth in the Bible—that they often avoid any careful treatment of the doctrine of the intermediate state. One pattern of avoidance is exemplified in Robert McAfee Brown's brief summary, in a 1958 theological handbook, of current views regarding biblical anthropology. The very title of Brown's entry is an indication of the metaphysical tone of the content: "Body (Soul)," which signals the view of composition that he sets forth, where the terms "body" and "soul" are each taken to refer to the whole person, without even a mention of the intermediate state.[16] Another option is a favorite strategy of Berkouwer's, who does raise the problem of the intermediate state but then resorts to a heavy reliance on the word "mystery."[17]

By way of contrast to those patterns, Cullmann's discussion is refreshingly nuanced. Indeed, as John Cooper points out in his extensive discussion of the issues I am touching upon here, while Cullmann is "often touted as a champion of biblical holism against

Greek dualism," he refuses to slip into the "conceptual ambivalence" that characterizes so many other recent commentators on this subject. Cullmann strongly criticizes Barth, for example, for using the "sleep" metaphor as grounds for insisting that the human person does not experience the passage of time between death and resurrection. Those who are "dead in Christ" do experience some sort of state of consciousness prior to the resurrection, Cullmann argues. They "are still in time; they, too, are waiting. 'How long, oh Lord?' cry the martyrs who are sleeping under the altar in John's Apocalypse ([Rev.] 6:10)."[18]

Nor does Cullmann shrink from facing the metaphysical implications of what he is allowing for here. It is fair to ask, he says, "whether in this fashion we have not been led again, in the last analysis, to the Greek doctrine of immortality." And the fact is, he continues, "There is a sense in which a kind of approximation to the Greek teaching does actually take place, to the extent that the inner man, who has already been transformed by the Spirit (Rom. 6:3ff) and consequently made alive, continues to live with Christ in this transformed state, in the condition of sleep. . . . Here we observe at least a certain analogy to the 'immortality of the soul,' but the distinction remains nonetheless radical." The key differences between the biblical and the Greek views remain, he insists. Death continues to be an enemy for the Christian; a residual consciousness after dying is not due to anything about "the natural essence of the soul." The interim state is, for the believer, a "waiting for the resurrection."[19] It is important to note explicitly here that everything Cullmann says on this subject applies exclusively to the Christian believer. He tells us nothing about the postmortem prospects of human beings in general. Indeed, he even stipulates that the Christian who has died enters into this "sleep" state by virtue of "a divine intervention from outside, through the Holy Spirit, who must already have quickened the inner man in earthly life by His miraculous power."[20] This too reinforces his insistence that there is considerable distance between the New Testament perspective and the Greek doctrine of immortality. Of course, it could be that God performs a somewhat different kind of miracle for those who die without having been transformed in their inner beings by the Spirit, perhaps sustaining in them a *fearful* waiting for the resurrection. But that is not a topic that Cullmann discusses.

However that may be, it is at least interesting to observe that Cullmann's discussion coincides nicely with Strawson's seemingly throwaway comment about the resurrection, cited earlier. Indeed, Strawson's ontology of personhood can be seen as fitting nicely with Cullmann's theological perspective. Personhood, on this view, is such that "spiritual" attributes can only be ascribed to an entity that also is constituted by physical reality. Any state of consciousness that is thought of as existing apart from a body, then, must of necessity be understood as a *disembodied* consciousness—that is, as consisting in a form of conscious life that can only be possessed by "a *former* person," an entity that once possessed both a bodily and a conscious life.

Whether this view is the correct account of what a human person must be like if the person is to be thought of as bearing the divine image is, of course, a question for continued debate. My own sense is that it has the advantage of allowing for a continued consciousness for the believer between death and resurrection while also emphasizing the fact that full personhood is only possible eschatologically when consciousness once again resides in a human body.

The idea of a disembodied consciousness, however, was subject to theological challenge at the very beginning of the Protestant movement, a challenge that was renewed by the Adventist movement of the nineteenth century and that has taken on new philosophical and theological sophistication in recent years by the advocates of a Christian version of "non-reductive physicalism."[21] Those who issue this challenge typically do not deny the truth of those biblical claims that seem to affirm a continued intermediate state of consciousness; rather, they interpret those claims—such as "absent from the body, present with the Lord"—in alternative ways. My own attention to these matters, in my philosophical and theological explorations, has been consistently guided by firm dualistic convictions on the compositional questions. I am well aware, of course, of the need to continue the arguments in the light of the emergence of new developments in brain science—as long as those much-needed discussions can keep a clear focus on the Bible's witness to the fact that human beings are created in the divine image.

## The *Imago* and Human Commonness

What I brought with me to my philosophical studies from Berkouwer's book was the strong sense that the biblical depiction of our humanness is a complex one. In exploring analytic philosophy's ways of addressing the topic of human composition, I was aware—an awareness stimulated for me in large part by Berkouwer's discussion—that I could draw upon a Christian perspective on human nature that offered important clues for pursuing a broad range of philosophical issues. I had come to philosophy from theological studies influenced by Paul Tillich's formulation of the relationship between the two subject matters: the Christian philosopher has to "correlate" philosophy and theology by taking the questions posed by theology and looking for answers in philosophy. In my own philosophical and theological studies, I came to see that this was too simple. Theology itself raises many questions and answers, and the exciting task, then, is to correlate those questions and answers with the equally complex questions and answers that show up in philosophical discussion.

The image-of-God theme is a case in point for that kind of theological complexity. For me, it has guided my thinking as I have explored issues of human composition. But I found it equally helpful as I looked beyond the focus on the metaphysical makeup of the human individual to broader questions of what it is that all human beings have in common.

Several decades ago, the self-described "postmodern" thinker Ihab Hassan set forth the case that we had arrived at "an antinomian moment" in which we must all recognize the need to "unmake" and "deconstruct" all "totalizing" accounts of the human condition; what this rejection of "the tyranny of wholes" means, he says, is that we must live with "an epistemological obsession with fragments."[22]

That call is an example of the way in which many of the thought leaders in Western culture have not only been observing a decline in convictions about human commonness but are actually at times celebrating *un*commonness. The realities they are highlighting are all too apparent, not only in the very visible tribal and ethnic conflicts that disrupt human life in so many parts of the contemporary world, but also in philosophical attacks on the very idea of unifying "metanarratives." There is no legitimate way, they insist, of articulating a basis for our common humanness because every such formulation is oppressive; the attempt to group all human beings under a common "story" is in fact nothing more than a brutal exercise of power, in which some groups exercise hegemonic control over others.

However we as Christians may assess the merits of this or that element of the epistemological or metaphysical aspects of this "fragmenting" perspective, at the very least we cannot simply abandon an emphasis on a God-created human commonness. The Christian intellectual tradition offers several significant resources for contemporary reflection on this subject: natural-law thought, the idea of general revelation, prevenient and common grace theologies, and so on. But surely the image-of-God idea continues to be a prime candidate for anthropological exploration.

There can be no ignoring the fact that in the past, a conviction that all human beings are created in the divine image has been a powerful force for good on the part of the Christian community. This point was made forcefully by J. H. Elliot, regius professor of modern history at Oxford's Oriel College, in a review published in the *New York Review of Books* of several historical studies of colonialism. Contemporary writers on early missionary activity frequently distort the motives of the evangelizers, Elliot argued. The sixteenth-century Spanish friars, for example, were, in his words, clearly "struggling to discover resemblances, not differences, in their pursuit of the not unworthy objective of establishing the common humanity of the human race."[23] This kind of observation has to be taken very seriously today. There is no question that what often compelled the missionaries of the past to enter into what were for them unknown territories, often at great risk to their own lives, seeking out human communities to whom they wanted to bring the gospel, both in word and deed, was a deep conviction about the innate dignity and value of the human person. They had the abiding confidence that they would not encounter any human being in any rural compound or village or city who was not created in the image and likeness of the God and Father of Jesus Christ. We need to find new ways today to sustain these convictions.

In our efforts to formulate a contemporary understanding of human commonness, however, it would be a mistake to ignore what advocates of "the postmodern turn" have been trying to teach us in recent decades about the need to focus on human diversity, including the human differences associated with such attributes as race, gender, ethnicity, nationality, and socioeconomic location. Here too, I suggest, we can draw on the resources offered to us by past theological discussions of the *imago Dei*.

One theologian whose treatment of the image of God has captivated me in a special way is Herman Bavinck, a younger colleague of Abraham Kuyper. Bavinck insisted that in addition to the fact that each human individual is created in the divine image, there is also a collective possession of the *imago*. The creation of humans in the divine image in the Genesis creation narrative, Bavinck observed, "is not the end but the beginning of God's journey with mankind." In mandating that the first human pair be "fruitful and multiply," said Bavinck, God was making it clear that "not the man alone, nor the man and the woman together, but only the whole of humanity together is the fully developed image of God," for "the image of God is much too rich for it to be fully realized in a single human being, however richly gifted that human being may be." Furthermore, this collective sense of the *imago*, he argues, "is not a static entity but extends and unfolds itself" in the rich diversity of humankind spread over many places and times. For Bavinck, this understanding of the image necessarily takes on eschatological significance when, in the end-time, "all the glory of the nations will be brought" into the new Jerusalem.[24]

For our present-day discussions, this suggests that we might think of the Creator as having distributed different aspects of the divine likeness to different cultural groups, with each group receiving, as it were, a unique assignment for developing some aspect or another of the divine image. Thus it will only be in the eschatological gathering-in of the peoples of the earth, when many tribes and tongues and nations will be displayed in their honor and glory in the new Jerusalem, that we will see the many-splendored *imago Dei* in its fullness. I first came across this idea of Bavinck's in reading Berkouwer decades ago. At the time it struck me as just one of many interesting ideas that I might pick up on someday. Today the idea of a shared, many-splendored image is an exciting one for me. Race, ethnicity, multinationalism, gender—these are topics that have come to loom large in my thinking, and in the practical realities of my life, in the twenty-first century.

Indeed, those realities of diversity have been writ large for me at Fuller Seminary, an academic community where in any given year I have been surrounded by women and men from at least seventy nations, as well as large numbers of North Americans representing a variety of ethnic and racial groups. To live and work in such a Christian context provides the blessings of a cross-cultural conversation undergirded by a spiritual bonding that is seldom available to scholars whose global contacts are available only through the usual academic networks. The privilege of participating in this extensive Christian network can nurture in us the attitudinal and communal resources to help us wrestle effectively with the facts of both commonness and diversity, even allowing us the freedom to linger a little more on the diversity side of things, while not abandoning our convictions about commonness.

This kind of philosophical-theological lingering is an important practice for me. It is helpful to take our time in the intellectual quest, to cultivate patience. Arthur Holmes, who had a wonderful career teaching philosophy at Wheaton College, put it nicely when he observed that in our lives as thinking Christians, we need to learn to live in the tension between "epistemic humility" and "epistemic hope."[25] The acknowledgment that only God possesses comprehensive knowledge of all things should inspire in us a strong sense of humility. But we have the promise from God that in the end-time, we will achieve that mode of perfect knowing that is proper to us as human creatures. So we can press on with patience, pausing to linger at key points along the way.

Socrates gives us some wisdom about cultivating the patience that is needed to stay the course. As Plato portrays him in the *Meno*, Socrates prods his friends with so many questions about the meaning of "virtue" that they are finally exhausted and want to give up in despair. They have been trying to come up with a unified definition of virtue as such, but instead, they say, all they have been able to produce is a "swarm" of virtues. At that point Socrates adopts a more pastoral tone. Don't get discouraged by the swarm, he tells them: in spite of appearances, "all nature is akin." This means, he says, that there is nothing to hinder us, having learned just one thing, from going on to find out about all the rest, as long as we do "not weary in seeking."[26]

I have often experienced that kind of frustration in trying to draw out the implications for the biblical idea of the *imago Dei* for important topics in philosophical anthropology. But all I have seemed to come up with is a swarm of possible questions and answers. As a Christian, though, I know that I have even stronger reasons than Socrates did for operating with the conviction that "all nature is akin." I can be confident that when the Bible makes a point of telling us that in the beginning humankind was fashioned in the very image and likeness of God, I have been given a piece of supremely important information, and that I ought not to grow "weary in seeking" to understand it more clearly.

# 4

## More Than Calisthenics

Isaiah Berlin famously divided the world of scholars into two categories: hedgehogs and foxes. He borrowed the image from an ancient Greek adage: "The fox knows many things, but the hedgehog knows one big thing." Hedgehog scholars, Berlin said, focus single-mindedly on one overarching idea, attempting to organize everything else with reference to that idea. Fox scholars, in contrast, go from one thing to another without worrying how to integrate all of it under a single umbrella concept.[1]

I'm not certain how properly to categorize my own overall scholarly interests in hedgehog-versus-fox terms. Obviously, any Christian scholar who believes that faith should have an impact on scholarly pursuits will be guided by the big idea that there is a God whose mind and will are the reference point for all truth and goodness. But how this gets spelled out will depend upon some other commitments. To believe in common grace, for example, is to be willing to wander a bit from one thing to another without being able to link what one finds immediately to a single big idea.

Those who are less inclined toward a common-grace teaching will function more consistently like hedgehogs.

Without charting my whole journey in fox-versus-hedgehog terms, it is certainly clear to me that my five years of graduate studies in philosophy, at the University of Alberta (MA degree) and the University of Chicago (PhD), were pretty much a "fox" period in my intellectual life. Both of those programs were dominated by British-American analytic philosophy. And while there is a kind of big idea at work in that school of thought, with its firm commitment to logical clarity, there is a lot of moving from one distinct topic to another, without always looking out for metaphysical or epistemological coherence. I took courses on, among other topics, Immanuel Kant's epistemology, Plato's later dialogues, Ludwig Wittgenstein's *Philosophical Investigations*, metaphysics of time, the ethics of utilitarianism, and Thomas Hobbes's social-political thought—without ever having anyone teach me how to weave it all together with reference to one big philosophical idea. To say that is not to complain. Rather, a willingness to scurry around a bit philosophically was an important rationale for my engaging in those programs in the first place. Submitting to the "fox" disciplines of analytic philosophy was a deliberate choice. David Hubbard, my immediate predecessor in the Fuller presidency, once told me that when he went off to the University of St. Andrews in Scotland to earn his doctorate in Old Testament studies, he did so with a deliberate decision to isolate himself from involvement in evangelicalism for the duration of that program, as a kind of test of his evangelical convictions. If he could make his way successfully in the broader world of biblical scholarship without having his sense of evangelical identity seriously undermined, he had decided, then he could reenter the evangelical academy with a clear conscience about his intellectual integrity. And at the end of that stage of his journey he found that he did indeed remain a committed evangelical.

I had made a very similar vow—not so much about evangelicalism but about religious interests in general. I wanted to be a

Christian scholar with the freedom to pursue a broad range of interesting intellectual topics. But I wanted to test my integrity by spending several years staying away from those specifically Christian scholarly pursuits. And while I had become convinced that the subjects pursued by most Anglo-American analytic philosophers did not particularly excite me as a long-range agenda for my own career, I did want to spend some time submitting to the rigorous patterns of thought that characterized their approach to philosophical topics. I saw this venture as something like the academic equivalent of doing calisthenics. In order for a quarterback to do well in a big stadium game—calling signals, passing, rushing into the end zone—he first has to do very different kinds of exercises: pushups, lifting weights, sprints, and so on. My time in graduate school was the calisthenics stage.

So I immersed myself in Anglo-American analytic philosophy. My main course work for my two years in Alberta, for example, was related to the philosophy of the "later Wittgenstein." For my more focused research I zeroed in on the "philosophy of mind," continuing with that concentration when I moved on to the University of Chicago. During those days, much of the attention in that area of study was on questions concerning human composition: of what, metaphysically, is a human being composed? The agenda for thinking about that topic in Anglo-American analytic philosophy had been pretty much set by Gilbert Ryle's *The Concept of Mind*, where Ryle's rejection of the "Ghost in the Machine" associated with metaphysical dualism was still a dominant reference point for discussions of the philosophical issues about human nature. Ryle himself seemed to espouse at times a fairly straightforward behaviorism, as in his suggestion at one point that we can construe consciousness simply as a set of dispositions to behave in certain ways.[2] I initially pursued the Rylean agenda by reading Wittgenstein, John Wisdom, Norman Malcolm, J. L. Austin, and others who did a lot with "ordinary language" analysis. But I soon moved on to what I saw as a more sophisticated address to the issues focusing on human action and related topics, particularly in the writings of P. F. Strawson, whom I have already mentioned, as well as Stuart Hampshire, Stanley Cavell, Elizabeth Anscombe, and Anthony Kenny.

The discussions of the relationship between "body" and "mind" also have direct connections to the question of "our knowledge of other minds," as raised in the past by René Descartes and the British empiricists, who asked whether, on the basis of observing another person's behavior, we can with reasonable certainty ascertain what is going on in that person's consciousness. And then there is the more radical question that some of them went on to raise: Can we justifiably believe with any degree of certitude, on the basis of what we can directly observe, that there actually *are* other minds?

To be sure, most people would insist that those are the kinds of questions that only a philosopher could take seriously. But to explore the questions is to reflect on some important conceptual issues. My (unpublished) 1971 dissertation, then, had the title *The Identification of Behavior and the Problem of Other Minds*, and I used the discussions of those questions as a springboard for exploring what I still think are interesting questions about human nature.

## "Order" and "Design"

As already mentioned, I had made a vow to myself that I would stay away, as much as possible in my graduate studies, from explicit attention to religious issues, and I have always thought of myself as having been faithful to that vow—except for a seminar, toward the end of my University of Chicago course work, on the ontological argument, taught by Alvin Plantinga, who did a stint in the department as a visiting professor. In thinking about what I would include in this book, I initially decided not to say much about the subject matter that occupied me in my graduate studies.

My memory was that, while the "calisthenics" were important for me to engage in, I really did not come up with much of substance that had any enduring influence on my intellectual life. But then I decided I would actually look at my dissertation, which had sat unopened on my bookshelf for over four decades. I was surprised to see that, while the topic of my dissertation had nothing explicitly to do with any religious topics, in my opening page I began by discussing the argument from design for God's existence, and I ended on the last page with a long quotation from a sermon by Bishop Joseph Butler. So I thought it a good idea to see what I discussed in detail during those first and last pages.

I began my dissertation by observing that quite often the case for a divine designer of the universe has been made by arguing that we can infer from the design we see in the natural world that there must be a divine designer. But this, I argued, is a confused way of proceeding, taking note of a helpful comment made by Philo, one of the characters in David Hume's *Dialogues concerning Natural Religion*. While we do indeed see an impressive degree of orderliness in the universe, Philo contends, the fact of *orderliness* does not establish *design*: "Order, arrangement, or the adjustment of final causes, is not of itself any proof of design."[3] Then later on, Philo— who is clearly speaking for Hume himself—allows that even if one can establish the presence of design, this does not confirm the existence of the kind of designer whose existence theists want to prove.[4]

A parallel distinction can be made, I argued, to the "other minds" discussions. I used a comment by Bertrand Russell to illustrate my point. In explaining the problem of other minds, Russell said that while we often say that we can see another person's anger, we don't actually see the anger; all that we can possibly see is the person's frown—from which we infer that the frown is expressive of a state of anger that is not itself directly observable.[5] My argument was that Russell had already conceded quite a bit, as an empiricist, in taking for granted that we can actually "see" frowns. Just as there is a gap between order and design, there is also a gap between observing physical movements and identifying those movements as *actions*. What we actually see, in the most basic sense, when a person is frowning or smiling, is a configuration resulting from some facial movements. But there have been experiments conducted where people are shown a picture of a person's face exhibiting the kind of configuration associated with smiling and are asked to identify what they see. They all say the person is smiling. But when the larger context of the photo is revealed, it turns out that the person is exhibiting deep anguish. Indeed, sometimes we argue about such things in interpersonal relationships.

> She: Why did you smirk when I told you about that?
> He: I *wasn't* smirking; I was frowning—I was identifying with your concern.
> She: It sure looked like a smirk to me!
> He: Hey, don't tell me what I was doing! You may not like the way I frown, but it was a frown. I know what I was doing!

No photo or video of what was on display on his face will resolve the matter. A frown and a smirk may use the same physical muscular movements. The difference is in what the actor *intends* by those movements.

In the case of the argument from design, once we have gotten to the point of identifying a certain kind of orderliness as design, we have already introduced the reality of some kind of designer. Similarly, when we stipulate that someone frowned or smiled, we have already ascertained something about a person's mental state. To be sure, we still need to acknowledge the possibility of pretense. A person may smile as a way of pretending to be happy or may frown to give the false impression of worry or anger. But to have gotten to those questions is already to be "behind the scenes" of consciousness. If a person is smiling, it is because the person either really is happy or is pretending to be happy. These days I would make my overall case with more attention to the phenomenological movement—a school of philosophical thought that was not very popular in my graduate programs. But in paging through my dissertation, I see that I did not completely ignore the phenomenologists. I quoted Maurice Merleau-Ponty along the way, and I made good use of his description of what is going on when we make an effort, in our very ordinary encounters, to understand another human being. In such an encounter, where we see the other human being as a *person* and not as a mere body, we inevitably commit what Merleau-Ponty describes as an act that "asserts more things than it grasps,"[6] an act whereby we take certain sounds and movements as "an intention, a thought or a project," a state of mind that has detached itself "from the personal subject and become visible outside him in the shape of his body."[7]

## Essentially Communicators

That notion of our bodies as the display areas where we go public with our intentions is, I think, a profound one. And I am impressed now with what I was working toward in making that case, even though much of what I argued in the form of examples about such things as groans and grimaces, smiles and smirks, I now find a bit pedantic. But I was pleasantly surprised in reading through what I wrote over four decades ago by the occasional theological point that I alluded to along the way. In the course of developing—by using some comments of Wittgenstein's—the idea of our purposive behavior as grounded in shared practices, I observed that I was "tempted by an even stronger picture," one that is suggested by "the Genesis account," where the Creator made a mate for Adam because "it is not good for the man to be alone." Maybe this points us, I suggested, to "something more profound than the thought that people enjoy company." Perhaps it is telling us that we are "essentially communicators" (I did the underlining in the original), that we "humans somehow have an 'instinct' for expressing

ourselves, for conveying, for placing feelings in the public arena."
"Instinct" does not quite do it for me now, but when I got to the
final chapter, I saw that it was not satisfactory for me then either.
On the penultimate page of that chapter, I got about as theological
as one could get in a philosophy dissertation at the University of
Chicago. I noted that John Calvin is "known to have asserted that
the true knowledge of one's self presupposes the knowledge of the
'righteousness' of God." For my present purposes, I observed, "it
takes perhaps no 'demythologizing' to see the important teaching here: that the self in its epistemological relations cannot be
properly understood or analyzed without introducing the *moral*
dimension, without considering the essential agency of the self,
an agency which cannot be conceived of apart from a network of
responsibilities and obligations."

Then, after a paragraph of illustrating why the failure to acknowledge that moral network leads to the horrors of concentration camps and ghettos, of napalmings and other "anarchic
gestures of destruction," I ended with this passage from Bishop
Joseph Butler's eighteenth-century sermon "Upon the Social Nature of Man—Rom. xii. 4,5":

> Men are so much one body that in a peculiar manner they feel for
> each other; shame, sudden danger, resentment, honor, prosperity,
> distress; one or another, all of these, from the social nature in
> general, from benevolence, upon the occasion of natural relation,
> acquaintance, protection, dependence—each of these being the
> distinct cements of society. And therefore to have no restraint from,
> no regard to, others in our behavior is the speculative absurdity of
> considering ourselves as single and independent, as having nothing
> in our nature which has respect to our fellow creatures. . . . And
> this is the same absurdity as to suppose a hand or any part to have
> no natural respect to any other or to the whole body.[8]

I still find wisdom in Butler's insistence that "in a peculiar manner" we human beings "feel for each other." We human beings can

understand each other in very basic ways because of our mutual participation in what Wittgenstein saw as shared "forms of life." Our bodies are the arenas for putting our inner lives on display, in accordance with shared meanings that are in turn embedded in shared practices.

But my use of that passage from Butler said something deeper to me as I reread those final pages of my dissertation. I had introduced those closing words from Bishop Butler by saying that the bishop was clearly stating what was for me "the sum of the matter" that I had been pursuing in my dissertation. In reading that, I had a profound sense that my younger self was sending a message to me today. I have often used the calisthenics image in too cavalier a manner in describing my graduate studies in philosophy. I have had a tendency to see those five years as taking a furlough from the kinds of questions that had drawn me to a serious intellectual life in the first place—questions about such things as the antithesis and common grace. But I have come to see something more: although in those years of graduate study I may have done more analytic plodding than I now am inclined to engage in, the plodding was not a detour from the path that has characterized much of the rest of my scholarly pursuits. Rather, it was in its own way a time of slow and careful moving ahead in the search for the common ground that allows for the experiences of a shared humanity.

# 5

## Lessons from the Philosophical "Moderns"

I HAD JUST BEGUN MY GRADUATE STUDIES AT THE UNIVERSITY OF Alberta when the chairman of the philosophy department took me aside at a Saturday-evening social gathering. "One of our instructors who has been teaching one of our sections in Introduction of Philosophy has to drop out. We need you to start teaching the class on Monday." The department offered multiple sections of the course, and the faculty all used a common set of texts, primary writings by key philosophers. I was to pick up my copies of the textbooks first thing Monday morning. In the meantime, he said, "Be ready to give a lecture Monday afternoon on Descartes's *Meditations*." I had not yet read Descartes's *Meditations*. English literature had been my undergraduate major, after which I had attended seminary. I had taken courses where I had read *about* Descartes and had heard references to him in lectures. In explaining his thought to my students in that course, though, I was barely a step ahead of them in my own encounter with what

Descartes actually wrote. The same was true that year of what I taught about the writings of Gottfried Wilhelm Leibniz, John Locke, George Berkeley, David Hume, and Immanuel Kant.

This was an important learning experience for me, and it benefited me greatly. A few years later, when I took my doctoral "prelims" at the University of Chicago, one of the four areas we were tested on—each was a four-hour essay exam—was the history of philosophy. I was one of a small group of about sixty taking the tests who passed all of them that year, and I received special commendation for my performance on the history of philosophy. My best essay, as I remember it, covered the material that I gave in my first lecture in Alberta on Descartes's *Meditations*. Preparing for those class lectures—and others, during my University of Chicago years, for philosophy courses that I taught at the new campus of the University of Illinois near the Loop—was really my main engagement with classical texts during my graduate studies. My actual graduate courses paid only scant attention to the works of the past. We would pick a specific passage from one of the classical thinkers and analyze it without paying much attention to the larger context of the person's thought.

One welcome exception to this pattern was the classes I took from Chicago's Alan Gewirth, all of them in ethics and social-political philosophy. Gewirth was demanding in his treatment of the classical works, and I was especially intrigued by the way he set the agenda for pursuing philosophical issues in social-political thought. He insisted that the three basic questions to ask are these: Why are human beings social at all? Why are we political at all? And what social and political arrangements are best for human beings?[1] Having set up the discussion in these terms, Gewirth laid out what he saw as the two basic options in social-political thought. One was a means-end justification of the social and political bonds—for example, the Hobbesian picture of isolated individuals sacrificing their right to "all and everything" in order to gain a measure of safety and stability. The other was the view, as in G. W. F. Hegel and Karl Marx, that sociality is somehow intrinsic to human nature.

I clearly was inclined toward the idea of an intrinsic sociality and spent a lot of time thinking (as I still do) about what constitutes healthy patterns for arranging and structuring our collective lives. When I discovered after joining the philosophy faculty at Calvin College in 1968 that there was a course on the books with the title "Social and Political Philosophy" but that it had not been taught in recent years, I jumped at the chance to teach it. This was right at the end of the activist 1960s, which had much to do with the fact that the course quickly became highly popular, and I continued to teach it each year until I left for Fuller Seminary in 1985. The more I got into the subject, however, the more I sensed the absence of serious attention to careful scholarly approaches in the evangelical community to basic issues in social-political thought. Much of my own writing in those early decades as a full-time faculty member, then, focused on helping to repair the situation, attending to both philosophical and theological issues.

## Social Contract Insights

In my studies under Gewirth's tutelage at Chicago, I cultivated an enduring interest in Thomas Hobbes, John Locke, and Jean-Jacques Rousseau. That trio is not very well liked in Christian circles, particularly because many Christians lump them together as social contract theorists who did much to move Western political thought in the direction of a thoroughgoing secularism. That understanding of the secularizing function of the views of Hobbes, Locke, and Rousseau is not restricted to the communities who regret their influence in the history of politics. It is also widely held by thinkers who celebrate secularist political views. A case in point is the portrayal of Hobbes in Mark Lilla's *The Stillborn God: Religion, Politics, and the Modern West*, a well-reviewed treatise chosen by the *New York Times* as one of the "100 Notable Books

of 2007." Lilla sees Hobbes as having led the way in the movement
that brought about "the decisive break" with previous political
thought.[2] Hobbes's classic 1651 work *Leviathan*, Lilla insists, "contains the most devastating attack on Christian political theology
ever undertaken and was the means by which later modern thinkers were able to escape from it." Nor was Hobbes's support for
this anti-Christian project inadvertent, says Lilla. His very aim
in writing the *Leviathan*, Lilla states, was "to attack and destroy
the entire tradition of Christian political theology."[3] That view of
Hobbes's project, once described by J. W. N. Watkins as "the orthodox undergraduate view of Hobbes,"[4] is certainly the one that
I was encouraged to adopt by my university mentors. When I was
assigned to teach two sections of an introduction to philosophy
course during my first year of graduate study at the University of
Alberta, I used a set of required texts that had been chosen by a
committee of senior faculty, and Hobbes's *Leviathan* was one of
the assigned books. We younger folks who were just starting out
in teaching philosophy were coached by various faculty members
about how best to exposit those texts. The faculty member who
mentored us on the teaching of Hobbes's thought told us to "skip
all the religious stuff." Hobbes, he said, was an enemy of religion
who nonetheless covered his tracks by using some pious rhetoric
on occasion to throw off his Christian critics. Later, when I dug
more deeply into Hobbes while studying with Gewirth at Chicago,
he too treated Hobbes's religious references as irrelevant to the
understanding of his intentions.

What troubled me at the time was the fact that a deliberate
decision to ignore the content of Hobbes's treatment of theological issues required one to pass over a fairly large segment of
what Hobbes had actually written. Books 3 and 4 of *Leviathan*,
where Hobbes conducts a detailed study of biblical-theological
matters, are roughly equal in length to the much-discussed first two
books. I was gratified to discover, when I later returned to a more
detailed study of Hobbes's thought, that the historian J. G. A.

Pocock directly addressed the ways in which my mentors had encouraged me to ignore the religious references in Hobbes's writings. The prevailing assumption in Hobbes scholarship about the philosopher's extensive treatments of religious questions, Pocock observed, "has traditionally been, first, that they aren't really there, [and] second, that Hobbes didn't really mean them." This poses the intriguing puzzle, says Pocock, of imagining why a notoriously arrogant thinker, vehement in his dislike of "insignificant speech," should have written and afterward defended sixteen chapters of what he held to be nonsense, and exposed them to the scrutiny of a public that did not consider this kind of thing nonsense at all.[5]

Pocock's challenge has special significance for Christians who study political thought. Ought we to view Hobbes as our ally or as our antagonist? If an ally, why is it that his expressed views on matters of religion have been so easily dismissed as not important to his overall perspective by so many of his interpreters? If an antagonist, does this mean that we are justified in simply ignoring his extensive treatment of biblical-theological themes?

My own inclination is to see Hobbes as an ally of sorts for Christian political philosophers. And I can take some comfort from the fact that this assessment is shared by some scholars who have studied Hobbes's thought in great detail. A. P. Martinich, who has written a fine biography of Hobbes, for example, gives detailed attention to the way Hobbes deals with matters of faith. Martinich draws heavily on Hobbes's personal correspondence, as well as citing some works that have not been examined by many previous commentators on Hobbes's thought.[6]

Martinich finds it difficult to doubt Hobbes's sincerity when the philosopher testifies, for example: "I take the sacrament of the Lord's supper to commemorate that Christ's body was broken and his blood shed for my redemption."[7] In noting that Hobbes insists that faith in Christ is essential to salvation, Martinich shows that this was not simply a comment that Hobbes tosses off in passing; having made the point in his 1640 *The Elements of Law*,

Hobbes returns to it frequently, insisting, says Martinich, that the essence of Christianity is the proposition that Jesus is the Christ. The formulas "Jesus is the Messiah," "Jesus is the Son of God," "Jesus is the only begotten son of God," "Jesus is the Holy One of God, the forgiver of sins, and is risen from the dead," and other familiar professions of Christianity are explications of the one, simple truth of Christianity. Hobbes would repeat this view in *Leviathan* and in some of his later polemical treatises.[8] Again, I find this fairly convincing. But even if the issue of Hobbes's actual personal relationship to the faith has to be left open, there are good reasons to call into question the depiction of his role in the widely accepted narrative of the history of political thought. There is certainly some evidence for the plausibility of seeing considerable continuity between Hobbes's outlook and those of several important premodern Christian thinkers.

It is at least important to ask, as I see it, whether Hobbes incorporated—consciously or unconsciously—some significant elements of the Christian past into his philosophical system. Martinich comes down clearly on the side of continuity. "Hobbes's fideism," he says, "is part of a respectable aspect of Reformation Protestantism."[9] Indeed, says Martinich, Hobbes should be seen as a "good English Calvinist"[10]—so much so in fact that "theological concepts, especially those of English Calvinism, are an inextricable part of his philosophy."[11] All of that needs more development and defense than I am going to pursue here. But it is enough to suggest that there are good reasons to look for continuities with earlier Christian political thought in Hobbes's philosophy—and also, I will propose, in Locke and Rousseau as well.

## The Theological Locke

The habit of ignoring Hobbes's extensive reflections on biblical topics extends to the study of Locke also. Students are regularly encouraged to learn about what he wrote in his *Second Treatise of Government* without paying any attention to what he covered in his *First Treatise*. In that earlier work, Locke offers a detailed refutation of the views set forth in Sir Robert Filmer's *Patriarchia* (1680), where Filmer argued in favor of monarchial power exercised by rulers who have inherited their authority from Adam as the primal parent of the human race.[12]

Locke not only found this perspective to be philosophically defective; he also saw it as based on a confused understanding of biblical teaching. He engaged, therefore, in a lengthy discussion of the "dominion" mandate of Genesis 1, the nature and extent of the fall into sin, the difference between parental and political authority, the creational status of women, and the biblical portrayal of the origins of national identities. Nor was all of that—and there is a lot of it in the *First Treatise*—the end of Locke's serious wrestling with biblical materials. One of his last writing projects, to be published after his death, was *A Paraphrase and Notes on the Epistles of St. Paul to the Galatians, Corinthians, Romans, Ephesians*, in which he confesses in his prefatory "Essay for the Understanding of St. Paul's Epistles by Consulting St. Paul Himself" that, while he "had been conversant with these epistles, as well as in other parts of sacred scripture," he now realized that he "understood them not," particularly "the doctrinal and discursive parts of them."[13]

It is especially instructive in this regard that Locke does give particular attention to Romans 13, the New Testament passage that is usually seen as the central text for Paul's understanding of the role of government. We are fortunate that Locke chose to comment on this passage, since it is the one that Christian critics of Locke typically point to in explaining the ways in which they see a stark contrast between biblical thought and the Lockean-type social contract perspective.

Here, for example, is the Calvinist philosopher Gordon Clark, who portrays the contrast in these terms: "The authority of magistrates does not derive from any voluntary social compact, but it derives from God."[14] A very similar way of putting the case was made by Robert Bellah and his associates in their influential 1985 book *Habits of the Heart*. John Locke, they say, was the key figure in setting forth a "radical philosophical defense of individual rights" of a seventeenth-century political perspective "that owed little to either classical or biblical sources." This way of viewing things, the Bellah team argues, "consciously started with the biological individual in a 'state of nature' and derived a social order from the actions of such individuals."[15]

Note that both Clark and the Bellah group employ the *derived from* formulation in describing the Lockean view: the authority inherent in the social and political bonds is *derived from* a contract made by individuals in a state of nature. But this is a view that Locke explicitly rejects in endorsing the Pauline conception as set forth in Romans 13. The apostle, he tells us, is pointing to the fact that God is the source from whom "all magistrates, everywhere, have their authority"; and Paul is also telling us, he says, "for what end they have it, and should use it."[16]

Locke is unambiguous on this point: all political authority comes from God. Paul had it exactly right, he says. But Locke then goes on to observe that there is a further issue that the apostle did not explore. In this Paul is following, he says, "the example of our Saviour, who refused meddling" in questions regarding *who* rightly holds the authority that comes from God alone.[17]

So, while for Locke political authority does come from God alone, the Scriptures are not clear—intentionally so—about where that authority properly resides. This question has to be decided on other grounds. This is exactly the kind of point that John Calvin made in treating the issue of political authority. When the Reformer insists that civil magistrates "have been invested with divine authority, and are wholly God's representatives, in a manner acting as his vicegerents,"[18] he explicitly warns that this does not settle questions about the merits of a specific form of government.

To get clear about those matters, Calvin says, "depends largely upon the circumstances."[19]

Here is the basic point. To insist—as we must—that all political authority comes from God does not yet tell us exactly where that authority "resides" in human collective relations. Or, to put it differently, if all authority comes from God, where does God primarily "deposit" that authority in political arrangements: a single ruler? a parliament? the citizenry? a constitution?

## The "Papacy" Parallel

I have found it illuminating, following the lead of Quentin Skinner in his magisterial study of the relationship between medieval and modern political thought,[20] along with Francis Oakley's detailed examination of the conciliarist tradition in Catholic thought,[21] to see the parallel between theories of political and papal authority. A much-debated question in Catholic discussions of the origins of the authority of the bishop of Rome is this: from where does the pope receive his authority?

One option—which many Protestants naively think is the only one for Catholic thought—is the monarchial one: the pope receives his authority directly from God. Another option is that God deposits that authority directly in the council of bishops, who then delegate that authority to the bishop of Rome—this is the conciliarist view. Yet another view is that authority is directly given to the whole church, as a cohesive body of members, who then delegate it to the bishops, who in turn delegate it to the pope. These views have some parallels in Protestant ecclesiology. A popular view (not an option in Catholic thought) is the "individualist" picture, where the church is seen as based on a bond among individuals who, having come to Christ by their personal decisions, agree to "fellowship" together for agreed-upon purposes. Congregationalist ecclesiology, in contrast, understands the gathered people, as a community, to possess primary authority. In presbyterian polity, a typical view is that ruling elders have a delegated authority, received from the congregation. And an episcopal system will often locate primary authority in a collective "house of bishops."

What is obvious in all of this is that a clear distinction must be made between the *exercise* of authority and the *source* of authority. In the monarchial view of the papacy, God is the source who delegates the right to exercise authority directly to a pope. In the conciliar view, God the source delegates the authority to a council of bishops who in turn delegate it to the bishop of Rome.

The parallels to notions of political authority should be obvious. A monarch is often viewed as getting authority directly from God. But a ruler can also be viewed in "conciliar" terms, where the authority exercised from that office is a delegated authority—from, say, a parliament, or even from the people themselves. And so on. Again, John Calvin was clearly sensitive to these distinctions, as were many of his followers who thought at length about the nature of political authority. The Scottish theologian Samuel Rutherford, for example, laid out the appropriate distinctions with much clarity. In his 1644 treatise, *Lex, Rex*, he argued that while "all Royal power is only in God," the Lord does use "the people as the instrument" for delegating his power. Thus, says Rutherford, "when the people maketh David their King at Hebron, in that very same act, God by the people using their free suffrages and consent maketh David King at Hebron."[22] The people's delegating the authority to David, then, an authority they had received from the Lord, simply *is* the way whereby God delegates authority to David. A very Lockean view of things!

None of this is to suggest that the kind of social contract theory associated with Locke, as well as the Hobbesian version, is entirely friendly to Christian thought. Whatever problems emerge from those ideas for Christians, however, are not with the idea of a social contract as such. When these philosophers talk about the transition from a "state of nature" to the social-political bonds, they mean to be engaging in a kind of philosophical fiction, imaginatively stripping us of our present networks of social relationships and speculating about what it is in our repertoire of pre-social desires and impulses that might reasonably motivate us to take on the obligations of citizenship.

The basic problem is that in so positing a gap between our natural selves and our social selves, social contract theorists often fail to account for an ambiguity in the word "natural" for Christian thought. On the one hand, "natural" can mean what we were *created* to be; thus we can say that it is a part of our basic nature to serve God and neighbor. But we can also think in terms of our *fallen* natures: we are by nature sinful and living out of harmony with God and our fellow human beings. Given these complexities, then, the real issue for Christians in understanding the basic obstacle to social harmony is not how to bridge the gap between our natural pre-social selves and our present lives as social beings. Rather, it is how to bridge the gap between our *sinful* social natures and the sorts of *God-glorifying* social relationships for which we were created. And in understanding this gap, I have received more wisdom from the social contract perspective of Jean-Jacques Rousseau—who is usually thought to pose, among my trio of "moderns," the most dangerous threat to Christian thought.

### A Genevan Accolade for Calvin

Since Rousseau has often been assigned an important villain role in Christian accounts of how things went wrong in the development of modern political thought, a favorable mention of him by a Christian needs special explaining. Not every Christian critic would put the anti-Rousseau case as strongly as Jacques Maritain did in his 1925 book *Three Reformers*, where the French Catholic philosopher identified Rousseau as one of three thinkers—Luther and Descartes were the other two—who "dominate the modern world, and govern all the problems which torment it."[23] But many

Christians would nevertheless include Rousseau in their lists of outstanding enemies of the faith.

I must confess that I have never been very sympathetic to this pattern of Rousseau-bashing. While I am not inclined to reverse the trend by nominating Rousseau for philosophical sainthood, I have always seen him as having some important insights into the fundamental problems that plague us as social-political beings. One pleasant surprise that I received when I first started reading Rousseau was his expressions of admiration for John Calvin. In discussing the role of the ideal legislator in book 2 of his *Social Contract*, Rousseau pays tribute in a footnote to the Protestant Reformer who had dominated public life in the city of Geneva two centuries earlier: "Those who know Calvin only as a theologian are poorly informed regarding the extent of his genius: the drafting of our wise edicts, in which he played a considerable part, does him quite as much honor as the *Institutes*. Until love of fatherland and liberty has been extinguished among us, we shall—whatever changes time may bring about in our religion—go on blessing this great man's memory."[24]

There is no reason to question the sincerity of Rousseau's explicit praise for Calvin's impact on Genevan life. But it does raise the question of what exactly Rousseau saw as the expressions of Calvin's political "genius." I have no decisive answer to that question, but I do think that Rousseau had some general sympathies for Calvin's way of understanding the gap between our depraved natures and the demands of citizenship. At the very least, Rousseau struggled in his thought, much more than Hobbes and Locke did in their systems, with the serious difficulties of moving from the "natural" condition to the benevolence toward others that is necessary for taking on the obligations of citizenship. As I have already observed, Hobbes and Locke assumed that we could imaginatively strip ourselves of our present network of social-political obligations and then ask what it would take for those "pre-social" types to offer a rationale for cooperative citizenship. For Rousseau, what it would take would be a miraculous transformation of the individual. In many familiar passages in *The Social Contract*, he emphasizes the need for a rather dramatic change in our views of both ourselves and our fellow human beings if we are to act out of that collective consciousness that promotes the goals of what he described as the "General Will."

Rousseau is much better at describing the gap, however, than he is in accounting for what it takes to bridge the gap. Usually he seems content simply to acknowledge that an extensive transformation of the way we think and feel must occur if we are to go from the state of nature to civil society. "The transition from the state of nature to the civil state," he remarks, "produces a quite remarkable transformation within—i.e., it substitutes justice for instinct as the controlling factor in [one's] behavior, and confers upon [one's] actions a moral significance that they have hitherto lacked."[25] Again, Rousseau clearly dissented from the more sanguine perspective on the transition from the state of nature to the social bond that we find in the writings of folks like Hobbes and Locke. The gap cannot be bridged simply by appealing to our self-interested calculations, he insisted. Something deeper must occur within the human spirit. And while the gap has to be seen in somewhat different terms from a biblical perspective, Rousseau was certainly correct in insisting on the need for transformative experiences if we are to gain the sort of consciousness that encourages constructive participation in civil society.

### Pursuing the Agenda

In my early days of teaching social-political philosophy at Calvin College, these were the kinds of questions I explored with considerable energy. It was, for me, exciting to be addressing this kind of scholarly agenda in an academic community where I was encouraged to teach and write about these matters with explicit attention to Christian perspectives. In giving that kind of attention to the philosophical topics that greatly interested me, however, I found myself looking more and more for helpful theological resources. Anglo-American evangelicalism did not provide much guidance in this regard. There had been the occasional plea in recent decades for more serious evangelical work on these kinds of issues—Carl Henry's important 1947 jeremiad, *The Uneasy Conscience of Modern Fundamentalism*, was a case in point—but by the end of the 1970s (I started teaching social-political philosophy courses at Calvin in 1969) the pleas had produced very little substantive material.

The next decade, however, was to see the beginning of some serious evangelical explorations of the theological underpinnings of a sustained address to social-political topics in the public arena. The occasion was the emergence of a new manifestation of evangelical social activism, which in turn stimulated new scholarly initiatives in an area of evangelical thought that had been long neglected.

# 6

## Commonalities in the Public Square

W HEN I RETIRED FROM MY TWENTY-YEAR PRESIDENCY AT Fuller Seminary, the community put on a large gala to honor our family. There were many surprises that evening, including one that brought me a little embarrassment, while causing much laughter in others.

Our son had conspired with the planners of the evening to collect old family photos, with many from the 1960s and '70s featuring me, bearded with long, shaggy hair. The pictures, displayed over and over again on a large screen, elicited much good-natured ribbing. One person put it this way: the collection could easily win a "Least Likely to End Up an Evangelical Seminary President" photo contest.

That piece of humor contained much truth. The pictures chronicled a period in my life when I experienced various degrees of alienation from evangelicalism. The estrangement began while living in western Canada, studying on a university campus where there was considerable political activism. At the beginning of my studies there, I checked out an evangelical campus group and was turned off by its fairly strong fundamentalism. So I became active in the more mainline—and very liberal—Student Christian Movement, and through that involvement I also became a leader in the Combined University Campaign for Nuclear Disarmament. This was a time also when the Vietnam War was a major issue of debate, intensified in this context by a more general Canadian resentment of the United States' military power, and I actively opposed the American military campaign in Southeast Asia. During my two years there, I served the United Church of Canada as a weekend supply pastor, which meant that I was almost completely cut off from any active engagement with evangelicalism.

I say "*almost* completely cut off" because I did continue to read *Christianity Today* and other evangelical periodicals, and I frequently returned to books written by Reformed scholars. But my political involvements created a strong sense of distancing from any association with evangelicalism as a movement.

When we moved to the University of Chicago, my focus quickly turned to my draft status. I corresponded at length with the New Jersey office of the Selective Service Commission, arguing that, while I was not a pacifist, I opposed the Vietnam War on just-war grounds. They were not impressed with my arguments, and it was only when we discovered that Phyllis was three months pregnant—a situation that automatically removed me from eligibility for being drafted—that those negotiations came to an end. I did stay active, though, attending meetings of New Left groups on campus and even participating in antiwar sit-ins.

I struggled with all of this, both spiritually and theologically. My experience with the Student Christian Movement and the United Church of Canada convinced me that I could not embrace liberal theology. I learned much from some excellent Vatican documents on social justice, but I was not drawn to Catholic theology or worship. My reconnection to evangelicalism was facilitated largely by discovering the *Reformed Journal*, a monthly periodical that

I was later to become intimately involved with, and through that
the Kuyperian tradition of social engagement. I already knew
Kuyper's theological thought, of course. But the writers I discovered in the *Reformed Journal*—Lewis Smedes, Nicholas Wolterstorff, Henry Stob, and others—opened up a new world of thought
for me, and my commitment to that world was solidified by my
reading, while at Chicago, Kuyper's Stone Lectures, delivered at
Princeton Seminary in 1898. Kuyper was a political activist par
excellence—shortly after delivering the Stone Lectures he would
serve for a few years as prime minister of the Netherlands—and
he grounded this activism in a deep commitment to Jesus Christ
as Savior and Lord.

## A New Activism

In 1971 Jim Wallis and a few of his fellow students at Trinity
Evangelical Divinity School visited the Calvin College campus,
where I was now on the faculty. They brought with them copies of
their new magazine, the *Post-American*, whose title communicated
the idea that, while others were talking about a post-Christian
America, some younger evangelicals were committed to a post-
American Christianity.

The vision Jim articulated was an exciting one for me. He also
had gone through much of the 1960s alienated from evangelicalism because of its failure to take up the pressing social issues of
the day. When, a few years later, the magazine changed its name
to *Sojourners*, I agreed to serve on the editorial board. This was
one of several magazines that appeared around that time in which
younger evangelicals, who had found one another after the spiritual
loneliness of the 1960s, began to speak out regarding questions
of social-political discipleship. When Paul Henry, the political-
scientist son of Carl F. H. Henry, joined the Calvin faculty, several
of us addressed the need for some scholarly discussions of these
matters, resulting in the first Calvin Conference on Christianity

and Politics in the spring of 1973. Out of that gathering came the plan for convening the group that published the 1973 Chicago Declaration of Evangelical Social Concern.

Several older evangelical leaders were present at the Chicago gathering, including Carl Henry. They gave their blessing to the declaration, even though many of us had the clear impression that Henry in particular was not altogether happy with everything the document affirmed—a fact confirmed by his reflections on the declaration in his autobiographical *Confessions of a Theologian*, published in 1986.[1] But the willingness of folks like Henry, Vernon Grounds, Frank Gabelein, and other senior statesmen in the evangelical movement to show support for this new activism meant much to many of us. And the national attention given to our declaration by the secular media was an added piece of encouragement.

### Theological Fragmenting

In retrospect, it is clear that the Chicago gathering was really the last time that many of us who were present could agree on a document of that sort. We would soon be engaging in serious debates among ourselves about matters of theology. Up to that point it had been encouraging simply to join with other evangelicals in letting it be known that from here on at least some evangelicals were going to be addressing structural-systemic societal issues.

It soon became clear to some of us, however, that being "activist" was not enough. We needed the kind of spiritual-ethical discernment that could come only from a more substantive theological grounding. And this is where we began to move in separate directions after that Chicago gathering. Some—influenced by John Howard Yoder's seminal 1972 book, *The Politics of Jesus*—looked to the Anabaptist tradition. Others worked at recovering relevant themes from the Wesleyan past. For some, the witness of Dietrich Bonhoeffer held promise for looking to Lutheran resources. Others of us found our inspiration in Calvinism, particularly as it was developed by Abraham Kuyper.

For my part, I took it as an important assignment to pursue with great diligence a dialogue with representatives of the Anabaptist perspective, particularly with John Howard Yoder. The issues that Yoder and I debated, both in print and in a number of public settings, went deeper than our obvious disagreement about pacifism versus just-war theory. Yoder once declared at one of the Calvin College conferences that when Jesus rejected Satan's offer of the nations of the earth if only Jesus would bow before him, the Savior was resisting the temptation to be a Calvinist! That assessment was Yoder's way—admittedly, not a very nice one—of pointing to important differences between the Reformed and the Anabaptist traditions regarding the permissibility of Christian participation in civil government as such. Yoder was calling for a Christian activism that stood over against the political-social-economic status quo. And the fact that he grounded this kind of active engagement in a strong "following Jesus" ethical emphasis was (and still is!) attractive to many evangelicals who were looking for a pattern of "radical discipleship" centered on a strong commitment to the person of Jesus Christ.

The passion that characterized these post–Chicago Declaration intra-evangelical debates demonstrated for many of us that it is not enough simply to pledge to work together as evangelical activists who focus primarily on a set of consensus convictions about issues in moral theology. Yes, there is much in liberal Protestantism and Roman Catholicism that desperately needs correctives grounded in our shared evangelical convictions. And yes, there is much in the "uneasy conscience" of our collective evangelical past that we can also work together to correct. But the more we look to the diverse theological-confessional traditions for much-needed wisdom for present societal challenges and opportunities, the more we will find ourselves arguing with one another about matters that have always loomed large in theological discussion. In an important sense, our talk as evangelicals about our shared commitment to "the historic Christian faith" masks the realities of what is more accurately thought of as the historic Christian *faiths*.

## The Biblical Drama

In 1974 I was invited to deliver some lectures at Regent College in Vancouver on the relationship between theology and social-political concerns. The inviters asked that I offer a clear case for my Reformed differences with the Anabaptist perspective, which was getting considerable attention in evangelical circles at the time. I worked hard on those lectures—they would become my *Politics and the Biblical Drama* (1976). I began my writing for the lectures by sketching out what I decided to call "the biblical drama," using Herman Dooyeweerd's schema of creation-fall-redemption as the three "acts" of the drama. But I soon decided that there needed to be a fourth act: eschaton. A clear distinction needs to be made, I became convinced, between the kind of renewal that is taking place under present sinful conditions and what we can gather from biblical revelation about what the new creation will be like. I followed Abraham Kuyper's proposal that if the fall had not occurred and if human beings had nonetheless done what is necessary to "be fruitful and multiply," eventually, given the development of large communities of human beings, some kind of political ordering would have been necessary. Take the traffic laws that require us to respect stop signs, traffic lights, separate lanes, and the like. Some people need those laws because they are hostile or reckless drivers. But most of us need them simply because we know that these regulations promote ordered expectations. A hundred drivers on the same highway, even if they were totally sanctified, cleansed of any sinful impulses, would still need to know how to avoid accidents. Unless they all communicated by the spiritual equivalent of extrasensory perception, they would have to make their way with agreed-upon guidelines. In a fallen world, governments need to enforce penalties to guarantee the good order of society. But even without the curse of sin, the regulation of our complex social interactions is a necessary feature of our collective lives. What the reality of sin introduces into our lives, then, is not the need for government as such but for a government that wields "the sword" of Romans 13—the threat of coercive measures that enables government to expedite its God-ordained task of rewarding those who do good and punishing those who do evil.

Having made that case, I went on to comment on how sin had introduced rebellion and unbelief, not only in the turning of our personal wills against the Creator, but also in the systemic dimensions of our collectives. This has profound implications, I argued, for our understanding of Christ's redemptive mission. Jesus came into the world to save sinners, and also to initiate a new program of renewal that touches all areas of our lives. He is Savior, and also Lord and King.

For my discussion of the eschaton, I made much of Revelation 21:24–26: "The nations will walk by its light, and the kings of the earth will bring their glory into it. Its gates will never be shut by day—and there will be no night there. People will bring into it the glory and the honor of the nations." In some mysterious way, I proposed, the political authority that belonged to Jesus all along, but has been so abused and misdirected for much of human history, is going to be acknowledged as his in the end-time: "So that at the name of Jesus every knee should bend, in heaven and on earth and under the earth, and every tongue should confess that Jesus Christ is Lord, to the glory of God the Father" (Phil. 2:10–11).

In working out what I saw as the implications of the "glory and honor of the nations" passage in Revelation, I was convinced I was developing a new line of thought that I had not come across elsewhere. When I gave that lecture at Regent College, a local Christian Reformed minister, trained in the Netherlands, attended. He came up after I had spoken to thank me for my lecture. "It was good to hear someone using Kuyper's interpretation of Revelation," he said. I was both surprised and gratified by his commendation. A year later, as I expanded my lectures into *Politics and the Biblical Drama*, I checked out Kuyper's commentary on the book of Revelation (I had not known he had written on the subject), and sure enough, my thoughts on the subject had been—as the Dutch would put it—*in de lijn van Kuyper* ("in the line of Kuyper").

## Engaging "the Powers"

One discussion that I added to my Regent lectures in preparing *Politics and the Biblical Drama* was a chapter on the Pauline "principalities and powers." This topic was central to the overall case made by John Howard Yoder in his *Politics of Jesus*, and for many evangelicals influenced by Yoder, this was their basic introduction to the topic.[2] Yoder made much of the cross as Christ's encounter with the powers, the personal angelic-type forces who oppose God's creating and redeeming purposes. These powers, who exert their influence on the structural-systemic patterns of collective life, used the visible authorities of the day—religious, economic, political, military—to crucify Jesus. The powers operate by coercion, and they lure human beings into their manipulative, often overtly violent designs. Jesus refused to accept their ways of "making things happen." Instead, he "accepted powerlessness," allowing them to do all they could by their violent means to attempt to destroy him. In emerging from the tomb on Easter morning, he made it clear that "accepting powerlessness" is the key to victorious redemption and renewal. As disciples of Jesus, then, we are called to live our lives, not by using coercion to influence events, but by seeing our lives as the effects of the cross. The fate of the powers was scaled by the victory of the cross. Our calling is to imitate Jesus in his willingness to suffer rather than to follow the ways of the powers.

I found—and still find—much of Yoder's approach illuminating and helpful. My dissent, as I expressed it in my book, had to do mainly with the implications of Christ's encounter with the powers for our patterns of discipleship. Significantly, in his exposition of the theology of the powers, Yoder made good use of a little book by the Dutch theologian Hendrikus Berkhof, *Christ and the Powers*, which Yoder himself had translated into English. In his own presentation of the implications of what Christ accomplished, Berkhof goes in a somewhat different direction than Yoder did. Because Christ conquered the powers, says Berkhof, they have now been "neutralized"—which means that we can reenter their territory "and follow God's call unhampered by external hindrances."[3]

Yoder likewise encouraged a reentry of sorts, but it was for him still a movement into hostile territory. The defeat of the powers had been sealed in the cross and resurrection, but for the present time the powers continue to goad us into adopting their coercive manner of operation. So we still must see our Christian involvement in public life as characterized by an over-against-ness. To be sure, Yoder saw himself as encouraging a new kind of political engagement. He meant to be updating the traditional Anabaptist ethic. Like Joseph, Daniel, and Mordecai, he argued, we can serve in the court of a pagan king. But it must never be done in a manner that makes us agents of the existing political systems. Like those ancient servants of the Lord, we must see our task as actively "witnessing to those in authority."[4]

Again, I considered all of that to be profoundly interesting and insightful. But in the end I concluded that we were still left with the older differences between an Anabaptist and a Reformed perspective. John Calvin saw political leadership as a very high calling. And Kuyper, in his years in Parliament and in the office of prime minister, certainly saw himself as working "within the system."

Because I meant my criticisms of Yoder as a means of inviting more dialogue between us, I was deeply disappointed with his initial response. He wrote me a letter detailing a few responses—very probing ones—but then added a personal complaint: he wished, he said, that I would stop trying to build my own reputation by criticizing him. Fortunately, though, his further actions took on a different character. I was invited, for example, to join a group of Anabaptist scholars for a conference devoted to discussing various aspects of *The Politics of Jesus*—biblical, ethical, political, and the like. At the end of the conference, Yoder was asked to respond, and in the middle of some rather grumpy comments, he said that he found it ironic that I understood what he was about better than many of his fellow Mennonites did.

Subsequently, he and I engaged in several public dialogues, where our discussions gradually expanded into more general topics of "Christ and culture." On one of these occasions, he provided me with a line that I have quoted many times in explaining the fundamental issue at stake between Reformed and Anabaptist theologies of culture. When an audience member asked Yoder if he could put in simple terms what he saw as the basic issue of disagreement between his views and mine, he answered: "Mouw wants to say, 'Fallen, but *created*,' and I want to say, 'Created, but *fallen*.'" Eventually, I would write a book elaborating on my own conviction that there is still much of God's good creation, as it was originally designed, that we can discern in the midst of fallenness. The book's title captures the gist of my arguments on this score: *He Shines in All That's Fair*. Yoder was less sanguine than I have been about our ability to see this "shining." He liked to argue that as an Anabaptist he took the noetic effects of the fall more seriously than Calvinists—in spite of our Reformed lip service to the doctrine of total depravity. In that regard, his criticisms of my Kuyperian endorsement of common grace are not far removed from charges lodged against that perspective within the Reformed community, as informed by a stronger emphasis on the antithesis than shows up in Kuyperianism. I take those concerns with utmost seriousness—to the point that I continue to worry a bit about my heavy reliance on commonness. I will come back to this concern later. Suffice it to say here that it has never led me to give up the quest for common ground, in the political sphere as in other areas of cultural life.

## Beyond Imitation

Another key disagreement I have had with Yoder's overall approach has to do with his portrayal of what was accomplished on the cross. In highlighting Calvary as an encounter with the powers, Yoder was emphasizing the ways we as Christians should follow Jesus in his resistance to the coercion-violence patterns associated with the general reality of fallenness. His "imitation of Christ" ethic was a clear advance over the "be like Jesus" teachings often associated with liberal theology. But if disconnected from other important aspects of the atoning work of Christ, it can end up as yet another reductionism.

To put it simply, while there is much that we must imitate in being faithful to the witness of Christ on Calvary—forgiving enemies, refusing to resort to unjust means of retaliation, and the like—there is also much in the death of Christ that we ought not to even try to imitate. On the cross, Jesus did something for us that we could never do for ourselves. He paid the debt for our sin and guilt. Because he suffered the most extreme penalty for sin, we do not have to endure that suffering. In this sense, the way of Jesus is *in*imitable, incapable of being imitated by the likes of us.

I make something of this for two reasons. The first is simply for the sake of orthodoxy. It is important to pay attention to various theories of the atonement, including the moral example theory, of which Yoder's is a very sophisticated version. But none of this should ever detract from a central emphasis on the once-for-all transaction that has traditionally been associated with the motifs of substitution, payment, and sacrifice. The second reason relates directly to the encounter with the powers. If Jesus in his suffering accomplished that which is unique and inimitable, so that we do not have to die for our own sins, it makes sense also to see his encounter with the powers as having a once-for-all character. Just as Jesus accomplished *the* encounter with sin and death, so he also brought about *the* encounter with the powers. We no longer have to fear death as he did in Gethsemane, and we no longer have to avoid those territories where the powers continue to lurk. Jesus has given new access to those regions in our efforts to promote the cause of righteousness.

## Cultural Discipleship

My differences with the Anabaptists have not been confined to questions of politics. They are grounded in more general disagreements about the theology of culture as such. I read H. Richard Niebuhr's 1951 *Christ and Culture* as an undergraduate.[5] I don't remember being overly enthusiastic about Niebuhr's case at the time, but his categories certainly stayed with me: Christ against culture, the Christ of culture, Christ above culture, Christ and culture in paradox, and Christ the transformer of culture.

Niebuhr's book has not exactly fallen off the sales charts in recent years, but there has been some slippage from its former status as the book that set the framework for discussions of Christian cultural involvement. Some of the slippage has to do with a shift of focus from the general to the particular: instead of spending much time on the notion of culture in general, contemporary explorations of religion and culture are more likely to concentrate on specific areas of cultural expression—film, popular fiction, hip-hop, politics, gender, and the like. Furthermore, to the degree that there *is* a continuing Christian scholarly interest in very general questions about culture, the focus has in large part shifted away from culture as a generic phenomenon to a more nuanced exploration of intercultural and cross-cultural concerns—we are more likely these days to talk about Christ and *the cultures* than we are to focus on God's concern for culture in general.

The fading influence of Niebuhr's discussion of the Christ-and-culture options cannot be attributed, however, simply to shifting foci. Niebuhr's book has also been subject to sustained critique during the past two decades by some scholars who do not see his past influence in wholly positive terms. In his recent exploration of Christ-and-culture topics from an evangelical perspective, for example, D. A. Carson—who expresses some appreciation for Niebuhr's typology—has helpfully pointed to places in Niebuhr's discussion where the argument tends to undermine historic orthodoxy, especially on the important issue of the unity of revealed truth in the Scriptures.[6]

Others, however, have insisted that the whole Niebuhrian project is a dangerous one. Most prominent in this group is John Howard Yoder himself, who argued that Niebuhr stacks the deck in favor of the transformationalist perspective, and in such a way that Niebuhr implicitly endorses certain culturally dominant values, ones that Yoder and others in the Anabaptist tradition see as inimical to faithful Christian discipleship. Here, for example, is one of several endorsements that appear on the cover of a book that sets forth a detailed critique of Niebuhr's overall scheme: "H. Richard Niebuhr's days are numbered," writes Mark Nation, a Mennonite ethicist. "Or so one can only imagine. This carefully argued and well-written book should bring the curtains down on the more than fifty-year reign of Niebuhr's typology in *Christ and Culture*."[7]

I still like Niebuhr's book. While I have my own criticisms of the way Niebuhr makes his case at several points, I think that his overall presentation of the issues of Christ and culture is a helpful one. Not only do his basic categories capture with rough accuracy the general tendencies among Christians in their relationship with their surrounding culture, but some modest version of his Christ-transforming-culture perspective—the one that he obviously endorses—is, I am convinced, the right way to view things.

One common way in which the anti-Niebuhrians make their case is by accusing Niebuhr of being entrenched in a "Christendom" understanding of the cultural place of Christians. My own inclination is to treat this kind of labeling with some suspicion. Terms such as "postmodern," "post-Enlightenment," and "post-Christendom" are used so frequently these days that they are sometimes treated as if they require little explanation. While there are important developments that are highlighted by the use of these labels, there is also a danger that they can become rhetorical tools that mask some important distinctions and nuances. This is certainly the case with "post-Christendom," a label that is frequently used interchangeably with "post-Constantinian," pointing to the serious drawbacks for the witness of the church that occurred when Emperor Constantine, having converted to Christianity, aligned the church so closely with political power that Christian identity and citizenship in the empire were virtually indistinguishable. I certainly don't want to defend all that has been associated with Christendom. At its best, the critique of Constantinian patterns has been associated with an exciting new "missional church" motif in present-day ecclesiology. The theologian who has inspired much that is associated with this theological perspective is the late Lesslie Newbigin, who served for many years as a missionary in India. When Newbigin returned to the British Isles after his retirement, he was shocked by the major cultural changes that had taken place there, as well as on the European continent and in North America. When he began his career, he had seen himself as being sent out from a Christian culture to a mission field. But now his own homeland was a mission field. Christians in the West, Newbigin observed, could no longer take a dominant Christian influence for granted. We are now "post-Christendom," and the church today—wherever the church is called to serve the Lord—must see itself as a missionary church.[8] This is an insightful analysis, and it should not surprise us that a book like Niebuhr's *Christ and Culture*, written over a half century ago, would see the actual contours of the larger culture quite differently than we do today. Niebuhr was a

representative of an older form of liberal American Protestantism that prospered at a time when the liberal churches thought
of themselves as "mainline," and even as constituting something
like a Christian "establishment" in their cultural contexts. Today
things have moved in a very different direction.

I have no problem, then, with critics who say that we have to
revise Niebuhr here and there if we are going to have a useful understanding of Christ and culture in our post-Christendom context.
I do worry, though, about what some of these critics identify as
the features of Christendom that they insist on rejecting, such
as employing military strategies to achieve certain social goals.
Now, there is nothing new about Christian disagreements on these
matters. The question of what it means for a Christian to be a
citizen of a nation, and the question of the moral legitimacy of
the use of violence—these were the subjects of passionate debates,
especially between Calvinists and Anabaptists, at the time of the
Reformation, and the debates have continued to our present day.
The Anabaptist perspective has been given new life in recent years,
particularly because of Stanley Hauerwas, whose writings have
had considerable influence both among evangelicals, who are attracted to the strong Christocentric themes in his perspective, and
in the broader Christian community, where many are disillusioned
with liberal theology.

## The Way of the Cross

In his fascinating study of the virtue theories developed by French
women thinkers in the last half of the seventeenth century, the
Jesuit philosopher John J. Conley observes that whatever their
particular ecclesial-confessional affiliation, these women emphasized the radical "specificity of Christian ethics." Conley offers
examples of their condemnation of those "vain virtues" that are
attractive to "a corrupt human nature," expositing their view that
Christian ethics should take "Christ's act of redemption" as its

starting point, in contrast to the notion that the Christian under-standing of the moral life should "be understood as an expansion or a deepening of a generic moral project."[9]

The views of the women in Conley's account comport nicely with Hauerwas's insistence that the way of Jesus is the exclusive normative reference point for the moral life.[10] Their emphasis on "our corrupt nature" suggests that since our fallenness has limited, perhaps even obliterated, our cognitive access to any divine ordi-nances that might have been discernible in the original creation, our only option is to create communities that follow the way of Jesus as set forth in the Sermon on the Mount and as displayed in his own radical willingness to take up the cross. In this kind of ethic, the only available revealed guidance for living the good life is to be found in our moral exemplar, Jesus of Nazareth. In becoming his disciples, and by immersing ourselves in the prac-tices of Christian community, we can cultivate the virtues that he displayed in his earthly ministry. And what Hauerwas makes clear in his account of the kind of community we are called to be is that our life together must embody economic, political, and social norms that are so antithetical to the patterns of collective life in the larger human culture that Christians are required, in effect, to create an alternative culture. Thus the Anabaptist-type call for the formation of a kingdom community living in separation from the practices of the larger human community, especially those practices that are closely aligned with the political assumptions of secular thought.

I'll say it again here: this is a powerful perspective from which I have learned much. It certainly exposes the confusions that can re-sult from a simpleminded application of Niebuhr's categories. One might be inclined, for example, to treat the Amish as a clear case of Christ-against-culture convictions. But Hauerwas's perspective suggests that the Amish might better be thought of as creating an *alternative* culture. They certainly do not reject farming—rather, they transform the typical patterns of farming. Nor do they reject technology as such, insisting instead on alternative technologies: the horse-drawn buggy is as much a piece of transportation technology as an SUV!

Furthermore, the present-day Anabaptists and their fellow pilgrims are right to call us to account for the ways we often identify Christian discipleship with specific political programs and ideologies. The church's record in aligning itself with political power, and in freely giving its blessing to various military campaigns, is not a noble one. For all of that, though, I am not ready to concede that the solution for Christian disciples is to abandon all efforts to employ the political means available to us as citizens to pursue Christian goals. Nor am I convinced that a thoroughgoing pacifism is mandated for Christian disciples. I will not argue these matters here, but I can at least point again to the witness of Lesslie Newbigin, whose influential call for a post-Christendom Christian witness in the West did not lead him simply to reject everything associated with the Constantinian arrangement. "Much has been written," he observes, "about the harm done to the cause of the gospel when Constantine accepted baptism, and it is not difficult to expatiate on this theme. But could any other choice have been made?" The Constantinian arrangement emerged, Newbigin argues, in a time of spiritual crisis in the larger culture, and people "turned to the church as the one society that could hold a disintegrating world together." What should the church have said in response? asks Newbigin. Should it simply "have refused the appeal and washed its hands of responsibility for the political order"? This is not to ignore the ways in which Christians "fell into the temptation of worldly power," he quickly adds. But do we really think that the cause of the gospel would have been better served "if the church had refused all political responsibility, if there had never been a 'Christian' Europe"? Newbigin's own answer: "I find it hard to think so."[11]

I agree with Newbigin, and I am convinced that his historical observation applies nicely to our own cultural situation. We live in a time of cultural crisis, and our obligation is to reflect carefully on how we can contribute to at least partial and temporary remedies for the ills that plague us. The prophet Jeremiah's counsel to the ancient people of Israel applies to us as well. When the Israelites found themselves newly exiled as "resident aliens" in the city of Babylon, he brought God's message to them that they must "seek the welfare of the city where I have sent you into exile, and pray to the LORD on its behalf, for in its welfare you will find your welfare" (Jer. 29:7).

To be sure, my Anabaptist friends would have a stern rebuke for me at this point. We don't begin, they would argue, by finding ways to improve things in the larger culture. To be obedient disciples is to worry not about effective actions but about faithful patterns of life. In a much-quoted phrase, Stanley Hauerwas says that the church does not *have* a social ethic; it *is* a social ethic. The primary Christian ethical task is for believers to "*be* a particular kind of people" so that both "we and the world [can] hear the [Christian] story truthfully."[12]

There is something to be said for Hauerwas's emphasis on "being" rather than "having." But it is also problematic. What is going on in this placement of "being" an ethic over against "having" an ethic? A church is called by God to "be" many things, and they cannot all be simply reduced to a social ethic. The church carries the memories of theological developments in its past. It evangelizes, catechizes, counsels, communicates with other churches, and much more—and most of this cannot simply be shaped by a social ethic that a particular church "is." Furthermore, while what Hauerwas wants the church to "be" is a countercultural community that consistently stands over against the political status quo, I am not prepared to give up on striving for effective political action in the world—in the standard worldly sense of "political." Indeed, I think that one of the reasons why Lesslie Newbigin could offer a somewhat different assessment of Constantinianism than we find in the Anabaptist critics is precisely his identification with the situations of Christians in the two-thirds world—contexts in which positive political striving is often necessary for the health of Christian communities and the larger culture in which they are called to serve the Lord.

A few years ago, while visiting in mainland China with a small group of Fuller Seminary faculty members, we engaged in a dinner discussion one evening with members of a provincial government's office for regulating religious affairs. When they discovered that two members of our group were psychologists, the government officials—all of them members of the Communist Party—began to share some candid concerns about trends in urban centers. While the introduction of a free-market system was beneficial in many ways, they observed, there were also some negative trends occurring: a rising divorce rate, increasing intergenerational conflict in families, and a rise in the number of suicides. "We are not equipped to provide the necessary mental health services," they told us. They went on to express the desire to have the church offer this sort of outreach—"but the churches are not equipped to do it either," they said. They wondered whether Fuller Seminary could provide the training of faith-based marriage and family counseling in China. Fuller took up the cause with much energy. Given the political realities of China, there is no way that this kind of service can occur without Christians closely aligning themselves with government regulations and policies. Is cooperating with the political powers in this case a "Constantinian" arrangement? If it is, my inclination is to say, "So be it." And as Christians in places like China seek theological guidance for their cooperative efforts in a larger culture shaped by non-Christian ideologies, the more basic theological issues of Christ and culture loom large. What norms should guide us in these cooperative activities? How do we view the continuities and discontinuities between Christian thought and non-Christian worldviews? What do we have in common with other human beings, apart from whether they share our most basic convictions?

## "Thick" and "Thin"

When in 2001 I was preparing an updated edition of my 1983 book *When the Kings Come Marching In*, I resisted the temptation to inject some criticisms of Stanley Hauerwas's views. The temptation came at the point when I read what I had written in the earlier version about human rights. Having referred to "the venerable tradition of appealing to 'creation' as a basis for treating every person as free and equal," I had observed that while this way of viewing things was not "completely misguided," I considered it nonetheless to be "an inadequate basis for opposing patterns of discrimination." Appealing to creation as a basis for equal justice is legitimate, I had written, but we must also view human equality "in the light of redemption."[13] I was glad to see, in rereading what I had written almost two decades earlier, that I had quickly gone on to reassure my readers that I was not in any way meaning to detract from the importance of working for justice for all human beings. But "at the very least," I said, "Christians should actively work to abolish patterns of racial and ethnic discrimination *within* the Christian community."[14]

While I did not give in to the temptation to criticize Hauerwas at that point, I was still a little nervous about the decision to let the 1983 version stand without saying more. I had become increasingly concerned about the influence among evangelicals of Hauerwas's insistence that Christian ethics must be grounded in the practices of a highly particularized Christian community whose moral discourse is radically discontinuous with that of the larger culture. The title of one of Hauerwas's books expresses the spirit of his views on this matter: *After Christendom? How the Church Is to Behave if Freedom, Justice, and a Christian Nation Are Bad Ideas*. While in that book Hauerwas obviously does not reject the idea of justice as such, he does worry that the presumption of an available common moral discourse signals that we have negotiated an unfaithful compromise with the fallen order.[15] But in *Resident Aliens* Hauerwas and coauthor William Willimon put the case in bolder terms. Can we really assume, they ask, that terms like "justice" and "peace" have core meanings that are understandable from a variety of worldview perspectives? How can Christians give meaning to such terms "apart from the life and death of Jesus of Nazareth"? It is only the biblical narrative regarding Jesus's mission that "gives content to our faith, judges any institutional embodiment of our faith, and teaches us to be suspicious of any political slogan that does not need God to make itself credible."[16]

My own sympathies are much closer to those of Max Stackhouse, who has defended a common public discourse by arguing that from a Christian perspective "human life has, at its root, a very profound *logos*, rooted in *theos*, that makes it possible for Jews, Christians, Hindus, Muslims and humanists to talk reasonably with one another and to live together in a society governed by a modicum of justice. Further, we can, in some measure, talk across boundaries and more or less discern what is valid and not valid in what others say. And we expect others to understand us and to challenge us when we do not make sense."[17]

The question I struggled with while revising *When the Kings Come Marching In* was how, given the fact that I fully endorsed the Stackhouse-type view about a shared public discourse, I could still say that a Christian understanding of public justice is "inadequate" without also looking at the issues "in the light of redemption." I am still inclined to stick with what I said in my book, but I do find it in need of some nuance.

Suppose, for example, I am engaged in a discussion with a Muslim and a secular liberal about a key question concerning the rights of undocumented immigrants in the United States. After considerable back-and-forth, we agree on a policy of immigration reform that advances the cause of justice. Our policy statement contains no explicitly theological language. We simply affirm what we agree to be a way of treating undocumented immigrant families that is fair, respectful, and compassionate.

Given what I have said about the importance of seeing these things "in the light of redemption," would I have to see what was accomplished in this joint declaration as legitimate but still "inadequate"? I think not. I would be happy to accept this statement of public policy as an accomplishment made possible by a careful exploration by persons who, in spite of serious worldview differences, possess a shared sense of justice grounded in a common createdness.

Where the "more" of redemption would come in, though, would be in my efforts to persuade many of my fellow Christians of the policy's justness. Suppose, for example, a fellow believer simply rejects any favorable depiction of the plight of undocumented immigrants by insisting that "they should go back to where they belong." Such a person may not disagree with me when I say that the immigrants in question are bearers of the divine image and that their Creator wants them to flourish as human beings whom he fashioned in love. "Fine!" my fellow believer responds. "I am all in favor of their flourishing as human beings—but not as people who have come to our country illegally. Let them flourish by going back to wherever they came from!"

At that point there is much to talk about in the "thick" language of biblical revelation. We can discuss God's call to his ancient people to offer hospitality to the "stranger in the land." Even more directly, we can reflect on God's reminder to the people of Israel that they had been strangers to him when he heard their cries for deliverance—a theme echoed in the New Testament's reminders that God reached out in love to us when "we were yet sinners" (Rom. 5:8).

To be sure, there is much complicated subject matter here, and no single appeal to biblical revelation will resolve all the issues. But within the Christian community we have a more complex theological narrative to draw upon in discussing issues of justice than what is possible when we are operating with the "thinness" of a shared public discourse in the larger human conversation.

The Lutheran theologian Ronald Thiemann rightly saw the opportunity for this "thick" intra-Christian conversation to be a
strength in dealing with the issues of public life when he argued
that local congregations should function as "'schools of public
virtue,' communities that seek to form the kind of character necessary for public life."[18]

The kind of pedagogy required for this was illustrated nicely for
me by a story told to me by a journalist who attended the Sunday
school class that Jimmy Carter taught in his local Baptist church
in Georgia. It was the Sunday morning after Carter had been
nominated for the presidency at the 1980 Democratic National
Convention, and the topic of the day was the acceptance speech
that Mr. Carter had given at the convention. The candidate took
the class through the main points of his speech, drawing connections to biblical themes. When he had talked about foreign
policy, he said to the class, he had in mind what Jesus said about
peacemaking. When he discussed poverty, he was informed by the
Old Testament prophets. And so on.

I don't know that I would have agreed with everything Carter
taught in that class, but what he did is for me an excellent example of a kind of *catechesis* for public engagement. Carter related
"thick" to "thin" by showing how a public address on policy matters can employ the language of a broad-ranging public discourse
while being able to link each key point to concrete biblical teaching.
It illustrates for me a workable principle: think "thick" within the
Christian community and then speak "thin" in the public arena.

# 7

## Preaching Civility

In MY FIRST BOOK, *POLITICAL EVANGELISM*, PUBLISHED IN 1973, I made a sustained case for a more activist evangelicalism, and I still agree with just about everything I said in that book. What those of us who were calling for an evangelical public activism in those days did not anticipate was the ways in which an aggressive activism took shape, especially in the 1980s, when evangelicals who had spent a half century thinking of themselves as a marginalized cognitive minority suddenly emerged as a bold "moral majority." For those folks, no attention was paid to the arguments between Anabaptists and a nuanced Reformed perspective. The shift to activism happened without much theological reflection.

There have been times, then, in recent decades, when I have wished I could be in a position to call the whole thing off, urging the evangelical community to return to its earlier posture of politically passive otherworldliness. But in my calmer moments I also know that there should be no turning back. Instead, the need is to move forward to a more mature understanding of the patterns of public engagement. And this includes the quest, I have come to see, for a new level of *spiritual* maturity. I have experienced a shift in my own focus, as an evangelical who cares about public involvement, from urging evangelicals simply to get involved in public life to encouraging them to work at exercising that involvement in the right *spirit*. This led, for me, to a sustained emphasis on the concept of civility in public life.

## Convicted Civility

I regularly get introduced to audiences as someone known for promoting the idea of convicted civility. I always feel obligated to make it clear that I did not invent that phrase. As I reported earlier, I came across it in a little book by Martin Marty, and the phrase "took" with me—so much so that I eventually decided I needed to write a book on the subject.

Even before I came upon the Marty phrase, though, I had already been stimulated by some important studies on the subject. One resource was a book I mentioned earlier, *Habits of the Heart*, published in 1985 by Robert Bellah and a team of fellow social scientists. Bellah and his associates argue at length—backed by extensive interviews—that an increasing individualism in American life was making it more and more difficult for people to express the kinds of commitments that are necessary to sustain a healthy public life. The older religious and civic visions of life were weakening in their influence, with the result that the public space devoted to civic dialogue was becoming cramped and crowded with individual interests. What is needed to correct this situation, they argue, is the recovery and reinforcement of those "communities of memory"—especially the churches and synagogues—where "there are still operating among us . . . traditions that tell us about the nature of the world, about the nature of society, and about who we are as a people."[1]

These traditions—these communal memories—are, according to the case set forth in *Habits of the Heart*, crucial to the health of a society. Thus the Bellah team calls for a public dialogue based on the shared assumption that the individual self finds its fulfillment in relationships with others in a society organized through public dialogue. The necessary dialogue can be sustained only by communities of memory, whether religious or civic, and it is symptomatic of the present state of American society that this vision remains sporadic and largely local in scope, though the larger implications are clear. These local initiatives may, however, be the forerunners of social movements that will once again open up "spaces for reflection, participation, and the transformation of our institutions."[2]

The observations of Bellah and his colleagues offer a very different picture of the relationship of religious belief to public space than the one often set forth by secularist thinkers. Bellah and his associates see the constrictions and cluttering that inhibit a broad public dialogue today as due not to religious dogma but to the fragmenting of interests that occurs when a society loses its vision of what community and citizenship are all about. And this is why they insist that the recovery of particularized religious understandings of the issues of public life is necessary for a much-needed opening up of our communal "spaces for reflection, participation, and the transformation of our institutions."

## Help from Calvin

I was inspired by the Bellah team's emphasis on the importance of worshiping "spaces" for keeping a healthy vocabulary of citizenship alive. And obviously, if I was going to follow through on their encouraging thoughts in this regard, I knew I had to square the efforts with my own "particularized" tradition, Calvinism. It was precisely on that quest that I received considerable perspective from Sheldon Wolin's brilliant 1960 book *Politics and Vision*.

On the face of it, Wolin's treatment of Reformation-era political thought was not so encouraging. Sixteenth-century Protestantism, he argues, gave expression to political ideas that threatened "to jeopardize a whole tradition of order and civility."[3] But, thankfully, Wolin exempts Calvinism from this charge, singling out John Calvin as the one Reformation-era thinker who "put forward a system of ideas which stemmed that flight from civility" that his fellow Reformers had encouraged.[4] Wolin sees the impulses that led early Protestantism to flee from civility as arising primarily out of Anabaptist and Lutheran thought. Both the Lutherans and the Anabaptists promoted the ideal of an ecclesial fellowship that was social without being political—a community that, since it was "a voluntary union bound by love, faith, and the worshipped presence of Christ, . . . could not generate power, domination, and authority."[5] These latter features were associated with the coercive patterns of political life, a way of ordering human affairs that both Lutherans and Anabaptists viewed with varying degrees of suspicion—sometimes even contempt—and that they certainly took to be completely inappropriate to the texture of ecclesial bonding.

Calvin, on Wolin's reading, challenged this perspective on two counts. First, he took a much more positive view of political life than did Luther and the Anabaptists. And second, he insisted that the church itself ought to display a kind of political ordering, since all communities require some form of institutionalized structuring if they are to maintain their coherence.

But Calvin was not simply observing that the church would do well to learn a few organizational lessons from political life. There is a larger perspective at work in his thought, one in which both the churchly and the political communities, in spite of their very different callings, possess commonalities and continuities that link them together in a broader unity. Calvin wanted this unity to become more visible in human affairs so that the links between ecclesial virtue and the virtue of the polis could be more clearly displayed in a social order. This social order would be, as Wolin puts it, "not a 'theocracy,' but a corporate community that was neither purely religious nor purely secular, but a compound of both."[6] There is obviously much that I could discuss about even that little bit of historical commentary by Wolin. But what I took away from my reading of Wolin—and from, I should add, some encouraging personal conversations I had with him when we were speakers together at a conference in the late 1980s at Loyola Marymount University —was some new thoughts about the importance of drawing on Calvin's overall perspective for seeing the church as a place in which we learn how to cultivate the kind of virtue that is appropriate and necessary for public life.

Wolin had insisted that Calvin saw the church and the polis as each having its own unique integrity—neither simply existed for the sake of the other in the divine order. This meant, Wolin observes, that for Calvin "there was a kind of virtue attainable only in the political order."[7] The polis "had a unique role to play" for Calvin. It gives us the arena for cultivating "a type of civility and discipline that could not be gained elsewhere."[8] In Calvin's own words, it is an important task of temporal government "to shape our manners in accordance with civil justice, to create concord among us, to maintain and preserve a common peace and tranquility."[9]

These public "manners," however, are not easy to come by. Thus it is one of the tasks of the church, as Wolin puts it, "to refashion Protestant man into a creature of order, or more accurately, to make him conform to a Christian image of civility."[10]

## Waiting for the Eschaton

My early thoughts on the topic of civility were also inspired by my reading of two good books written by John Murray Cuddihy on the subject. The title of his 1978 book, *No Offense: Civil Religion and Protestant Taste*, came from a conversation about religion he overheard in a public setting, where one person said, "No offense, but I'm a Catholic." Cuddihy rightly took this to illustrate the difficulty many people have in reconciling strong convictions with a desire to be civil toward folks who do not share those convictions. And the title of his 1987 book, *The Ordeal of Civility*, acknowledges the hard work that has to go into maintaining convicted civility.

In my own speechmaking and writing on civility, I have regularly emphasized that "ordeal," quoting the older translations of Hebrews 12:14, where we are told to "strive" to live at peace with others. Convicted civility does require significant effort. Cuddihy, a Catholic thinker, proposes a Christian strategy for coping with this "ordeal" that entails adopting an "ethic for the interim," which prescribes patience as we await God's future victory over the forces of unrighteousness. Christian discipleship, Cuddihy suggests, "puts a ban on all ostentation and triumphalism *for the time being*, before the Parousiatic return, at which time alone triumphalism becomes appropriate and fitting." For Christians to attempt to claim our glory here and now "is precisely vainglory—it is vulgar, empty, and in bad theological taste. 'Whosoever shall exalt himself shall be abased; and he that shall humble himself shall be exalted' (Matt. 23:12)."[11]

Cuddihy cites approvingly Glenn Tinder's recommendation that Christians look at the present age with a sense of "resignation," a trait that is outwardly indistinguishable from a "Machiavellian" attitude. But this is not as cynical as it might seem at first glance. Both Tinder and Cuddihy mean to stress here the *outward* appearance of a similarity to Machiavellianism. Our Christian resignation, Tinder insists, is only "provisional; and fundamentally it is neither Machiavellian nor ethical, for it is subordinated to a limitless hope."[12]

I found this helpful. Both Cuddihy and Tinder rightly emphasize that the Christian's hope for the future is profoundly communal in nature. If taken seriously, this vision of a glorious future is not passive acceptance of the status quo but an active longing—of the sort described in Hebrews 13:14: "Here we have no lasting city, but we *seek* the city which is to come" (RSV, emphasis added).

I did put my own positive spin on this line of thought, however. I did not want to give the impression that civility is something we cloak ourselves in because we have nothing better to do while we are waiting for the future consummation. Rather, our civility is grounded in a genuine conviction that we have much to do by way of preparing for the city that is to come. Practicing a calm and steady humility is not merely a way of biding our time until the end-time arrives. It is itself a crucial way of anticipating the final chapter of the narrative, an important *preparation* for the eschaton. Indeed, a yearning for the future glory should make us bold to join others in the larger human quest for a healthy public space. In my decades of reflecting upon the contours of Christian civility, I have come to see the importance of the role of the local church as providing the necessary spiritual nurture for cultivating a spirituality of civility. The late Ronald Thiemann of Harvard put it well when he proposed, as I noted in the previous chapter, that local congregations function as "'schools of public virtue,' communities that seek to form the kind of character necessary for public life."[13] To be sure, that isn't all that the local church must be about. These days I also worry that the church is not doing enough in the area of catechesis, which includes the careful teaching of sound doctrine. But here too the connection to civility is obvious. A proper spirituality for public life cannot require us to hold our core convictions with little or no depth or intensity. The challenge is to cultivate a spiritual outlook that is fed *by* those strong convictions.

## Spiritual "Schooling"

In emphasizing the hard work of cultivating civility, I have drawn heavily on my Calvinist pietism. The formation of moral character does not always proceed smoothly, because we are sinners who are prone to self-deception. The process must include transforming

moments when we are forced to look directly at our own depravity. Often we need to be shocked into an awareness of the motives
that really shape our thoughts and actions, and we must respond
to these revelations by pleading for the mercy that will allow us
to repair our ways. All of this must happen in contexts where the
basic issues of sin and grace are openly displayed in the worshiping
life of a community. And unless that community explicitly attends
to the need to be formed—better yet, *transformed*—for our lives
as citizens, little good can be expected of Christians vis-à-vis the
crucial issues of public life.

The requisite spiritual transformation surely includes a continuing inner renewal of our individual inner lives. In my discussions
of civility, I have been fond of quoting what John Calvin wrote
in the *Institutes* on the subject of warfare. In spelling out his own
version of just-war theory, Calvin urges civil magistrates who were
thinking about attacking an enemy to engage in serious reflection
before going to war. One thing they must do, he says, is examine
their own motives, to be sure to "not be carried away with headlong
anger, or be seized with hatred, or burn with implacable severity."
They must also, he insists, "have pity on the common nature in
the one whose special fault they are punishing."[14] Calvin, I have
remarked, was a good Calvinist—he knew that as sinners we need
a spiritual strategy for dealing with our sinful tendency to put the
best possible interpretation on our own motives while putting the
worst possible interpretation on those of our opponents. So he
advised magistrates to do two things: look into yourself to see if
you are being guided by some sinful motive, and be sure also to
reflect on the humanity you share with your enemy.

## Rousseau's Festival

Among social contract philosophers, Rousseau was the one who
paid close attention to the "spiritual" dimension of civic bonding. As I mentioned earlier, he insisted on a large gap between

our "natural" selves and what we need to be like in order to take on the obligations of shared citizenship, and he puzzled over the ways to bridge that gap. And when he did directly address the question of how this transformation to civil consciousness might actually happen, it should not surprise us that Rousseau—pagan that he was—would look to nature festivals to find ways to create the necessary bonds. In one account, for example, he imagines how a sense of shared citizenship might be called forth during a community festival in a town where the leaders have planted "a stake crowned with flowers in the middle of a square"; there the people can gather, he says, at a time when the sun's rays and some gentle breezes flow over all the participants, energizing them in such a way that they "become an entertainment to themselves," to the point that "each one sees and loves himself in the others, and all will be better united," thus producing the kind of "patriotic drunkenness . . . which alone can raise men above themselves."[15]

There is much wisdom in what Rousseau is proposing here. He is insisting that an awareness of a shared humanity will not be generated by enlightened self-interest, nor will it simply happen by teaching individuals to accept a theoretical account of the essential features of human nature. The awareness of a shared humanity is just that: an *awareness* of what we have in common, wherein, in his apt phrasing, "each one sees and loves himself in the others," so that "all will be better united." A more recent example of a non-Christian recognition of the need for a kind of spiritual reinforcement of a sense of civic solidarity was offered by the philosopher Richard Bernstein, in the course of explaining Hannah Arendt's notion of public community. Writing about the worship-like character of a gathering of African American participants that he—himself a secular Jew—personally witnessed during the civil rights movement in the 1960s, Bernstein reported the following:

> The experience I want to relate occurred in the Morningstar Baptist Church, the headquarters [of the Mississippi Summer Project] for the Easton precinct of Forrest County. Many of those who came

to Mississippi this summer knew that they would be returning to
the safety of their homes at the end of the summer. But no one
then knew what would happen to the local blacks who identified
themselves with the civil rights movement. It took an enormous
amount of courage and risk [for them] to participate. After several
weeks of voter registration, the moment had arrived when it was up
to the local blacks to meet and publicly elect their representatives.
That meeting was one of the most impressive political gatherings
I have ever attended. . . . As you might imagine this gathering had
something of the quality of a religious meeting. And there were two
things that deeply impressed me—that I was witnessing the creation
of just one of those public spaces that Arendt describes, and that
what gave the participants the courage, hope, and conviction to
participate was informed by their religious communal bonds.[16]

In explaining this occurrence, Bernstein uses a Rousseauean
image: this is the kind of thing, he says, that sometimes just
"springs up" in a public gathering. But I want to insist that something much more is going on. The African American civil rights
activists had been "schooled" in a pedagogy of public spirituality.
We can hope that when this pedagogy is taken seriously by Christians it can succeed in making an impact on the larger human
community. But even when it fails in that regard, it bears witness
to the kind of profound vision that was described powerfully by
the Catholic bishops gathered at the Second Vatican Council, in
their declaration *Gaudium et Spes*, adopted in 1965. That document, especially these words, has given me much inspiration on
this topic:

> The joys and the hopes, the griefs and the anxieties of the [people]
> of this age, especially those who are poor or in any way afflicted,
> these are the joys and hopes, the griefs and anxieties of the fol-
> lowers of Christ. Indeed, nothing genuinely human fails to raise
> an echo in [our Christian] hearts.[17]

# 8

## Depravity: Less Than "Total"?

WHEN I ACCEPTED THE INVITATION FROM CALVIN THEOlogical Seminary to give the 2000 Stob Lectures, I had no hesitation about what my topic would be. I had been looking forward to thinking through some aspects of common grace theology, and a return to Grand Rapids seemed an excellent opportunity to publicly test my thoughts on the subject. Overall, the lectures went well. The auditorium was packed, and what I had to say generated some lively discussion.

I was a little taken aback, however, by the reactions of a few of my friends. It wasn't that they disagreed with this or that point in my presentations but that they seemed puzzled, maybe even a little embarrassed, that I had chosen the topic. One of them put it bluntly. It felt like "an exercise in nostalgia," he said. "We put these issues to rest long ago." Why, he wondered, would I try to dredge them up again?

My friend was right in observing that in my lectures I had rehearsed topics that had been passionately debated in Grand Rapids in the 1920s. In 1924 the Christian Reformed Church's

Synod had affirmed that there is a nonsaving grace that signals an attitude of divine favor toward all human beings. It takes the form of the bestowal of natural gifts, such as rain and sunshine, upon creatures in general; a providential restraining of our sinful tendencies, so that unredeemed humans do not produce all the evil that their depraved natures might otherwise bring about; and the ability of unbelievers to perform acts of civic good. These points were rejected by a brilliant pastor-theologian, Herman Hoeksema, who then led congregations and pastors out of the Christian Reformed denomination to form, in 1925, the Protestant Reformed Churches.[1]

My friend was obviously seeing this dispute as nothing more than a stage on which the Christian Reformed Church had engaged in a theological processing of its struggles to find its cultural place in North America. The denomination had switched to English as its primary ecclesiastical language not long before. A younger generation was finding its social commonalities with its fellow citizenry. The theological question of what the redeemed hold in common with the unredeemed was closely tied to the question of what a community of recent immigrants had in common with its new neighbors. There is no question that those kinds of sociocultural concerns were clearly at work in the Dutch-American Calvinist debates of the 1920s. But the theology of those debates cannot simply be reduced to the categories of disguised sociology or social psychology. The practical struggles with matters of cultural accommodation brought enduring theological issues to the fore. That this was the case was reinforced for me by the fact that when an expanded version of my lectures was published, as *He Shines in All That's Fair* (2001), it was received well, even with some enthusiasm, beyond the Reformed community. One Pentecostal scholar expressed gratitude to me for shedding light on topics that were crucial for understanding what a healthy Pentecostalism would look like.

## An Intrafamily Dispute

One of the things I discovered in exploring the common grace debates of the 1920s was that the opponents of common grace were sometimes accused by their fellow Calvinists of being "Anabaptist." One Christian Reformed minister, for example, wrote a pamphlet in which he applied the term to Herman Hocksema's theology. He was chided by a member of the Calvin Seminary faculty who, while expressing agreement with the pamphleteer's critique, told him that he "would have done better to leave out that epithet 'Anabaptist,' which here can serve only as a scornful word." And the fact is, the professor wrote, much of what Hoeksema argued against common grace theology could also be found in the writings of "the old theologians of Reformed scholasticism."[2]

That observation was a case in point for a portrayal of Reformed-Anabaptist relationships that John Howard Yoder and I had set forth in an essay we wrote together in the late 1980s. Our cooperative effort grew out of a brief exchange in print, where I responded to a short article that Yoder had written.[3] Yoder was pleased with what he (rightly) took to be a friendly affirmation on my part, and he suggested that we explore the subject further together in a coauthored piece.[4] The point we expanded upon at some length was that arguments between Calvinists and Anabaptists should not be construed as disputes between radically different theological types. Rather, they are better understood as displays of an intrafamily argument. The high intensity of these disputes, we concurred, is due to the fact that the differences between the two groups are of a more intimate character than are either of their arguments with, say, the Lutherans or the Catholics. Anabaptist thought is, in effect, a radicalization of some key Calvinist themes.

At the time of the Reformation, the Calvinists had begun their depiction of the human condition with a stark portrayal of human depravity. Having started there, though, they quickly began to introduce the sorts of modifications that made room for their endorsement of some of the things going on in the larger culture, especially the workings of civil government. The Anabaptists jumped on this, accusing the Calvinists of inconsistency, insisting that a negative assessment of unregenerate human nature required a strict posture of separation from the world.[5] Here the Calvinist response featured the kind of condemnatory language we saw being used in the Belgic Confession's insistence that Reformed Christians are to "detest the Anabaptists and other seditious people, and in general all those who reject the higher powers and magistrates, and would subvert justice, introduce community of goods, and confound that decency and good order, which God hath established among men."[6]

Yoder and I knew that it might come across as a bit odd—even a bit offensive—to suggest that the other streams within the broad evangelical community should see the kinds of arguments that he and I had been involved in as having implications for Lutherans, Pentecostals, Restorationists, Wesleyans, Baptists, Congregationalists, and others. But we were convinced that the lines were most clearly drawn when Reformed and Anabaptists have debated the kinds of issues that are also regularly discussed in those other traditions—issues such as war and peace, Christ and culture, church and state. More recently, this contention has been reinforced for me by witnessing up close the serious disagreements in Chinese Christianity between "registered" and "unregistered" churches. The arguments are often set forth as if the matters at stake are fundamentally about the church's relationship to what is seen as a particularly hostile government. The same impression could be gotten from the earlier twentieth-century debates between the "registered" and "unregistered" Baptist churches in the Soviet Union. The fact is, though, that the arguments have come up historically in a variety of contexts, as in the Reformation-era debates between the Anabaptists and other communities, and in the debates between many Puritans and the Anglican establishment in England. Significantly, for my present purposes, the same kinds of issues caused divisions within the Calvinist community in the nineteenth-century Netherlands. In the 1830s a group of separating (*afscheiding*) congregations declared independence from the government-sanctioned church, resulting in over a decade of persecution: their services were declared illegal, and some of their pastors were imprisoned. When this group of congregations was finally offered legal status in the 1850s, though, some within the group refused it as a matter of theological principle; the church has no business, they argued, seeking legal recognition from a civil government.[7]

That a dispute of this sort could take place within Calvinism lends credence to the "intrafamily" thesis that Yoder and I insisted upon. My own support for this thesis drew much inspiration from the views of Leonard Verduin, a Christian Reformed pastor whose affection for the Anabaptists was well known in the Mennonite community, particularly because of his efforts in translating the works of Menno Simons into English. Verduin argued that there were close similarities between the "believers' church" emphasis of the Anabaptists and Verduin's own "experiential" strain of Dutch Calvinism. Mennonites, he pointed out, will only baptize people who have had an experience of conversion, while experiential Calvinists would only baptize children whose *parents* have had an experience of conversion.[8] The Dutch Calvinist pietists' view of baptism was linked to broader ecclesiological convictions: they advocated for a "gathered" church versus a "territorial" (parish-type system) church.[9] In this emphasis—an expression of a strict antitheticalist adherence to total depravity, Verduin argued—they were in fundamental agreement with the Anabaptists in rejecting "Constantinian" Christianity and calling for the formation of a church that would stand over against the present order of things.

What Verduin did not explicitly address, however, is the fact that this kind of pietist Calvinism, when it takes the shape of careful theological formulation, often steps back from an unqualified endorsement of an Anabaptist type of spiritual epistemology. This is certainly the case in the thinking of the one determinedly antitheticalist Reformed thinker in recent years who most closely approximates the Anabaptist perspective: Klaas Schilder, especially as he sets forth his case in his little book *Christ and Culture*. While Schilder explicitly rejected Kuyper's brand of "cultural transformation," he still maintained a strong notion of a broad creation-based cultural mandate. In advocating an "abstinence" from aggressive cultural engagement with fallen humankind, Schilder distinguished two kinds of cultural abstaining. The one he condemned was the variety that "originates in resentment, laziness, diffidence, slackness, or narrow-mindedness." His preferred mode was a "heroic" withdrawal, a strategy that conforms to Christ's call for his disciples to "make themselves eunuchs for the Kingdom of heaven's sake and not in order to avoid this Kingdom."[10] This self-limiting pattern is not anti-culture as such, but it does restrict the territory in which we carry out our cultural activity under the condition of fallenness. By insisting that Christians concentrate on a cultural formation that occurs primarily within the Christian *koinonia* (communion or fellowship), then, Schilder comes close to an Anabaptist position. Significantly, though, he does acknowledge a Christian obligation to attend to the preservation of "a *sunousia*, a being-together, among all men."[11] Christians cannot simply ignore the life of the larger human community, Schilder says, because in the midst of human rebellion we can still discern the "residues" of what was originally "given in the paradisal world."[12] Here Schilder is recognizing God's continuing purposes for his creation as such. And what Schilder concedes grudgingly, I have wanted, following Kuyper, to celebrate: that all people, redeemed and unredeemed alike, live within the lawful structures of God's creation—a creation that is heading for renewal rather than a final destruction. This means that we have a mandate to promote the common good.

## Creation and Fall

Schilder's acknowledgment of a continuing *sunousia*, a shared human being-together, is an important reinforcement for spiritual epistemology that allows for a broader cultural conversation. My aforementioned worries about Stanley Hauerwas's views on the Christian's relationship to the public arena have to do with his failure to clearly acknowledge this kind of *sunousia*, thus not leaving much room for exploring commonalities with people who profess very different worldviews than the one we embrace as Christians.

But like Schilder—yet without Schilder's insistence on the *sunousia* concept—Hauerwas cannot completely stay with his "no shared language" thesis. This is why some folks who have been deeply influenced by Hauerwas have criticized him for conceding too much to the possibility of a common language. Robert W. Brimlow, for one, highlights some comments in Hauerwas's writings where Hauerwas seems to allow for some sort of "translation" of particularistic Christian language into terms that make sense to non-Christians. These concessions, argues Brimlow, blunt the force of Hauerwas's emphasis on radical discipleship.[13] Brimlow calls Hauerwas to return to an uncompromising insistence that Christians "are called to the margins; we are called to be weak and separate and to view ourselves as such. We therefore must turn our back on all that is incompatible with the Gospel."[14] John Howard Yoder himself acknowledged on occasion the need for a larger moral perspective than is available in an exclusive reliance on the way of Jesus. At one point in his major work *The Politics of Jesus*, he expresses the need to draw on a wider variety of ethical resources. We cannot hope to gain "a specific biblical ethical content for modern questions," he says, without also making use of "broader generalizations, a longer hermeneutic path, and insights from other sources."[15]

It is significant, I suggest, that these Anabaptist thinkers hedge a bit on the claim that the New Testament witness to the way of Jesus is our only resource for understanding God's guidance for the task of cultural discipleship. As I see things, it is important to see the way of Jesus against the background of the purposes that shaped God's original creative activity. In that sense, what Jesus taught and did cannot be isolated from the designs of the good creation. With the necessary aid of biblical spectacles, we can still discern vestiges of the original created order. No matter how perverse the processes and products of cultural formation have become, human beings still work within the structures of the good creation. And working within these structures, we can approach our fellow human beings in the confidence that we are bonded to them in a continuing *sunousia*.

## The Barthian *Nein*

The present-day appropriation of an Anabaptist countercultural perspective is enhanced for many by an appreciation also of the stern "*Nein!*" that Karl Barth pronounced against natural theology in his debate with Emil Brunner during the 1930s.[16] Barth was offering a theological critique of the "culture religion" that prepared the way for the widespread German acceptance of Hitler's ideology. Hauerwas, for one, has endorsed the Barthian critique. Barth, he says, was able to see that the theologians in Germany "who had spent their careers translating the faith in terms that could be understood by modern people" had thereby rendered themselves "unable to say no" to the Nazi threat.[17]

I certainly have no desire to defend the Nazi-era theologians who were the targets of Barth's condemnation. In issuing his "*Nein!*" Barth was clearly speaking out against a theological system that was seriously—even horribly—defective. The important question to ask about that wicked accommodation to Nazism is whether its evils were, to use H. Richard Niebuhr's apt formulation, expressions of "evil as perversion" or of evil as "badness of being."[18]

I see Barth as rightly speaking a clear word to a specific historical situation in which an identifiable culture, reinforced by a theology that supported that culture, had generated evil practices.

He correctly saw that a certain "translation" project had gone terribly awry. Where Barth and his present-day fellow "*Nein!*"-sayers go wrong, however, is in taking that specific cultural situation to be a paradigm that reveals, precisely because of the clarity of the crisis that characterized it, the inevitable defects of any theological approach that attempts "a generic moral project."[19]

When Barth and Brunner debated the question of natural theology in the 1930s, each accused the other of betraying the basic aims of Reformation thought. This was to be expected in an argument between two Reformed theologians, each of whom was calling for a return to something that had been betrayed in recent history. While Barth insisted that the return required a firm rejection of natural theology as such, Brunner issued a more modest call for "our generation to find the way back to a true *theologia naturalis*,"[20] one that avoids the pitfalls of what Brunner set forth as the Roman Catholic version. Again, it is understandable that two Reformed theologians would each go out of his way to argue that his views are consistent with those of Calvin and his fellow Reformers. And it is understandable that each could find support in Calvin's writings for his own viewpoint, since Calvin seems to nod in each theologian's direction at various points in the *Institutes*. While Barth acknowledges the presence of favorable comments by Calvin about the possibility of a "natural knowledge" of things divine, he dismisses their importance. Calvin, Barth insists, was misled by Augustine, failing to see "the extent to which . . . [Augustine] has to be regarded as a Roman Catholic theologian."[21] But we should not allow "that little corner which has been left uncovered in Calvin's treatment" to lure us into an endorsement of natural theology.[22] Instead, we must recognize that "what Calvin wrote in those first chapters of the *Institutes* has to be written again and this time in such a way that no [present-day natural-law theologians] can find in it material for their fatal ends."[23]

Brunner obviously sees things differently. And the kind of reading of Calvin that he offers is presented in the form of a detailed historical scenario by Stephen Grabill in his book-length study of Reformed natural theology. "While Calvin neither constructs nor sanctions a robust natural theology," Grabill argues, "he certainly does not deny the formal possibility of developing subsidiary doctrines of natural theology and natural law on the basis of God's reliable but obfuscated natural revelation within creation, design of the human body, and conscience." This direction in Calvin's thought was taken up by other Reformed theologians—rather immediately, in fact, by Calvin's contemporary Peter Martyr Vermigli, who "formulated a more sophisticated doctrine of natural law on the basis of a modified Thomist understanding of the natural knowledge of God."[24] This theological project was then expanded and solidified by subsequent generations of Reformed thinkers, such as Johannes Althusius and Francis Turretin, with the result that an appreciation for some sort of "natural knowledge" of God found a place in much Reformed theology. When Barth arrived on the scene, however, things took a different course in Reformed thought. And for many, the Barth-versus-Brunner debate poses a basic choice for Reformed theology: either a robust natural-theology/natural-law approach or an alignment with Barth's negative verdict.

## The Dutch Neo-Calvinist Alternative

The fact is, however, that for at least some thinkers in the Reformed tradition, Barth versus Brunner is a false choice. They refuse to utter the Barthian "*Nein!*" against "natural knowledge," while expressing reluctance to endorse the kind of robust advocacy of "natural knowledge" that was developed by many of the Reformed theologians who came after Calvin. This is true particularly of those of us who have drawn heavily on the Dutch "neo-Calvinist" thinking represented in the theological writings of Abraham Kuyper, Herman Bavinck, and G. C. Berkouwer. I was a little surprised, then, that Stephen Grabill, in his otherwise insightful study of natural theology in the Reformed tradition, does not see the Dutch neo-Calvinists as providing a distinct third option on the Reformed spectrum. Instead, he treats neo-Calvinism as a somewhat muted version of the Barthian "*Nein!*" Grabill sets the stage for his characterization of the neo-Calvinist approach to natural-law thinking with this brief summary account: the kind of critique of a robust natural theology set forth in this school of thought can be found, he reports, in the writings of "Herman Dooyeweerd and G. C. Berkouwer, a devotee of Barthianism for much of his long career at the Free University of Amsterdam, and is reiterated at points in Henry Stob's and Richard Mouw's treatment of natural law."[25] The suggestion of a significant Barthian influence is repeated a little further on when Grabill observes, with reference to Stob's perspective, that "it is possible to detect the influence of a Barthian-style actualism in his mature criticism of natural-law ethics, most likely filtered through the anti-scholastic and Christocentric theology of G. C. Berkouwer that was popular in Christian Reformed circles during the 1960s and 1970s." Furthermore, says Grabill, Stob's views "had a significant influence on such philosophers and ethicists in the Dutch Reformed tradition as Richard Mouw, Lewis Smedes, and Nicholas Wolterstorff."[26] Thus he suggests that the perspective at work here is basically a Barthian one.

To put my surprise at Grabill's suggestion in personal terms, I was actually more than a little shocked to see my name appear in the context of a Barthian rejection of natural theology. My first contact with Barth's thought, as I reported at the beginning of this book, was when as an undergraduate I read Cornelius Van Til's writings, where Barth is portrayed as a representative of the older modernism in a new disguise. I was cured of that way of understanding Barth by reading G. C. Berkouwer's much more charitable study of Barth in *The Triumph of Grace in the Theology of Karl Barth*. But I was never tempted thereafter to think of myself as a Barthian. In seminary I read a lot of Paul Tillich, and while I certainly never became a Tillichian on any substantive theological matter, I clearly sympathized with his critique of Barth's "keryg-matic" approach from the perspective of Tillich's own "method of correlation."

Nor have I ever taken theologians like Berkouwer and Stob to be in the Barthian camp. Berkouwer may have been a Barth "devotee" on some issues, but only some. On many key topics, including Barth's handling of the biblical material regarding general reve-lation, he was quite critical of Barth. Of Barth's treatment of the key Pauline passages in Romans 1 and 2, for example, Berkouwer notes that Barth's "exegesis is more the result of an *a priori* view of revelation than of an unprejudiced reading of the text itself."[27] Furthermore, Barth's account of unbelief, says Berkouwer, "is in contradiction with the permanent confrontation of man with God's revelation," and Barth's "characterization of the universal element of all religions as unbelief is a distortion."[28] Here is Berkouwer on Barth's treatment of the first chapter of John's Gospel: "It is remarkable that Barth does say that John mentions a cosmological function of the Logos, but, nevertheless, neglects this in favor of the soteriological aspect."[29] Significantly, when Berkouwer states his own positive views, he points to a sense of the divine in human beings that "is preserved by God in the human heart" in a manner that "does not relieve the darkness, but it does help explain how it is that religions still arise in a fallen world and how it is possible that these false religions bear a marked semblance of order."[30]

The fact is that Berkouwer and Stob, and others significantly influenced by them, were drawing primarily on a fairly well-defined pre-Barthian strand of thinking about these matters. While the most immediate theological influence was the neo-Calvinism of Abraham Kuyper and Herman Bavinck, Berkouwer and Stob also appealed directly to Reformation-era themes that have not figured prominently in the Barth-Brunner kind of debate. And in doing so, they were representing a perspective that counts as a distinct alternative to both a robust natural theology and a firm rejection of such a theology.

## The "Extra-Cognitive"

A central matter of contention between Barth and Brunner was the merits of Calvin's notion of the twofold knowledge—the *duplex cognitio*—of God. While this focus on the possibility of at least two ways of "knowing" about God is certainly important, it is not the only subject that deserves attention in reflecting on the possibilities of some sort of moral and spiritual awareness that Christian believers share with their fellow human beings. In the Christian tradition in general, and in the Reformed tradition in particular, attention has also been given to other motifs for understanding that awareness of the divine: the *imago Dei*, the *sensus divinitatis*, the *semen religionis*, and common grace, among others. And not all of these resources have to do with *cognitio*. The almost exclusive focus on the part of Barth and Brunner on the possibility of a natural *knowledge* is, from the perspective of some strands of Reformed thought, somewhat myopic. This is certainly the case for the Dutch neo-Calvinists. Kuyper and Bavinck addressed moral and spiritual continuities between believer and unbeliever by appealing to the notions of common grace, while Berkouwer departed from Barth by expressing a positive appreciation for the notions of general revelation and the *semen religionis*. Unlike natural theology, these resources can be thought of as extra-cognitive, since they do not attribute to the believer any sort of clear cognitive access to correct information about God's nature or about God's will for moral behavior. Because they have wanted to avoid the more optimistic views of fallen human nature as set forth by Catholics and others, the neo-Calvinists have been reluctant to concede too much by way of a "natural knowledge" to the unregenerate consciousness. In this regard it is important to distinguish clearly between the Kuyperian understanding of common grace and the notion of "prevenient grace" that is popular in other traditions. The neo-Calvinists see the appeal to prevenient grace as a way of downplaying the extent of human depravity by positing a kind of automatic universal upgrade of those dimensions of human nature that have been corrupted by sin. To put it much too simply, the goal of prevenient grace *is* the upgrade; it is to raise the deeply wounded human capacities to a level where some measure of freedom to choose or reject obedience to God is made possible. Common grace, in contrast, is typically set forth by the neo-Calvinists as a divine strategy for bringing the cultural designs of God to completion. Common grace operates mysteriously in the life of, say, a Chinese government official or an unbelieving Parisian artist to harness their created talents to prepare the creation for the full coming of the kingdom. In this sense, the operations of common grace—unlike those of prevenient grace—always have a goal-directed ad hoc character.

The appeal to Calvin's notion of the *semen religionis* is similarly noncognitive. One can have a vague awareness of—to use Carol Zaleski's apt phrasing—being "hunted down by the God who instills transcendent longing,"[31] without necessarily knowing that it is in fact the deity who is doing the pursuing. Similarly, the *sensus divinitatis* need not be a "sense" that is capable of cognitive articulation. The great Jewish theologian Abraham Joshua Heschel makes this point eloquently when he describes the Genesis scene where Adam and Eve, having eaten of the forbidden fruit, hid themselves from the presence of God. The Lord comes looking for them, and he cries out, "Where art thou?" (Gen. 3:9 KJV). That call, says Rabbi Heschel, is one "that goes out again and again. It is a still small echo of a still small voice." It may not be "uttered in words" or "conveyed in categories of the mind," but all human beings, as children of God, regularly hear it in the deep places of their being: "Where art thou?"[32]

What looms large for those of us in the neo-Calvinist camp, however, is the confessional address to the question of a "natural" awareness of the divine. Because we stand in a tradition that places a strong emphasis on fidelity to the Reformation-era confessions, we take the relevant confessional passages to have a direct bearing on our theological formulations on a given subject. In this case much attention has been given to article 2 of the Belgic Confession, which has the heading "By What Means God Is Made Known unto Us":

We know him by two means; first, by the creation, preservation and government of the universe; which is before our eyes as a most elegant book, wherein all creatures, great and small, are as so many characters leading us to contemplate the invisible things of God, namely His power and divinity, as the apostle Paul says, Rom. 1:20. All which things are sufficient to convince men, and leave them without excuse. Secondly, he makes himself more clearly fully known to us by his holy and divine Word, that is to say, as far as is necessary for us to know in this life, to his glory and our salvation.[33]

The felt obligation to square any assessment of a continuing consciousness of the divine presence on the part of sinful humanity with this confessional statement disinclines us from endorsing the Barthian "*Nein!*" But neither have we seen this article as requiring the acceptance of a natural theology as such. For one thing, the article does not require ascribing cognitive access to the divine: the manner in which the "characters" in creation's "book" are to be thought of as "leading us to contemplate the invisible things of God" need not be taken as providing us with knowable information about God. For another, the article simply stipulates that, on the basis of what is made available by means of nature's "book," the unregenerate consciousness is "without excuse" in its willful disobedience.

## The "Voluntarist" Factor

While Grabill puts us neo-Calvinists with the Barthians in posing his polar options, he does observe that our fondness for the doctrine of common grace allows for, at best, a "hesitant juxtaposition" of common grace to natural law.[34] In his brief attempt to explain this hesitancy, he rightly points to the neo-Calvinist attraction to a "voluntaristic" insistence on God's unrestricted sovereign will. He refers to my defense of a divine command ethic as a case in point for a depiction of the God-human relationship in basic "will-to-will" terms. On this voluntaristic view, he observes, God's moral legislation has its origins in the divine sovereign freedom, which means that the requisite human response to this legislation is a volitional "mirroring" of the sovereign freedom of God.[35]

It is difficult to see how this will-to-will depiction of the most basic character of the God-human relationship can simply be expunged from Calvinism. I certainly have not been able to do the expunging. One would expect that a follower of John Calvin would always be nervous about any tendency to see God as somehow "bound" by, or "subject" to, a law that is coeternal with his own being. As Bavinck put it: "God does not stand outside of nature and is not excluded from it by a hedge of laws but is present in it and sustains it by the word of his power."[36]

And this being-present-to character of God's relationship to the creation in general has to be highlighted in a special way with reference to God's relationship to human beings. The notion of human lives, including rebellious human lives, as lived inescapably *coram Deo* is a standard feature of Calvinist portrayals of the human condition—beginning, of course, with Calvin himself, who in the opening paragraphs of the *Institutes* emphasizes the need for us to know ourselves, not by thinking thoughts about God and his law, but by scrutinizing ourselves before the "face" of God.[37]

To be sure, human beings are subject to a cosmic legal system that is the expression of a sovereign divine will. But ultimately we are accountable, not to the law as such, but to the law's Author, who calls us into a covenantal relationship with himself, one to which we must freely respond. It is significant that the Canons of Dort, often thought of as the harshest of the Calvinist confessional documents, nonetheless make much of the role of the human will in responding to God. The section where the folks at Dordrecht address this is my favorite in the document. "This grace of regeneration does not treat men as senseless stocks and blocks," the authors of the Canons insist, "nor take away their will and its properties, neither does violence thereto; but spiritually quickens, heals, corrects, and at the same time sweetly and powerfully bends it, that where carnal rebellion and resistance formerly prevailed a ready and sincere spiritual obedience begins to reign."[38]

Calvinism's critics have regularly raised the charge that the God of Calvinism operates in a fundamentally ad hoc fashion, issuing arbitrary and disconnected commands in the manner of a despot. And the fact is that many Calvinists have operated with an understanding of their relationship with God that closely conforms to this picture. Indeed, for many Calvinists this extreme moral voluntarism is bounded by an even more poignant soteriological voluntarism. There is a strong strand of Calvinist piety that views God as arbitrary not only in his moral negotiations but also in the manner in which he distributes his redemptive benefits as such. Thus the phenomenon of pious Calvinists who fret about their elect status as individuals at the mercy of a deity who dispenses his saving grace in a purely arbitrary manner.

What is missing in such a perspective, of course, is a sense of lawfulness. While the Calvinists who endorse this picture of things may actually make frequent use of the *word* "law," for them this divine law actually functions as a series of arbitrary, disconnected, fiat-type commands, with no obvious unifying pattern of rational coherence.

## A Lawful Ordering

It is precisely in our understanding of divine law that we neo-Calvinists have intentionally distanced ourselves from the more arbitrary versions of Calvinist voluntarism. Because God regularly speaks and acts lawfully, believers do not need to stand in primitive fear before a divine despot whose ways are totally unfathomable to human beings. The harsher tones of the divine mystery have been softened by God's own publicly announced commitment to juridical fidelity. The God of the Bible—so insists the neo-Calvinist—has committed himself to acting toward his creation in ways that are reasonable and reliable. He is a faithful God who redeems his people so that they may come to understand and obey his ordinances. Thus divine sovereignty is administered in accordance with lawful patterns. This emphasis looms so large in neo-Calvinism that the philosophical movement associated with Herman Dooyeweerd's thought labeled itself *de wijsbegeerte der wetsidee*—the philosophy of the law-idea.[39]

In our shared human nature we have been designed by the Creator to respond in obedience to this lawful ordering of reality. But in our sinful rebellion our response has become one of disobedience. The redemptive mission of Christ was required to make it possible for depraved sinners to be redirected toward paths of obedience. The moral life that Christ came to inaugurate, then, is on this view not something brand-new. Rather it is the reclaiming and restoring of that which had been seriously marred by original sin. Kuyper makes the point forcefully in a much-quoted passage in his Stone Lectures:

> Can we imagine that at one time God willed to rule things in a certain moral order, but that now, in Christ, He wills to rule it otherwise? As though He were not the Eternal, the Unchangeable, Who, from the very hour of creation, even unto all eternity, had willed, wills, and shall will and maintain, one and the same firm moral world-order! Verily Christ has swept away the dust with which man's sinful limitations had covered up this world-order, and has made it glitter again in its original brilliancy. . . . The world-order remains just what it was from the beginning. It lays full claim, not only to the believer (as though less were required from the unbeliever), but also to every human being and to all human relationships.[40]

While this lawful ordering of the creation "lays full claim" on believer and unbeliever alike, this does not mean that the unregenerate consciousness has a clear cognitive access to this ordering. The most that can be said is that unbelievers are "without excuse" with regard to the divine expectations because they are in the presence of that which they refuse to acknowledge. As Gordon Spykman summarized the neo-Calvinist perspective on this matter, "The creation order establishes an ontic commonality and solidarity among all peoples, even in the midst of the radical noetic polarities among differing faith communities."[41]

This emphasis on a "commonality and solidarity among all peoples" that is "ontic" but not "noetic" should make it clear that the neo-Calvinist position is indeed a distinct alternative both to the natural-law tradition and to the Barthian rejection of natural law. Human beings are seen as inescapably confronted with God's ordering of the creation in which they carry on their lives. This confrontation includes an awareness of this creation order, albeit one that falls short of cognitive access—thus the neo-Calvinists' very un-Barthian appeal to the notions of general revelation and common grace. In this scheme of things, a lawful moral ordering of reality is not only acknowledged; it is a central theme. In that sense, the disagreement with the natural-law tradition concerns not the "ontic" but the "noetic."

## Covenant and Moral Reality

The neo-Calvinist understanding of a general human awareness of the reality of the divine, then, draws on a medley of concepts, including the *semen religionis*, the *sensus divinitatis*, ethical volitionalism, and a creational law-structure that is ontic in character. And the volitional and the law-structure, as I view things, need each other in order to avoid the unnuanced volitionalism that often manifests itself among Calvinists in the form of a despotic-type understanding of God's relationship to the creation. But I must also confess to some personal nervousness with the way the idea of God's creational law-ordering has sometimes functioned in

neo-Calvinist thought. The worrisome tendency shows up particularly in the way Dooyeweerd and his followers featured "the
conception of the lex as the *boundary* between God and the creation."[42] As Henk Geertsema of the Vrije Universiteit, himself a
proponent of Dooyeweerd's overall perspective, once observed at
a neo-Calvinist gathering in the Netherlands,[43] this emphasis on
law as *the* "boundary" between Creator and creature can give the
impression that our individual relationships with God are always
in some sense "mediated" by laws—a tendency that, Geertsema
also observed, has been on display in frequent criticisms of various
forms of pietism by thinkers in the Dutch "law idea" (*wetsidee*)
tradition. What Geertsema was insisting upon was that Calvinism cannot relinquish the "I-Thou-ness" of the individual's relationship to God—the very aspect of Reformation thought that
Alasdair MacIntyre complained about when he criticized Calvin
and Luther for having produced in their theologies the ancestor of
the postmodern "emotivist self," the de-roled individual, stripped
of all social characteristics, who stands alone before God.[44] The
danger of this "I-Thou" conception is, of course, the unnuanced
"despotic" Calvinism I have already complained about. But we
can avoid this danger by insisting that we retain—in a way that
John Calvin himself would surely celebrate—a strong reliance on
the idea of *covenant*. In Reformed theology the covenant motif
has also, along with the stress on lawfulness, made an important
contribution to the kind of "softening" of Calvinist soteriology
that is necessary if an unnuanced voluntarism is to be avoided.

   In this regard the work of Max Stackhouse has been helpful
to many of us in the neo-Calvinist movement. While endorsing
many of the key concepts of neo-Calvinism in his approach to
public theology, he has given significant attention to the covenantal
motif, not only as it applies to specific moral relationships, such as
marriage and family life, but also as it relates to the fundamental
character of moral reality as such. Stackhouse takes special note
of those thinkers in the Reformed tradition who have posited

the existence of a covenant between God and human beings—typically referred to as the "covenant of works"[45]—that operated in the pre-fall garden. On this view, says Stackhouse, a covenant is not just a handy device for structuring a salvific arrangement; rather, a covenant is "given by God to Adam in the very fabric of creation," so that "the primal relationship of God to humanity is covenantal."[46] This insight can motivate us to be on the lookout for "the presence of covenant-like possibilities in many, perhaps all, cultures," and this in turn "suggests that in the very structure of human relationships we find traces of what God graciously revealed to humanity in the fabric of creation."[47]

The idea of covenant helps us to retain the nonnegotiable voluntarist component in the Calvinist view of selfhood, while recognizing that *trust* is a key feature in a covenant. Covenantal trust is more open-ended than the sort of trust that characterizes contractual arrangements. In a contract the trust is more limited; it is bracketed by clearly defined expectations. In a covenantal relationship the promise is not so much to be faithful to a set of conditions; it is a commitment to be faithful *no matter what*.

Human beings, as volitional creatures, do have a special relationship to law. Unlike animals and plants, which are also subject to God's lawful ordering of the creation, human beings have the choice of obeying or disobeying the divine ordinances. To understand this is to discern the nature and reality of our sinfulness, as a willful rebellion against the divine Lawgiver. It is also to grasp the basic pattern of God's gracious provision of a remedy for our fallenness: Jesus as the incarnate Son of God fulfilled the demands of the law on our behalf and made the payment that was necessary to purchase our redemption. By accepting this substitutionary work on our behalf, we enter into a renewed covenant with our Creator.

Since this covenant is initiated by the Triune God, it is important also to see the role of law in its trinitarian context. The First Person is indeed a lawgiver, but this does not mean that we experience him in that way in all aspects of our relationship with him. In the

Old Testament, God is portrayed in numerous ways that seem to supplement, rather than to be subordinate to, his legislator status. While a human parent makes the rules that "govern" the life of a child, a child can also experience the parent as a caregiver, nurturer, teacher, guide, and even playmate. Similarly, the God who is the legislator is also portrayed by the biblical writers as a father who showers tender mercies upon his children, and as a mother who gives birth to us and protects us by drawing us close to herself in times of danger. In both the human and the divine cases, the juridical framework may never be completely absent, but there are times—importantly so—when law stays in the background and more intimate, face-to-face dimensions of the relationship come to the fore. This intimacy is intensified in our relationship to Christ, who as the incarnate Son descended to our station "under" the law, experiencing the pain, abuse, and temptation that are part and parcel of our fallen brokenness (Heb. 2:10–18). In Jesus we experience God, not so much as Lawgiver, but as one who became one of us in order to qualify as a fellow law-obeyer.

And the Holy Spirit functions in our lives not so much as a legislator but as a guide and enabler to obedience. The Spirit's place in reference to the law is not above the human self, as Lawgiver, but alongside those who have received the law, as their divine Comforter.

# 9

## Our "Direction-Setting"

ONE OF THE HOT TOPICS WE DEBATED QUITE A BIT IN GRADU-
ate school was "minds and machines." None of us had
our own computers in those days, but there was a sense that we
were on the brink of experiencing new technologies that would
significantly affect our lives. One of the big philosophical questions for those of us focusing on "philosophy of mind" was the
question of whether a computer could ever come to a point in
its operations where we would say that it was actually capable
of *thinking*. If so, could such a computer so closely approximate
human patterns of reasoning that we would have to decide that
it had a *mind*?

Some philosophers had no problem with the idea of a thinking
machine, since they had a rather low—a naturalistic or reduc-
tionistic—view of the human person. One rather flippant way in
which some of them put it at the time was that human beings are
simply machines that happen to be made of meat.

Others, however, were concerned to maintain the uniqueness
of the human person by insisting on a qualitative difference—an

113

unbridgeable metaphysical gap—between human minds and the bearers of so-called artificial intelligence. The argument of these opponents of a robust "computer intelligence" made much of the fact that computers, even when, as in a chess game, they are "reasoning" very quickly, nonetheless are always sorting out and eliminating possibilities. A favorite example here was how a computer would determine the meaning of "Time flies like an arrow." The first option an actual computer came up with was that there was a species of flies, called "time flies," who were fond of arrows; a second option was that of a command (where "time" is the verb)—as in telling someone with a stopwatch to "time flies like an arrow" in order to determine how long a fly would take to travel a certain distance. Only after checking out these options would the computer zero in on the more metaphorical meaning. Not so with the human mind, the argument continued. Human consciousness can focus directly on the correct meaning without assessing possible alternatives. We are capable in such situations of "just getting it."

The debates could get quite passionate. What was clear, though, was that beneath the obvious disagreements, there was a shared assumption at work. Both sides agreed that what fundamentally defines the human person is rationality. Where they disagreed was on the question of whether the human kind of rational intelligence could be replicated in a computer.

I was always uneasy about that shared assumption. It seemed to me that there was something deeper at stake than simply the question of whether machines could "think." The grounds of my uneasiness became clear to me when I got around to seeing Stanley Kubrick's 1968 film *2001: A Space Odyssey*. In it, the crew members of a Jupiter space mission rely on the deliverances of a computer they have named "Hal." There is no question that Hal, as depicted in the film, is highly intelligent. But what was more important for me was the fact that Hal is devious. He rebels against the crew and plots their demise. Yes, this is science fiction. But as such it provides an important insight. A computer would finally come close to being like us, not simply in being able to think like us, but in having the capacity to elicit trust and to betray that trust. To put it in explicitly biblical terms, it was not so much Hal's capacity for rational understanding that made him so humanlike, but rather it was that he was the kind of entity to which one could legitimately preach, "Trust in the LORD with all your heart and lean not on your own understanding" (Prov. 3:5 NIV).

The biblical language is important here. The "heart" is typically seen by the biblical writers as the center of our humanness. In our fallen condition, "the heart is deceitful above all things, and desperately wicked: who can know it?" (Jer. 17:9 KJV). To be cured of sinfulness, something important must happen in the sinner's "heart." The direction of our lives—either toward the Creator, glorifying him in all that we do, or toward something other than the true God— is determined in that deep place in our being.

### Locating "Heart"

But what is the character of that deep place in which our life-direction is determined? How are we to understand "heart" in relation to the kinds of accounts that philosophers have given to the dynamics of human consciousness?

In the *Republic*, Plato offers a tripartite picture of the "parts of the soul": each soul is composed of the logical, the "spirited," and the appetitive—or, as it is usually presented, reason, the will, and the passions. In a properly functioning soul, Plato insists, reason will rule or guide the passions by means of the will. A common picture of this is a chariot, where the driver, who is reason, is using the will to harness the passions. This tripartite picture continues today in less "soulish" form with what are often described as three "aspects" of human consciousness: the rational, the volitional, and the affective.

In teaching my undergraduate students about Plato's views on this subject, I always contrasted his views with the biblical perspective. Rationality itself is instrumental, I would tell them. It is—and here I would use a common Calvinist image—like a weapon. In the hands of a lunatic, it can do much harm; when used by an agent of justice, it can promote good things. This kind of imagery would suggest that wherever else a Calvinist might want to locate the direction-setting center of the human person, it is not going to be in the intellect. Our intellectual pursuits are guided by a prerational direction-setting. And that seems to be the overwhelming consensus of those who have explored this topic from a Reformed perspective.

But it is not a universal consensus. Some Calvinists have insisted that the biblical "heart" is actually to be identified with the intellect. This comes out clearly, for example, in some comments made by Elizabeth Clark George, the daughter of the late evangelical philosopher Gordon Clark, in a published reminiscence on her father's antipietist orientation. She takes note of what she sees as "the aggravatingly careless use of the terms 'heart' and 'head' which are tossed about in Christian conversation today." What many people don't realize, she says, is that, properly speaking, when people disparage "the 'head' they are actually denouncing the 'heart'" since "the 'heart' is not superior to the mind . . . [because] the heart *is* the mind." She continues: "The mind is not dry, dull, and spiritually detached; nor does the heart produce some emotional frill that supposedly substantiates salvation. The head and the heart are synonyms, regenerate in some people, unregenerate in others. And out of the abundance thereof, the mouth speaketh."[1]

Needless to say, the real issue here is often clouded by some unfortunate rhetoric on both sides. Elizabeth George reports, for example, that many evangelicals accused her father of being "all 'head,' no 'heart,'" even intending thereby to call his eternal salvation into question. She, in turn, finds it easy to dismiss those who want to posit a distinction between "heart" and "head" as grounding their salvation in "some emotional frill."

I don't find this insistence on the primacy of the intellect to be convincing. Up until quite recently I have insisted in my teaching that the heart is not to be identified with any of the three aspects in the tripartite scheme; rather, it is pre-cognitive, pre-volitional, and pre-affective. And if I had to abandon that contention in favor of one of the aspects, I would have gone for the volitional: since it was the willful decision to "be as gods" in Genesis 3 that got the whole mess of sin going, it would make some sense to see the fundamental event for restoring the right direction for our lives as a surrendering of our wills to God. But I have now been convinced by Bavinck that the heart should be identified primarily with the affective. Here is Bavinck in his 1909 Stone Lectures at Princeton Seminary:

> Man tries to give direction to his life by his consciousness, but that life itself has its origin in the depth of his personality. It must not be forgotten . . . that though reason is necessary to guide the ship of life, feeling is the stream that propels it. Beneath consciousness there is a world of instincts and habits, notions and inclinations, abilities and capacities, which continually sets on fire the course of nature. Beneath the head lies the heart, out of which are the issues of life.[2]

In his *Reformed Dogmatics*, Bavinck expands on this by depicting what he sees as a plausible sequence for how the workings of regenerating grace operate on the complexities of our consciousness. On one level, says Bavinck, we come to faith by hearing the Word proclaimed. "But that knowledge of God penetrates the heart and arouses there an assortment of affections, of fear and hope, sadness and joy, guilt feelings and forgiveness, misery and redemption." And then, he contends, "through *the heart it in turn affects the will*," which then becomes "manifest in works." All of this brings about the following result, says Bavinck: "Head, heart, and hand are all equally—though each in its own way—claimed by religion; it takes the whole person, soul and body, into its service."[3]

To be sure, what all this tells us is that it is not easy, from a biblical perspective, simply to divide the human person into three distinguishable "parts." Elizabeth George herself seems to be acknowledging this implicitly when, in defending her father's view on the primacy of the intellect, she tells us that "the mind is not dry, dull, and spiritually detached," thereby building some affective elements into her conception of cognition.

## Uses of the Tripartite Scheme

The biblical "heart" may be more fluid a notion than our tripartite labels can capture. But I am not prepared simply to abandon the kinds of distinctions those labels afford. At the very least they help us to sort out actual differences in the ways people set forth their accounts of what is distinctive to the human quest.

Take, for example, the ways in which thinkers in recent years have described "the Enlightenment project." In many accounts of where the Enlightenment went wrong, it is assumed that the defining feature of the Enlightenment was the insistence that enlightened human reason is the highest standard for deciding issues of truth and goodness and beauty. What this way of construing the Enlightenment ignores is the presence of Romanticism during the same period. And while we are certainly free to treat Romanticism as a separate movement, it is nonetheless the case that the romantics also were committed to "enlightenment." It also then makes good sense to see, say, a rationalist like Descartes and a romantic like Coleridge as sharing a common assumption—namely, that the highest standard of truth, beauty, and goodness in the universe is *enlightened human consciousness*. Their fundamental disagreement, then, is whether enlightened reason or enlightened affect ought to be the driving force in human consciousness. To see both views as covered by the Enlightenment label is to recognize the "faith" stance of each. Neither side can win the argument by appealing to enlightened consciousness as such. One chooses the cognitive and the other the affective—and each critiques the other by its own standard of what is primary in an enlightened consciousness. And to these arguments we can add the contentions of, for example, someone like Friedrich Nietzsche, who rejected both the rational and the affective in favor of the enlightened naked human will as the supreme arbiter: true enlightenment comes when—recognizing that there is no divine will over our individual wills—we each issue our own sovereign fiat: "Let there be light!"

## Three "Calvinisms"

Where I have found it especially helpful to use the tripartite scheme, though, is in the effort to understand actual differences within the Christian community, even within the boundaries of evangelical orthodoxy. I can illustrate this by a presentation that has given me much help over the years in understanding not only my own spiritual identity but also what I see as the basis for maintaining a robust neo-Calvinism.

In the mid-1970s, my colleague Nicholas Wolterstorff—we were both teaching philosophy at Calvin College at the time—delivered an address, sponsored by a Christian Reformed congregation in Grand Rapids, in which he set forth a typology of different "minds" within the conservative Dutch Calvinist community in North America.[4] He employed three labels: the doctrinalist, the pietist, and the Kuyperian. These labels signified, for him, three different perspectives on the kind of book the Bible is. For the doctrinalist, the Bible primarily sets forth religious teachings— *doctrines* to which we must give our assent. For the pietist, the Bible tends to be treated as a devotional handbook, the reading of which is meant to generate certain godly experiences and to form important subjective dispositions. And for the Kuyperian, the Bible is meant to give us our cultural marching orders, instructing us in the ways of discipleship in the collective patterns of life in the larger human community.

These three views of the Bible, Wolterstorff argued, generate three different basic tests for what it means to be faithful to what the Bible intends to convey. For some, the fundamental question has to do with doctrine: What biblical truth-claims must we accept about God and God's will for humankind? For others, the decisive test is about piety: Have I appropriated experientially what the Scriptures address to me in the deep places of my own personal being? For still others, it is about being aligned with God's culture-transforming purposes in the world.

Wolterstorff's typology has wider application than simply to Dutch Calvinism, a fact that George Marsden recognized when he adapted it for broader use by substituting the label "culturalist" for Wolterstorff's "Kuyperian"[5]—thus recognizing the reality of the kind of evangelicalism that emphasizes working for cultural renewal without linking that theologically to the influence of nineteenth-century Dutch writers.

This broader applicability of the typology is evident in the fact that most of us can easily imagine a conversation in which one Christian makes much of the importance of doctrine and another challenges that person by warning of the inadequacy of "mere head knowledge" for entering the kingdom; after all, the pietist will remind the doctrinalist, the devil has a fairly orthodox theology, but he still is a citizen of hell. The doctrinalist will then respond that our feelings, our subjective states, can be misleading unless they are grounded in a solid grasp of the truth. Suddenly a third party enters the conversation to point out that a person can have an orthodox theology and a strong personal piety and still be a racist or a perpetrator of economic injustice. At that point, predictably, the doctrinalist and the pietist together will respond with a warning against "works righteousness." And the arguments go on and on.

Wolterstorff was certainly correct, then, in identifying some obvious strands that often stand in tension. But I do have my own problems with his use of the "Kuyperian" label. For Wolterstorff it was a shorthand for characterizing what he would advocate in subsequent writings as "world-formative Christianity."[6] I certainly have strong affinities with that kind of culturalist emphasis; indeed, I have been much influenced by it. But in the final analysis, I am a pietist. And truth be told, I think Abraham Kuyper was also a pietist. I do not see Kuyper as a "Kuyperian" in Wolterstorff's sense of the term. This is not to deny that the great nineteenth-century Dutch theologian and activist called for the kind of Christianity that takes cultural transformation seriously. Many folks who know very little about Kuyper's life and thought can at least quote some version of his famous bold declaration that "there is not a square inch in the whole domain of our human existence over which Christ, who is sovereign over all, does not cry 'Mine!'"[7] But Kuyper also actively opposed the liberal theological teachings of his day—to the point that he even led a major exodus from the large mainline Reformed denomination in the Netherlands. And during his many decades as an important public and ecclesiastical leader, he regularly wrote profound, and very pious, meditations on biblical themes. The spirit of these meditations is nicely captured by the title of the large volume containing many of them—almost seven hundred pages in length—*To Be Near unto God*, a very "pietist" title, taken from the final verse of Psalm 73: "But as for me, it is good to be near God" (NIV).

For those of us who identify with the pietist tradition, there is no better example of what we are about than John Wesley's well-known testimony regarding his Aldersgate experience. As Wesley told the story, he attended on May 24, 1738, a meeting at Aldersgate, where someone read from Luther's preface to the Epistle to the Romans. Wesley reported that at the point where Luther in his text "was describing the change which God works in the heart through faith in Christ, I felt my heart strangely warmed. I felt I did trust in Christ, Christ alone for salvation; and an assurance was given me that He had taken away my sins, even mine, and saved me from the law of sin and death."[8]

The kind of very direct and datable experience that Wesley was describing has a link in my own spiritual journey to the fundamentalist "altar calls" of my youth. Typically there would come a point in an evangelistic service when the preacher would intone, "Every head bowed, every eye closed. No one looking around, please." And then the people present would be asked to search their individual hearts. Those who had not yet come to faith in Christ were urged to accept him right then. But it was also a time of self-examination for the rest of us, who were given the opportunity to look into our hearts anew and reflect honestly about our relationship to the Lord. And in those moments we sang hymns as well. "Is your all on the altar of sacrifice laid?" "I surrender all." "Just as I am, without one plea, but that thy blood was shed for me." "Jesus paid it all, all to him I owe." Those moments, and those hymns, were a crucial element in my own spiritual formation. They were occasions when I stood—in ways that I have never quite experienced elsewhere—face-to-face with eternity. Whatever else the "sawdust trail" meant to me—not all of it positive—it was for me in those moments a sacred space, of the sort that I have not been able to find with the same profundity in other regions of the Christian world.

### Pietism's Weaknesses and Strengths

Ernest Stoeffler was a scholar who devoted his life to the study of pietism in its many forms: Lutheran, Reformed, Anabaptist, Moravian, Puritan, Wesleyan, and the like. His magnum opus, *The Rise of Evangelical Pietism*, still stands as the best overall survey of pietism as an international movement. Not only does Stoeffler chronicle the various manifestations of pietism in great detail, but he does so with an obvious love for his subject matter, which means, among other things, that he draws attention to strengths in pietism that are often ignored by others. Indeed, in his study of American pietism he insists not only that there was a social conscience at work in many pietist subgroups but that the movement in general was an influential force for creating the environment for important twentieth-century gains in the promoting of social justice. He is convinced, he says, "that the Pietist understanding of life, which regards every fellow believer as 'sister' or 'brother,' helped to begin the process of breaking down the rigid barriers associated with ethnic origin, race, and sex, which Americans originally inherited from Europe."[9]

While he does much to highlight pietism's strengths, Stoeffler is not insensitive to the movement's weaknesses. He specifically singles out three of what he describes as its "less admirable" traits or tendencies: namely, an "escapist" mentality that puts "the emphasis on blessedness in the hereafter rather than justice for all in the here and now"; "a certain anti-intellectual atmosphere"; and a "pronounced tendency toward sectarian fragmentation."[10]

Stoeffler is right to point to these tendencies in pietism, but he clearly does not think than they are inevitable or intrinsic traits of a pietist orientation. And he is right about that also. When, for example, early in my intellectual journey I read Carl Henry's 1947 jeremiad *The Uneasy Conscience of Modern Fundamentalism*, I saw Henry, in his critique of fundamentalism, as focusing on traits that I later identified with the tendencies Stoeffler pointed out. Henry clearly condemns the "escapist" mentality that had come to dominate the evangelical mood in the first half of the twentieth century. He also worries much about a lack of nuanced evangelical engagement with the important intellectual issues of the day. And he certainly also regrets the separatistic patterns that had produced a fragmented evangelical movement. Henry was joined in looking for remedies to these defects by Harold John Ockenga, who wrote an introduction to Henry's book in which he emphasizes the same concerns.[11] Particularly on the point of countering the fragmentation of evangelicalism, it is no accident that Ockenga and others who founded the National Association of Evangelicals chose to name the association's magazine *United Evangelical Action*—a motif that also came to characterize Billy Graham's program of "cooperative evangelism."

I have spent a good part of my own participation in the evangelical movement working to remedy those traits that Stoeffler singled out as dangerous tendencies in pietism. This is still an important agenda today, even though the defective tendencies—and their attempted correctives—may show up in new ways in our present context. Having said all of that, I have long been convinced that it would be a very bad move to try to remedy these defects by moving in a completely opposite direction. We do not correct anti-intellectualism as Christians simply by slipping into a thoroughgoing rationalism. Nor is an uncritical accommodation to the dominant cultural patterns of this present world a proper antidote to otherworldliness. And an "anything goes" ecumenism is not the right way to counter the spirit of separatism. In saying that, I am affirming what I consider to be the spirit of a proper sort of pietism. Our intellectual lives, our cultural engagements, our relationships with others in the body of Christ—all of these must be guided by a personal and communal godliness, by hearts that desire the kind of holiness without which none shall see the Lord.

# 10

## Paying Attention to Context

I N THE LATE 1970s I WAS INVITED TO LEAD A WORKSHOP AT A large conference on urban ministry. In order to ensure some uniformity in the format of the workshops, the conference planners asked each leader to choose a title by filling in the blanks of this formula: "A _____ theological perspective on urban _____." The first blank was meant for a label that identified the leader's theological perspective; the second was for singling out the specific area of urban life that would be discussed. I had no difficulty filling in the blanks: I wrote "Reformed" for my theological perspective and "politics" for my area of focus.

When I received the official program for the conference, however, I was struck by the ways in which the other workshop leaders identified their theological perspectives. Some had chosen, as I had, a label that had long had some currency in theological discussion: "A Lutheran theological perspective on urban law." "A Catholic theological perspective on urban education." "A Mennonite theological perspective on urban community." But others chose very different sorts of labels: "A black theological perspective on urban family

life." "A feminist theological perspective on urban economics."
"An Asian American theological perspective on urban church life."

What took me by surprise then has now become common-
place in theological discussion: the labels associated with what
we have come to think of as "identity theologies," where ethnic,
gender, and national identities are now widely acknowledged to
have theological relevance. The significance of this newer labeling
system was impressed upon me with even more poignancy not
long afterward, when I attended an ecumenical consultation that
focused on the question of eucharistic fellowship. When the time
for discussion groups came, the participants were divided into
the standard confessional groups: Catholic, Orthodox, Anglican,
Free Church, and so on. I was in the Reformed group, and at the
outset of our discussion the one female member described her
discomfort in being in our group. "In my church," she said, "I am
not allowed to officiate at the Communion service. Because of that
I feel that I have much more in common with the Catholic nun in
the next room than I do with you men." The one black member of
our group quickly joined her protest: "In my part of the country,
Communion services are still racially segregated—and that's true
whether your theology is Reformed or Catholic or Methodist!"

People who were claiming the newer "identity" labels were
pointing to the inadequacy of a theological agenda consisting
primarily of the issues debated among the classical Orthodox,
Catholic, and various Protestant traditions. A much richer understanding of the scope of our theological differences, they have been
insisting, emerges when we give explicit attention to the theological
relevance of such factors as race, gender, class, and geography.

These matters are now taken for granted in most theological
circles. Recent theological discussion has rightly devoted considerable attention to the relation of the gospel to diverse cultural
situations. The term "contextualization," like its close kin "indi-
genization," is emphasized by thinkers who want to draw sympathetic attention to the different ways in which the Christian

message is received, appropriated, and interpreted in a variety of cultural contexts. It is not uncommon to be challenged to take an honest and critical look at the ways in which the transmission of the gospel to the non-Western world has been weighed down by a close association with colonialist programs, as well as with the values of a technocratic-scientific worldview. Nor has this kind of emphasis been viewed as necessarily hostile to the core beliefs of traditional Christian communities. Indeed, contextualization issues have been given much positive attention by thinkers who represent the more orthodox theological perspectives, especially evangelicals and Roman Catholics; it is the representatives of these traditions who have also been in the forefront of recent missionary activity, continuing to evangelize persons from non-Christian groups long after that has ceased to be a high-priority activity among mainline Protestants. Consequently, the more conservative Christian groups have been forced to struggle with contextualization issues because of the challenges presented to them by their own converts, who often combine a deep interest in cross-cultural questions with a strong commitment to theological orthodoxy. To repeat: it is a good thing that Christian thinkers have become sensitive to such matters. Indeed, for many of us in the Christian world, our first awareness of contextualization themes was a liberating experience. This has certainly been true in my journey. Attention to these themes has helped me to appreciate the fact of cultural diversity, both within the Christian community and in the larger human community as such.

## Philosophy and Context

When I was introduced to Anglo-American analytic philosophy as a graduate student in the 1960s, the kinds of approaches and issues that received much attention were shaped by a reaction against the older logical positivism. While only a small subgroup of analytic philosophers at that time would identify with the "ordinary language" school, there was nonetheless a widespread focus on our everyday uses of language. By paying attention to "what we say" in this or that situation, philosophers hoped to explicate the underlying "logic" that operates when, say, people make predictions or express appreciation for a work of art. The "we" whose uses of language the philosophers discussed referred, of course, to the philosophers themselves as well as to other people who were very much like them. This meant that it was not necessary to engage in carefully constructed research projects about linguistic practices, since "we" were all quite the experts on what "we" were saying about this or that subject. Reference was seldom made, therefore, to actual empirical studies of linguistic usage. Rather, the creative energies of philosophers were directed toward imagining how "we" would adjudicate matters in hypothetical circumstances.

Sometimes these imaginative exercises would consider cross-cultural matters. But when that happened, the emphasis was seldom on actual data from other cultures. Instead, a philosopher would propose a hypothetical situation involving an encounter with another cultural context. Ludwig Wittgenstein, whose later (i.e., post-*Tractatus*) writings were highly influential during this period, was a master of constructing these sorts of examples. He regularly engaged in what we might think of as "fictional anthropology." Here are a few typical passages in his *Philosophical Investigations* and *Lectures and Conversations*:

> Suppose you came as an explorer into an unknown country with a language quite strange to you. In what circumstances would you say that the people there gave orders, understood them, obeyed them, rebelled against them, and so on?[1]

> Ask yourself: Would it be imaginable for someone to learn to do sums in his head without ever doing written or oral ones?— "Learning it" will mean: being made able to do it. Only the question arises, what will count as a criterion for being able to do it?—But is it also possible for some tribe to know only of calculation in the

head, and of no other kind? Here one has to ask oneself: "What
will that be like?"[2]

If you came to a foreign tribe, whose language you didn't know at
all and you wished to know what words corresponded to "good,"
"fine," etc., what would you look for? You would look for smiles,
gestures, food, toys.[3]

Nothing in these probings would require any knowledge on Wittgenstein's part of actual cross-cultural data. Indeed, in his writings
these imaginings were of the same order as examples that he often
posed about hypothetical visitors from other planets.

This pattern of considering hypothetical examples for the purpose of philosophical analysis was evident also in the ethical writings of the period. In the 1950s and '60s many Anglo-American
moral philosophers were especially interested in the question of
moral "objectivity." They explored questions about whether moral
judgments—"Stealing is wrong," "Honesty is good"—are capable
of being shown to be true or false, or whether such locutions are
in some sense grounded in subjective states to which the categories
of truth and falsehood are not applicable. As they explored these
matters, they slid rather quickly over the substance of ethical diversity, showing little interest in the actual moral convictions and
practices of other cultures. For example, R. M. Hare concluded
his book *Freedom and Reason* with a chapter titled "A Practical
Example," in which he discussed race relations at length. But while
he obviously had South African apartheid in mind, there was not
a single citation of any work dealing with the actual situation in
South Africa. Instead Hare chose to offer examples "of arguments
that *might be used* by people when faced with conflicts between
races."[4]

While most of the major ethical thinkers during this period
seemed concerned to avoid an open endorsement of ethical relativism, a careful examination of their writings shows that they
were not very convincing on this matter. Philosophers like Hare,

Stephen Toulmin,[5] Kurt Baier,[6] and others were clearly committed
to accounts that were essentially relativistic in nature. Typically
they diverted attention from this consequence of their views by
insisting that while certain kinds of ethical disputes are, to be
sure, ultimately irresolvable, we can consign such matters to the
periphery of ethical discussion—as Hare did in the aforementioned
chapter by treating Nazis and defenders of apartheid as "fanatics."[7]

An important shift away from a reliance on these tactics occurred, however, in the work of Peter Winch. In his 1958 book, *The
Idea of a Social Science and Its Relation to Philosophy*, a work that
became a reference point in philosophical efforts to relate action
theory to broadly social scientific issues, Winch had demonstrated
a willingness to look directly at the writings of social psychologists
and sociologists. But in a critical essay on Winch's book, Alasdair
MacIntyre—who stands out in Anglo-American philosophy for his
consistent (and in recent years, quite successful) urging of his colleagues to broaden the range of philosophical dialogue—challenged
Winch to interact more extensively than he had with the kind of
anthropological study that E. E. Evans-Pritchard had undertaken in
his work *Nuer Religion*.[8] Winch took up this challenge in his 1964
essay "Understanding a Primitive Society,"[9] and Anglo-American
philosophers subsequently followed his lead by taking an increasing
interest in cultural anthropologists' reports on such phenomena
as Zande witchcraft, cargo cults, Dinka deities, and the political
systems of the Burma highlands. The results of this shift can be
seen in the very rich discussions of cultural diversity in two col-
lections of essays, one published in 1970 and the other in 1982, in
which Anglo-American philosophers and anthropologists explore
together cross-cultural perspectives on rationality.[10]

At the very least, this philosophical openness to anthropological data has meant that more recent philosophical discussion has
been enriched by a new store of examples. In ethical literature,
for instance, rather than tossing out unsubstantiated allusions
to, say, cannibalism or polygamy, moral philosophers now seem

to sense an obligation to describe the actual cultural contexts in which such practices are embedded.

But it is also obvious that in attending to such matters in more detail than they have in the past, philosophers are much less reluctant these days to promulgate straightforwardly relativistic accounts in ethics. And even where there remains a commitment to viewing ethical disagreements as in principle decidable with reference to cross-culturally binding standards, there is a sensitivity to the fact that we cannot assess ethical beliefs and practices in isolation from their larger cultural contexts.

## Fragmentation

Just as the philosophical discussion of ethical and other matters has been enriched by an emerging interest in the data of cultural anthropology, so the awareness of contextualization can be celebrated for the ways it liberates Christian theology from some insular—and imperialistic— patterns of thought. At the same time, however, my own enthusiasm for this kind of attention has been moderated by worries that I have about some aspects of the overall project. The major risk that I see in this emphasis on cultural shaping is what I consider to be an obvious one for anyone who takes seriously the central Christian insistence that there is a revealed Word from God that comes to humankind as such: the threat of relativism. Relativistic thinking is nothing new. But it appears these days in new guises, especially in the fragmentation that regularly comes along with an emphasis on diverse "narratives," accompanying charges that sexual and linguistic minorities have been oppressed by "totalizing" accounts of the issues of human life. Each cultural unit is urged to construct its own narrative as a means of maintaining control over its own destiny. And these groups must be vigilant in opposing any overarching "metanarrative" that is designed to place these distinct "identity" narratives into a common interpretive framework.

It should be obvious that the core convictions of traditional Christianity do not fare well in the eyes of the fragmentation celebrants. From that perspective Christian orthodoxy is a message of oppression. To insist, for example, that the Christian gospel calls all human beings to repent and to accept Christ as the unique Savior and as Lord of the worldwide church only serves to control the epistemological "have-nots" by imposing upon them a narrative that will simply reinforce their marginalization. And this controlling function is not seen merely as an accidental feature of traditional Christianity. It is taken to be intrinsic to its portrayal of reality. My own struggle has been to oppose these themes while at the same time admitting some truths that are associated with the overall perspective. The fragmentationist point of view may be wrong, but it is not *simply* wrong. It has appropriated some important insights in a distorted manner, which means that we must be sensitive to the insights even as we reject the distortions.

Wrestling with the fragmentationist outlook can be an important aid in exercising the "hermeneutics of suspicion," allowing us to move beyond a precritical state of consciousness. This involves an inevitable experience of something like fragmentation, a distancing from that which we have previously accepted as an integral whole that is directly "given" to our understanding. It is a good thing to experience this critical distancing with reference to our own cultural location. Thus it is helpful for us to see that which we previously experienced as a coherent unity now broken up into fragments, so that we are confronted by the fact of a seemingly disconnected set of cultural contexts. Not only can this cognitive distancing help us better understand our own cultural contexts, but the attention to cultural location can itself be a means for gaining clarity about the larger issues of life. As the anthropologists George Marcus and Michael Fischer have pointed out, both "epistemological critique" and "cross-cultural juxtaposition" are important methods of "de-familiarization."[11] And as another anthropologist, James Peacock, puts it, we have not yet appreciated the benefits of cultural anthropology until we recognize the ways in which that discipline "joins philosophy and other fields that push us to examine our conduct, our values, and our lives to consider the premises that guide us and the consequences of actions, probing these matters as deeply, critically, and broadly as we can."[12]

Becoming aware, then, of the diversity of cultural contexts and of the manner in which our own cultural location shapes our way of viewing the world is an important means of gaining a critical perspective on reality as such. Approaching the "givens" of our experience, including the ways in which we understand God and God's relationship to humankind, in a manner that features defamiliarization and fragmentation—this can be a healthy thing. But if it is to be genuinely healthy, the experience of fragmentation should not comprise an end state. It should be seen as a clarifying "moment" in our consciousness and not as a permanent mode of being in the world.

## Identifying Cultural Units

For me, the errors of fragmentationism are grounded in the fundamental problem of identifying the kinds of cultural units whose particular narratives we are going to treat as irreducible. I have found the social scientist Barbara Frankel helpful in exposing this problem. We might think of a human being, she suggests, as living "within a set of Chinese boxes, . . . a social universe composed of contexts of ever-widening extent, from the dyad to the world-system, and from microseconds to millennia."[13] There are an infinite number of ways in which we can combine characteristics to identify ourselves: age, gender, hair color, sexual orientation, neighborhood, city, state, nation, hemisphere, and so on. How then do we specify with any degree of precision, she asks, the appropriate context for defining, say, the cultural identity of a person or group?

A similar kind of critique has regularly been formulated in the history of philosophical critiques of ethical relativism. An excellent example is the case made in the 1930s by the Princeton philosopher W. T. Stace, who examined the version of relativism that holds that while we cannot adjudicate differences *between* cultural groups, we can make moral judgments *within* such groups, since there is typically a set of standards accepted as applying to all members of the group. "But," Stace asks, "is even this minimum of moral judgment really possible on relativist grounds?" He argues that it is not. "Perhaps the blessed phrase 'social group' will be dragged in to save the situation. Each such group, we shall be told, has its own moral code which is, for it, right. But what is a 'group'? Can anyone define it or give it boundaries?"[14]

Stace goes on to argue that any attempt to provide a definition will surely be subject to challenge. Are gangsters to be criticized morally for departing from the standards of their society? They can simply insist that they have their own group within that larger social unit. Even within an assemblage of gangsters, a moral disagreement can simply be construed as the presence of two "groups" where we thought at first glance there was only one. "It means in the end," says Stace, "that every individual is to be bound by no standard save his own."[15]

And, I want to add, even when we focus only on the individual, it is difficult to draw boundaries. Some "postmodern" psychologists have been arguing in recent years that the problem of identifying legitimate identities occurs even on the microlevel of the individual, within an individual psyche—and, they argue, there is no solution to it. This is the case made, for example, by Kenneth Gergen in his book *The Saturated Self: Dilemmas of Identity in Contemporary Life*. He argues that traditional conceptions of how to understand personhood—the notions, for example, that we have unified selves and that human beings have "intrinsic worth" or "inherent rationality"—have been discredited by "the postmodern turn" as having no basis in reality. They are merely ways of talking about human beings, and they are in fact bad ways of talking. We simply must accept the fragmentation of selfhood and learn to enjoy what Gergen calls "a free play of discourses" about ourselves. This means, furthermore, he says, that we help people best by inviting them into what he labels an "endless wandering in the maze of meaning." He even suggests that we may need to write a new postmodern hymn with the title "Mazing Grace."[16]

Gergen does go on to recommend that we learn how to have "internal dialogues" among our multiple selves so that we can learn how to wander in our internal mazes in productive ways. But it is not clear exactly what the standards are that will guide this wandering in a world in which all comparative judgments are arbitrary. Why should my sports-fan self have any less status in my life than the self that senses a need to serve the poor? Why should I prefer any instinct or preference over any other one? In such a world, what is the difference between a healthy and an unhealthy self? What would keep each of us from simply proclaiming, like the young demoniac whom Jesus encountered, "My name is Legion; for we are many" (Mark 5:9)? To be sure, it is always open to the fragmentationist to accept these criticisms as legitimate and simply insist that he or she is willing to live with the chaos of incoherence—this is, in fact, the response that many present-day thinkers give to these sorts of criticisms. And it is difficult to know how the argument can continue once that point is reached. But we will still want to pay close attention to the ways in which such people speak and act, in the hope of finding further points of contact to pursue.

Here is an example of what I have in mind: A few years ago, Jacques Derrida—a philosopher well known for making fragmentationist prescriptions—became embroiled in a controversy over the publication of one of his essays in a volume published by Columbia University Press. Derrida did not like the translation (or the translator), so he took legal action to keep the volume from appearing. The *New York Review of Books* gave considerable space to the charges and countercharges, labeling the dispute "L'Affaire Derrida." At one point in the exchange, Derrida expressed considerable frustration over his critics' allegations. He regretted having to respond again, he said, but it was necessary nonetheless "to recall a few stubborn and massive facts" that should not be ignored.[17]

This is one of a few times that I have taken delight in something written by Derrida. His formulation here ("a few stubborn and massive facts"), with its clear insistence that there are binding standards for assessing our claims about reality, is intriguing and worthy of broader application. My own sense of the need to press the issues with those who seem content with disconnected narratives is reinforced by regular signs, like this formulation of Derrida's, of a deeper yearning for commonality and consensus—signs that are often there to be seen, if we are willing to pursue the conversation long enough to find them.

## Babel and Pentecost

In his important treatise in moral philosophy *Ethics after Babel*, Jeffrey Stout characterizes our contemporary cultural situation as one for which the biblical image of Babel can serve as "a trope."[18] Stout focuses specifically on how the kind of thinking that I have associated with fragmentationism affects our moral discourse, but his observations are also instructive for understanding our broader intellectual and cultural climate.

The Babel trope is indeed an apt image for our present-day mood. In Stout's account of our moral situation, the Babel of our moral diversity is haunted by three "specters" that threaten the bonds of our communal lives: "skepticism, nihilism and relativism."[19] I think it is obvious that these three "isms" are also at work in the broader, more-than-moral reaches of our private and public lives. Now, of course, if the fragmentationist view of reality is the correct way of seeing things, and if we want to be honest people, we will simply have to live with some version of our contemporary confusion of tongues. Stout, however, refuses to concede the case to the thoroughgoing skeptics, nihilists, and relativists—even though he still assumes the backdrop of Babel, arguing that we can piece together a workable moral discourse by a pragmatic process of what he describes as moral bricolage.[20]

Reading Stout on the Babel trope influenced my own thinking, while it also stimulated me to propose a more explicitly biblical alternative to Babel. The culture of Babel takes the confusion of tongues for granted; it sees no clear alternative to the acceptance of irreducible diversity. In such an understanding of our cultural condition, the Christian metanarrative can only be viewed as scandalous. But the Scriptures present a remedy for Babel's confusion. Pentecost was God's reversal of Babel. There the confusion of tongues was transformed into mutual understanding: "Are not all these who are speaking Galileans? And how is it that we hear, each of us, in our own native language? . . . In our own languages we hear them speaking about God's deeds of power" (Acts 2:7–11).

This is, I believe, a contrast that has profound importance for contemporary debates over "multiculturalism." If we take the Pentecostal alternative to Babel seriously, we cannot allow multiculturalism simply to be defined in terms of the Babel experience. Babel represents one kind of multiculturalism. Babel is an extreme picture of an irreducible diversity, of the loss of common patterns of understanding; Babel confuses, divides, and erects barriers. Pentecost, in contrast, represents a very different kind of multiculturalism. The Pentecostal experience does not eliminate the diversity of tongues, but it provides us with the ability to communicate across linguistic and cultural boundaries. Pentecost heals, unites, and promotes understanding. From this perspective, the fundamental question about cultural diversity today is this one: Are we going to think about this diversity against the backdrop of Babel or against the backdrop of Pentecost? In an important sense, of course, we are faced here with a sheer act of faith. Indeed, the fragmentationist mood highlights the reality of the basic

faith choice in a very special way. The great Jesuit thinker John
Courtney Murray recognized this fact already in the 1960s in his
Yale lectures; the postmodern thinkers, he said, have forced the
fundamental issues back into a "biblical mode."[21]

> The issue is drawn. Which is the myth and which is the reality?
> Is the myth in Nietzsche or in the New Testament? Is it in Marx
> or in Moses? Is it in Sartre of Paris or in Paul of Tarsus? Is God
> dead, as the prophet of the postmodern age proclaimed, or is he
> still the living God of more ancient prophecy, immortal in his
> being as He Who Is, deathlessly faithful to his promise to be with
> us all the days, even to the end of the epoch within which both
> the modern and the postmodern ages represent only moments in
> a longer dialectic of history?[22]

## Created Diversity

What we need is the negation not of cultural diversity as such
but of the cultural diversity of Babel. Pentecost brings its own
version of diversity. Because the Spirit is building the church by
saving persons from every tribe and tongue and people and nation, we must reflect carefully on the way that Spirit reaches out
to us in the cultural locations in which we find ourselves. The
gospel is addressed to a rich variety of human cultural contexts.
To acknowledge this kind of contextualization can be a fruitful
way of exploring the riches of Pentecostal power.

I reported earlier about the ways I have been influenced by several Dutch theologians—Bavinck and Berkouwer in particular—on
the subject of the image of God. They helped me to think about
the ways in which each human individual is created in the image of
God. There is also a "collective" possession of the divine image.
The Lord distributes different aspects of the divine likeness to
different cultural groups. Each group receives, as it were, its own
assignment for developing some aspect of the image of God. Only
in the eschatological gathering-in of the peoples of the earth,

when many tribes and tongues and nations will be displayed in their "honor and glory" (Rev. 21:26) in the new Jerusalem, only then will we see the many-splendored *imago Dei* in its fullness.

I came to realize the need for some careful nuancing in developing this approach, however, during my engagement in active opposition to South African apartheid during the 1970s and '80s. When the black anti-apartheid activist Steve Biko was killed by the South African police, I authored a letter, signed by most of my Calvin College faculty colleagues, to the faculty of one of the Afrikaner Reformed universities. In urging them to take a stand against the continuing oppression of the apartheid regime, I quoted what I thought to be a convincing biblical text, from Acts 17:26 (KJV): the Lord "hath made of one blood all nations of men for to dwell on all the face of the earth." I found out later, to my chagrin, that this verse was a favorite of the apartheid advocates, since it goes on to say that God "hath determined the times before appointed, and the bounds of their habitation." "One blood" was no problem for the apartheid defenders to admit—as long as the diverse peoples were kept within the assigned proper "bounds of their habitation."

One of the most prominent theological architects of apartheid thought, Nic Diederichs, was known for his insistence that the Creator dislikes "deadly uniformity"—which is why, he said, the world contains a plurality of cultural groups.[23] That statement, taken out of the South African context, would certainly have been endorsed, not only by Herman Bavinck, but also by the people who have made us more conscious in recent years of cultural contextualization. We human beings, in all our cultural diversity, display a mysterious richness. Theology in the Pentecostal mode can be an important way of gathering the splendors of this mystery into the church of Jesus Christ, drawn from every tribe and tongue and people and nation. We are privileged, with our ever-increasing opportunities for global awareness, to enjoy the gifts of this gathering-in. Our affirmation of the wonders of this gift, though, must be properly nuanced if we are to avoid new forms of racism and ethnocentrism.

## The Scope of Contextualization

But again—and I am eager to keep making this reminder—those nuances should not be allowed in any way to detract from the importance of cross-cultural explorations on the part of the Christian community. We miss the real message of the contextualizers if we hear them saying that it is merely permissible to translate gospel themes into the terms of a specific cultural context. Their point is a much stronger one: *all* of our preaching and theologizing are inevitably contextualized. None of us escapes the formative influence of our cultural situation in our understanding of the biblical message.

The Bible's message is many-faceted. As God's Word to us, it must never be confused with the cultural contexts in which we receive that Word. The black South African theologian Allan Boesak made that point clearly in his critique of certain varieties of black theology. What are commonly referred to as "the black situation" and "the black experience," Boesak argues, do not *within themselves* have revelational value on a par with Scripture." These contexts are simply "the framework within which blacks understand the revelation of God in Jesus Christ. No more, no less."[24] This last comment is a telling one. The black experience, Boesak says, is not itself divine revelation; rather, it is no more than the situation in which blacks have received that revelation. But neither is it *less* than a situation to which God has revealingly spoken. This means that while the black historical experience is not on a par with scriptural revelation, it is at least on a par with *white* historical experience, which must also be denied revelatory status.

This clearly implies, though, that in order for us to understand God's revelation in a way that does not confuse it with the cultural contexts in which it is received, we must study those cultural contexts carefully. The examination of the contents of "identity" theologies, by sifting and sorting their various claims, can be an important process for getting at the riches of divine revelation. The Catholic philosopher Albert Borgmann has argued that, for all its celebration of diversity, the "postmodern" consciousness often limits its attention to the *surfaces* of the complex reality that it claims to understand so well. Borgmann addresses this malady with a call to rediscover "the eloquence of things" in their particularity, in order to recognize "the things that command our respect and grace our life" as we get glimpses of "the depth of the world."[25] The Christian study of diverse cultural contexts can be a vibrant response to this kind of mandate.

Not that cultural diversity has to do with *mere* surfaces. Many of the differences run deep. But we are indeed "made of one blood." And the common predicament of our shared rebellion also requires the "one blood" remedy that God has graciously provided at Calvary. When we probe, then, into the deepest places of the shared human condition, we eventually come to a grace beyond which there are no further depths.

# 11

## Reformed and Evangelical

SHORTLY AFTER MY RETIREMENT FROM MY STINT AS PRESIDENT
of Fuller Theological Seminary, a friend from a denomination-
ally sponsored theological school asked me this question: "How in
the world did you manage to lead such a diverse school as Fuller? I
mean, how did *you* manage it—a self-declared Calvinist, presiding
over a student body from all over the evangelical map: Mennonites,
Presbyterians, Methodists, Anglicans, Baptists, 'emergent' types,
and Lord knows what else? How did you pull it off?"

I did not have a very detailed answer to offer. Basically, the challenge for leading any diverse community is to find value in that diversity while also constantly exploring the underlying commonalities
that brought people to that diverse community in the first place. And
I learned much in the process of attempting to "pull it off" at Fuller.

### Belonging to the Movement

My father was a pastor in the Reformed Church in America, but
his theology was more generically evangelical than it was Reformed

in character. He had come to a saving faith in Christ through the ministry of the Star of Hope Mission, a wonderful urban mission in Paterson, New Jersey, and immediately joined the staff there, preaching in prisons and conducting services in what were then called "old-age homes." When he met my mother, a daughter of strict Dutch Calvinist immigrants, he moved in a more Reformed direction, but he never completely abandoned the Scofield Bible dispensationalism of his Star of Hope training. While the local church was an important part of our family life, we supplemented that with extensive involvement in the parachurch networks of evangelicalism, often of the more fundamentalist variety: summer Bible conferences, evangelistic crusades, subscriptions to *Moody Monthly* and *Eternity,* and faithful listening to Charles Fuller's *Old Fashioned Revival Hour* and Donald Grey Barnhouse's *Bible Study Hour.*

There came a point in my late teens when I rebelled against much of that, but in God's providence a good part of my rebellion was theological. I became a convinced Calvinist, with a special love for the Canons of Dort. Fortunately, I also became very fond of Spurgeon's sermons on election and related topics. So, although I argued with my parents much on points of doctrine, Spurgeon helped me to see that classic Reformed doctrines could give depth to the kind of preaching that issued from a strongly evangelical "heart for the lost." This was reinforced for me eventually by discovering that Abraham Kuyper—who, having been trained in liberal theology, had a profoundly evangelical conversion during his first pastorate—not only cared deeply about politics and economics but also wrote wonderful devotional meditations on the need to spend time concentrating on the Lord's presence. Thus I was never tempted simply to draw lines in the sand between Reformed thought and evangelical piety.

When I joined the Calvin College faculty in 1968, I found that many of my Reformed colleagues there expressed a distaste for much of evangelicalism. The Christian Reformed community at the time understood itself in "third-party" terms. We Dutch-American

Calvinists were neither evangelicals nor liberals. Ours was a theological perspective that integrated the best of those other two parties while rejecting their errors. The third-party self-identification
could also be found among other groups with a recent history of
immigration—the Mennonites and Missouri Synod Lutherans,
for example. Several of us, mostly young faculty who had come in
from "outside" the Christian Reformed denomination—George
Marsden, Ronald Wells, Paul Henry, and Mary Stewart Van Leeu-
wen were my fellow travelers in this regard—argued that we Grand
Rapids Calvinists should see ourselves as part of the evangelical
mix. Eventually that viewpoint won the day, due in part to Calvin
College's decision to increase enrollment by serving a broader
constituency. And Paul Henry's creative leadership in founding
an annual conference on Christianity and politics did much to
establish Calvin as a convener of evangelical scholars for serious
discussions of timely topics.

The decision that Phyllis and I made to move to Fuller Seminary
in 1985, after seventeen marvelous years on the Calvin faculty,
was a decision on my part to work at a slightly different mix of
Calvinism and evangelicalism. Fuller was and is the epitome of
broad-based evangelicalism, a community representing a spectrum
from Anglicanism to Pentecostalism to "none of the above"–type
worshiping bodies with names like Mosaic and Living Waters
Fellowship. When my friend Lewis Smedes was ready to retire
from the Fuller faculty—he had left Calvin for Fuller right when
I joined the Calvin faculty—he lobbied for me to serve as his
replacement. He and I both saw my joining the Fuller faculty as
a continuation of his role as a representative at the seminary of
Kuyperian Calvinism.

That worked fine for the first four years at Fuller, until David
Hubbard asked me to serve as provost in 1989, which was followed
by my move into the presidency in 1993. This meant that I had to
begin speaking with a more "generic" evangelical voice, a challenge that I took on with considerable enthusiasm.

## Articulating Neo-evangelicalism

The early Fuller leaders had been my youthful heroes. One of my thrills soon after I entered my teens was shaking Charles Fuller's hand when our family, on a vacation trip from New Jersey to California, attended a live broadcast of the *Old Fashioned Revival Hour* at the Long Beach Auditorium. Harold John Ockenga, Fuller's founding president, was another household name in my early years. I heard him speak many times in my childhood, at youth rallies and Bible conferences. And, as already mentioned, I was very familiar as an undergraduate with the writings of Edward John Carnell; the one time I saw him in person was when I sat in the audience at the University of Chicago's Rockefeller Chapel the evening he appeared on a panel, in 1962, with Karl Barth. I was also influenced early on by Carl Henry's writings.

I found it easy as president, then, to articulate the kind of "neo-evangelical" vision that Fuller stood for over the decades. Fuller came into existence, I have often observed, because of a desire to promote in post–World War II evangelicalism a commitment to solid scholarship, cultural engagement, and spiritual renewal. That was an agenda I could not only endorse; I could preach it with some passion because it was in essence the story of my own spiritual-intellectual journey.

But I also deeply appreciated how the early neo-evangelical leaders were profoundly committed to what they had brought with them from fundamentalism. They were unwavering in their commitment to the full and supreme authority of the Scriptures. They cared passionately about evangelism. They were uncompromising in their commitment to what they rightly saw as nonnegotiable basics: the reality of our sinfulness and our desperate need for a Savior, the substitutionary atonement, the "blessed hope" of his return, and so on. These convictions were at the heart of generic evangelicalism. And Fuller, with its student body from seventy denominations and nondenominations, along with its global vision for theological education, has been generic evangelicalism at its best.

None of that in any way diminished my own commitment to Reformed theology. Indeed, being at Fuller reinforced my conviction that a "thin" generic evangelicalism has to be strengthened by taking seriously the various "thick" confessional streams that feed into the evangelical movements,[1] especially the streams that I have associated with four "re-" movements: Reformation theologies, restorationism, revivalism, and the Pentecostal-charismatic renewal.

Again, I am not opposed to the idea of a broadly based evangelical movement that is bonded together by a shared commitment to such things as the supreme authority of God's Word, a passion for evangelism, and a firm desire to honor the Lord Jesus as the heaven-sent Savior who alone can save. Indeed, I love that kind of theological consensus. My problem is not with a transconfessional, transdenominational evangelical theological consensus as such. But I do worry about a movement in which the only operative theology is of a generic evangelical variety. Take the example of our views about the nature of the church. Evangelicals are often accused of having a "weak ecclesiology." That is certainly a legitimate observation if we focus primarily on what we evangelicals do or do not say when describing what we hold in common. Billy Graham has said little about the nature of the church in his wonderful ministry. The National Association of Evangelicals does not require its members to subscribe to a detailed ecclesiology. Nor has *Christianity Today* focused much on what we Reformed types label "the marks of the true church." Among influential evangelical scholars, F. F. Bruce and James Houston were formed by the Plymouth Brethren Movement, while James Packer and John Stott have ministered as Anglicans. The ecclesiological spectrum evident in those examples is a broad one.

None of that should mean, however, that "thick" ecclesiology is not important for the evangelical movement. Indeed, my own conviction is that the impression we often give about a lack of robust ecclesiological understanding is in fact based on a genuine weakness in evangelicalism. As a matter of sheer social history, Alister McGrath was right when he responded to the charge that evangelicals have an "under-developed ecclesiology" by suggesting that maybe "it is others who have over-developed ecclesiologies."[2] We evangelicals have long worried about ecclesiological perspectives that are so highly detailed and all-consuming that they crowd out other important theological concerns. And so we respond by emphasizing some things, such as the need for a personal relationship with Jesus Christ and the need for evangelizing the lost, that are often neglected by people who delight in detailed ecclesiologies.

Fair enough. But without careful attention to ecclesiological details we can get into serious theological trouble. There is plenty of evidence today that when we start with a theology that only features the shared evangelical convictions, we are left with a movement that can easily be blown about by every wind of doctrine. A consensus evangelical theology is a weak basis for sustaining biblical orthodoxy. Much to be preferred is an evangelicalism that, sharing some fundamental convictions that are ignored and even explicitly denied in the larger Christian community, eagerly enters into a freewheeling discussion of what we can best draw upon from the "thick" confessional traditions of the past in addressing urgent questions today about the church's life and mission.

I am convinced that the argument for "thickness" needs to be stressed much in the present. Unfortunately, the rich discussion of various historical traditions that engaged many younger evangelicals in the wake of the Chicago Declaration is less visible on the contemporary scene. Insofar as attention is given to historical traditions, much of it is highly selective. Many younger evangelicals engage in a kind of "designer" theology, a bricolage project wherein we find elements drawn from the monastic tradition, alongside some Anabaptist themes, with an atonement perspective that draws heavily on the European post–World War II explorations of the "principalities and powers." There is also a discernible "post-evangelical" trend that features the rejection of the substitutionary atonement along with long-held evangelical convictions about sexual morality.

To be sure, some kind of mixing and matching of elements from various theological traditions is inevitable for those of us who recognize an unnecessary wall-building in our own historic camps. When I read, for example, the Stone Lectures that my theological hero Abraham Kuyper delivered at Princeton Seminary in 1898, I frequently bristle at some of his uncharitable comments regarding Catholicism, the Anabaptists, and Lutheran thought. I have learned much from those traditions, incorporating elements of each in my own Reformed theological perspective. But I do see myself as bringing those diverse insights into a perspective that has coherence as a system of thought that differs significantly on key points from those other traditions.

All of this is background for my saying that as Fuller's president I worked for twenty years at a balancing act between the "thick" and the "generic." I made no effort to hide my own Calvinist loyalties. At the same time, though, I encouraged, with considerable success, an increase in the numbers of serious Anabaptist scholars at Fuller. And I promoted the idea of Fuller as a thriving center for Pentecostal and Wesleyan scholarship. When the seminary received complaints about a couple of my colleagues who seemed to be denying the reality of "the intermediate state" as a condition of continuing consciousness between the death of a believer and the final resurrection, I mentioned my own friendly arguments with the colleagues in question, while also defending our taking that perspective seriously within Fuller's theological mix: Luther said things along those lines, I pointed out, and the doctrine of "soul sleep" was featured in the growth of Adventism. In a present-day context in which new questions are posed to theology from research in neuropsychology, I argued, we need to look to evangelical debates of the past as resources for the present. Serving as president of Fuller Seminary forced me to clarify my thinking about "thick" and "generic" in evangelical life and thought. And I continue to struggle to hold the two together, even when I no longer have to do so as a designated institutional leader.

## Enriching Calvinism

I have been emphasizing the need for evangelicalism to be fed by the specifics of various "thick" theological traditions, and I have made it obvious that I think my own Calvinist tradition has much to offer in this regard. I wrote an entire book, *Calvinism in the Las Vegas Airport*, about why I find Calvinism so compelling, and I will not try to cover that territory here. Furthermore, as I approach the end of this book, I will say some things about how I struggle with the fact that Calvinism itself is a pluralistic tradition—which means that I have engaged in my own *intra*-Calvinist debates, some of them characterized by considerable passion, and even not a little rancor.

As I reported earlier, when I arrived at Calvin College in 1968 as a new faculty member, I discovered that many of my colleagues wanted to maintain a serious distance from the Anglo-American evangelical movement, and that some of us countered that spirit with pleas for closer alliances with evangelicalism. Those calls, as I saw the situation, were not based on mere pragmatism—the practical need, for example, for broader patterns of student recruitment. Those of us who made those pleas were convinced that a healthy Calvinism needs to draw upon the strengths of evangelicalism. There are, of course, some standard ways of saying why it is a good thing to interact with people with whom we disagree: "Iron sharpens iron," or "Discussions with people from other perspectives have helped me understand better what I believe." There is nothing wrong with these formulations. They do capture some of the benefits of interacting with traditions other than one's own. The problem with sticking with these kinds of responses, though, is that they are quite compatible with a strong defensive mentality. Those who emerge from a battle with an enemy, for example, can rightly claim that "iron has sharpened iron," that what it took for them to defeat their enemy made them stronger in their commitment to their cause—ideological, say, or patriotic—than if they had never gone into the battle. What my daily exposure to such a rich evangelical diversity has taught me, though, is to look at more than the theology a person professes in judging his or her value to the kingdom of God. As I testified in *Calvinism in the Las Vegas Airport*, Charles Spurgeon has been a positive model for me in this regard. He loved Calvinist doctrine, and he could on occasion be severe in criticizing alternative theological systems. As a case in point, he disagreed strongly with some of John Wesley's teachings, so much so that he confessed, "I detest many of the doctrines that he preached." But he immediately went on to say, "Yet for the man himself I have a reverence second to no Wesleyan." And then this:

> The character of John Wesley stands beyond all imputation, self-sacrifice, zeal, holiness, and communion with God; he lived far above the ordinary level of common Christians, and was one "of whom the world was not worthy." I believe there are multitudes of men who cannot see these [Calvinistic] truths, or, at least, cannot see them in the way in which we put them, who nevertheless have received Christ as their Savior, and are as dear to the heart of the God of grace as the soundest Calvinist in or out of Heaven.[3]

Two analogies have helped me much in thinking about the positive aspects of theological differences. One is the notion of medical specializations. A practitioner of preventative medicine looks at things differently than a surgeon does. Oncologists focus on different aspects of our physical being than gynecologists do. In the big picture, all medical specializations have their place. This is why it is always important to consider getting a second opinion when dealing with a medical problem. And in weighing conflicting professional recommendations, it is necessary to take the specializations of the recommenders into account.

Specialization is also a good thing in theology. I have to confess that I have not given much attention in my career as an ethicist to the Sermon on the Mount. I am much more of a "Sinai commandments" thinker when it comes to charting out the proper paths of a godly moral life. My Mennonite friends, however, focus intensely on the Sermon on the Mount. I have learned to take them seriously on this subject, as a corrective to the relative lack of attention given to these teachings of Jesus in my own tradition.

A second helpful analogy is the system of religious "orders" in Catholicism. It is misleading to contrast—as often happens—the "unity" of Catholicism with the "dividedness" of multidenominational Protestantism. Catholicism encompasses many different orders, each with its own set of special vows, and each promoting unique missions and virtues. Jesuit life and thought are different from what characterizes the Franciscans. Dominicans are different from Carmelites, and Benedictines from Claretians. I see my own commitment to Calvinism as something like both committing to a theological specialization and taking some special spiritual-theological vows.

A high school student wrote to me recently for advice on the differences between Calvinists and Arminians. She was being educated in a Calvinist context but wanted, in a term paper she was writing, to put the differences in the most "civil" manner possible (she had read my book on civility). I told her that I think of the differences in this way: We Calvinists have taken a special vow to protect at all costs the idea of God's sovereignty, whereas Arminians have taken a special vow to protect the idea of human free will. This means that we Calvinists would rather run the risk of limiting human freedom than give the impression that we are detracting from God's sovereign control over all things, whereas Arminians would rather risk challenging God's sovereignty than deny our responsibility for our basic choices in life. But when these respective vows are working in the best way, each side knows when it goes too far, acknowledging that we have to live with some mystery on the subject. (She liked my answer—and asked me to pray that her Calvinist religion teacher would like it as well when he read her paper!)

My experience in the diversity of spiritualities and theologies of the evangelical world has been greatly enriched by seeing things in these terms. Lutherans are an "order" organized around a strong commitment to the idea of justification by faith alone. Pentecostals have taken a vow to honor the power of the Holy Spirit in a special way. Wesleyans want to remind all of us of the biblical call to "holiness unto the Lord." Mennonites model for all of us what it means to walk "the way of the cross." And so on.

None of this is meant, of course, to deny that there are some very bad theological ideas at work in the world—and certainly within evangelicalism! But when I encounter a teaching that I find strange, and even offensive, I try to remind myself to ask what specialization might be at work in the other person's way of viewing things and how I might learn from it. To be sure, many of my fellow Christians will see that as much too messy a way of dealing with theological disagreements. But I have also learned to be content with a certain degree of messiness in my theology.

# 12

## When Truth Is Distorted

IN MY 1989 BOOK *DISTORTED TRUTH*, I SUGGESTED THAT EVERY Christian who thinks about serious intellectual matters ought to have a favorite error. What we believe is very important to us, I wrote, but so is what we do not believe. Often the viewpoints that we reject most energetically tell us something about the manner in which we embrace our own positive beliefs. I wrote that in the chapter where I discussed nihilism. And I confessed that of all the basic worldviews that I reject, the nihilistic perspective was my favorite. I said that some of my favorite thinkers are folks whose views border on nihilism, and I named Friedrich Nietzsche, Albert Camus, Jean-Paul Sartre, and Simone de Beauvoir as examples of thinkers whose wrongheadedness I was especially fond of.

I still agree with that assessment. Each of those thinkers is associated with the existentialist movement, a school of thought that was quite popular in intellectual circles when I was an undergraduate. Sometime during my last two years of college, I read William Barrett's *Irrational Man*, and it motivated me to read more widely on the subject. I wrote a college term paper on Søren

Kierkegaard, and in graduate school I departed a bit from the analytic-oriented agenda of one seminar and did a fairly lengthy comparison of Augustine and Sartre on selfhood—a paper I wish I could find and read, to see how I handled the subject.

Sartre especially loomed large in my philosophical development. The people I studied with in my graduate programs were for the most part not interested in his thought. But I treated reading Sartre as a kind of side hobby, and when I began teaching introductory philosophy courses, I made a point of regularly assigning Sartre's *Existentialism Is a Humanism* as a required text. I consider it a nice, readable statement of the basics of Sartre's version of existentialist thought.

I'm not sure what happened to existentialism. No one in the academic world seems to say much about it anymore. People do still read and write about Kierkegaard and Nietzsche, and Heidegger continues to get much attention. But nowadays each of those three is seen as important in his own right—with little attention given to how each prepared the way for the philosophical ideas associated with existentialism as a movement. In contrast, Sartre's philosophical writings seem to stay pretty much on the shelf these days. I'm not quite sure why his thought has gone out of style. In the past few decades, I have read my share of writings by the more recent postmodern types: Derrida, Foucault, and the like. I know that those thinkers have their quibbles with Sartre, but they still seem to me basically to be carrying on some of the key emphases of Sartre's philosophical project.

One reason I find Sartre fascinating is that he serves nicely as a kind of foil for Calvinist ideas about human selfhood. He laid out in stark terms the issues at stake between a Christian worldview and a straightforward rejection of the basics of the biblical perspective on the human condition. This use of Sartre as a foil is expressed succinctly by the Dutch philosopher S. U. Zuidema, as he moves toward the conclusion of his critical discussion of Sartre's system, in a booklet published as part of a Calvinist series on modern thinkers. Sartre's thought, says Zuidema, is "a tissue of plagiarism and perversion of religious ideas. His idea of freedom is a perversion of the sovereignty of God, his idea of self-election, a perversion of God's election, the idea of inter-human society as conflict, a borrowing from ancient polytheism, his idea of self-foundationing man taken from the *aseitas* of God, who is his own foundation." What all of this amounts to, then, says Zuidema, is that Sartre's "deepest intent is an apostate *Eritis sint Deus*, you shall be as God, by forsaking God and justifying that which the Bible teaches as the fall into sin."[1]

I basically agree with Zuidema's portrayal of Sartre's overall project. But while Zuidema's "tissue of plagiarism" rhetoric points us to something important in Sartre's thought, it can also keep us from learning lessons from Sartre. And the fact of those lessons is another reason why I find Sartre's brand of existentialism fascinating.

### Perverting "God-Likeness"

The great Jesuit thinker John Courtney Murray puts the point well in his 1965 book *The Problem of God* (a book that has also strongly influenced my own thinking!): Sartre and other atheist existentialists, says Murray, have performed the important service of returning the formulation of the basic issues of the human condition to a "biblical mode."[2] Like Zuidema, but in less harsh terms, Murray sees Sartre as endorsing the serpent's "You shall be as God" of Genesis 3.

Other non-Christian philosophers have been less direct than Sartre in opposing biblical thought. They may ask us to place our ultimate trust in our own rationality, or in an enlightened imagination, thus ruling out God's revelation in the Scriptures as our only reliable authority on the important issues of life. But thinkers like Sartre and Nietzsche explicitly go to the heart of the matter. The nonexistence of God, they say, means that there is no sovereign divine will that called the universe into being. And since an objectively ordered reality—a cosmos—would require a divine "let there be" to create and sustain it, reality is, properly understood, a chaos. But there is a hope of sorts to be found in all of this, they argue. Our own individual spirits can brood over the chaotic waters, and we can issue our own version of the divine "let there be." But this requires the recognition that we are alone. Any good that can be found must be created by our own wills. And this means acknowledging our radical freedom to create.

To be sure, within the Sartrean framework there are obvious limitations on what I am free to create. I cannot create a world in which there are no heart attacks. I cannot choose to be a rhinoceros. And so on.

I find it most helpful to think of what Sartre means by radical freedom in terms of roles and relationships. Each of us inhabits a variety of roles. I am a husband, a father, a grandfather, a professor, a church member, a sports fan, a consumer—and more. Each of these embodies a certain pattern of behavior. I inhabit these roles, but Sartre would insist that in doing so I am exercising a fundamental freedom. In each of these roles I am free to say no to the role in question, casting it aside by refusing to acknowledge that it has any power over how I live my life. Suppose I am presented with the opportunity to act in a certain way, but I refuse to do so, saying, "I can't do that; I am a Fuller Seminary professor." In seeing my professorial role as restricting my choices, I am, Sartre would say, living in "bad faith." I am refusing to acknowledge my radical freedom. I am failing to acknowledge that I am free to say no to the *Fuller professor* role. But, I might reply, for all sorts of reasons it would be irresponsible for me simply to abandon the behaviors and expectations that go with my professorial role. True enough, Sartre would say, but I still have the freedom to say no to the more basic *responsible human being* role. I am always free to choose to be irresponsible.

That is fairly elementary existentialist thinking about freedom. And I see it as an accurate way of viewing the human situation—except for one extremely important factor. As a Christian I have to insist that there is one role I cannot escape: my fundamental human status as a creature of God. Even here, of course, I have a kind a basic freedom: I can choose to rebel against being "contained" within that role, or I can choose to accept who I am, as a created person who lives my life *coram Deo*.

That is exactly our fundamental situation as human beings as portrayed in the first three chapters of Genesis. We are created in God's image, "to glorify God, and to enjoy him forever," according to the Westminster Shorter Catechism. But the serpent presents us with the challenge to "be as a god" to ourselves. What could be a more stark contrast with Christian thought than that? Glorify the one true God or be your own god. Submit to divine authority or sit on your own throne.

It is precisely this kind of radical conflict between opposing worldviews that led me to think about the notion of *distorted* truth. Actually my ideas on this issue were inspired by a comment from H. Richard Niebuhr, alluded to earlier, in his discussion of the Christ-transforming-culture perspective. In arguing for the continuing presence of the cultural ordering of creation that God intended from the beginning, Niebuhr maintains that under fallen conditions "culture is all corrupted order rather than order for corruption. . . . It is perverted good, not evil; or it is evil as perversion and not as badness of being."[3]

That way of viewing the relationship between created and fallen culture has profoundly influenced my own theology of culture. And I have extended that basic insight to questions of truth and falsehood. I find it helpful to see the kind of non-Christian thought that overtly opposes Christianity to be a distortion of something true, rather than simply false in an unqualified manner.

To be sure, we have to allow that it is difficult to see exactly what truth is being distorted in some situations. The same holds for the Niebuhrian claim about culture. There may be certain cultural practices, artifacts, or patterns where it is difficult to see the difference between "evil as perversion" and evil as "badness of being." Similarly, some claims put forth by thinkers may be so perverse that it is not worth spending time probing for a truth of which their claims may be a distortion.

But I still take Niebuhr's point as a trustworthy insight, in matters both of culture and of truth. On the falsehood question, for example, I think the distorted truth formulation applies helpfully to what many of us see as the basic falsehood in the history of humankind: the claim made by the serpent to Eve in Genesis 3. He told her that if she ate the fruit from the forbidden tree, "You will be like God" (Gen. 3:5). The clear intent of the serpent's claim is that the human pair need not acknowledge God's supreme authority over their lives. They could prosper best by claiming that authority for themselves.

Unlike folks from other Christian traditions—my Eastern Orthodox friends, for example—we Calvinist types see the endorsement of this serpentine thesis as the event that got us into the ongoing mess that only sovereign grace through the atoning work of Christ could remedy. "You will be like God" is the fundamental falsehood that led to our fallen condition. But in the light of the creation account of Genesis 1, the falsehood of Genesis 3 is a distortion of something true. In the act of creating human beings, God's declared intention was to fashion them "in our image, according to our likeness" (Gen. 1:26). In her unfallen state Eve was already in a very important sense "like God." The serpent was now tempting her with a distorted understanding of her God-likeness. Instead of being like God in ways appropriate to her humanness, she was being encouraged to ascend to an understanding of herself as *being* God by appropriating to herself the kind of authority that belongs to God alone. But she could succumb to this temptation to *be* God precisely because of her capacities as a being who was created to be God-*like*.

Zuidema is right, then, to see the Sartrean conception of a radical human freedom as a "plagiarizing" of the biblical account of our created nature. What he fails to be explicit about, though, is the fact that the plagiarism is itself a misappropriation of a profound truth.

## Learning from Falsehoods

Much hangs on whether we see the falsehoods set forth by non-Christians as falsehoods-as-such or as distortions of the truth. At least this has been the case for me. The distorted-truth approach has created for me a presumption that I can learn something from thinkers with whom I radically disagree on important topics.

I once heard a preacher start off a Mother's Day sermon by quoting the opening lines of Albert Camus's novel *The Stranger*: "Mother died today," the fictional narrator wrote. "Or maybe yesterday. I can't remember." This is a good example, the preacher said, of the decline of respect for motherhood. It is certainly understandable, he allowed, that a person in the 1950s might momentarily forget whether his mother died, say, in 1943 or 1944. But to "forget" whether it was yesterday or today—a person has to be pretty nonchalant about his mother's passing to make that kind of admission, said the preacher.

The sermonizer missed the profundity of what Camus was portraying. Camus's fictional character was not so much alienated from his mother as he was alienated from himself. Camus was taking it as a basic fact that our relationship with our mothers is a very intimate aspect of our self-identity. The narrator of his novel was looking at that very reality of mother-son intimacy—the bonding of his own self with that self's mother—as a manifestation of his deep alienation. His reality is as a son who sees himself as *this* mother, the mother who is now dead. But he now sees that intimacy from an existential distance. He sees his ordinary self in this instance as "the stranger."

The point Camus is making in this fictional portrayal is not too different from what Sartre was getting at in his constant refrain that "existence precedes essence." We can think of a person's "existence" in Sartre's thought as the radically free self, with the "essence" as consisting of the kinds of roles that we often make reference to in "defining" ourselves. These roles never really capture who we are as existential agents.

Someone says to me, "Tell me about yourself," and I respond by identifying myself in terms of my basic relations—son, husband, father, academic, church member, and so on. To assume that I have somehow captured who "I" am in this list of roles, as I noted earlier, is to engage in what is for Sartre "bad faith." I am, he insists, radically free not to "be" any of these things. To be sure, I cannot change the simple facts that I was born into a certain family in a certain place at a certain time. But I cannot allow these factors to impinge on my freedom. What I cannot legitimately say is something of this sort: "I can't help it; that's the way I was raised," or "As a husband and father my options are limited." My radical freedom means that I can say no to these factors as limiting my choices. I have the freedom to choose not to be determined by how I was raised or by specific social roles. The biblical parallel to this Sartrean portrayal of selfhood is clearly set forth in Psalm 139—one of the great *coram Deo* passages in the Scriptures. Since God knows our motivations and thoughts better than we do, we ask the Creator: "Search me, O God, and know my heart; test me and know my thoughts" (Ps. 139:23). We live inescapably under God's gaze. Denying the reality of that gaze does not make it go away. The apostle Paul describes the rebellion of those who deny the existence of God in blunt terms: "for though they knew God, they did not honor him as God or give thanks to him, but they became futile in their thinking" (Rom. 1:21).

Christian critics of Sartre's perspective on the self often complain that all of this is radically "individualistic" in a way that clearly runs counter to the biblical perspective. I agree with that assessment, but in a manner that places a strong emphasis on the "radically" part of the criticism. In my book *The God Who Commands*, I include a chapter titled "On Being Fair to 'Individualism,'" in which I argue that there is an ineradicable emphasis in the Bible on the importance of the human individual. As I conclude the chapter I acknowledge that the perspective I am defending would inevitably bring charges of being "individualistic," and I profess that I simply refuse to be intimidated by that kind of accusation. When someone accuses a position of being "individualistic," I argue, it usually means that the position in question places too much of an emphasis on the individual self. Thus understood, I maintain, the charge does not actually prove anything. What it signals is the need to look carefully at the status of the human individual in the overall scheme of things.[4]

In this regard I quote James Cone's marvelous study of the African American slave spirituals, where he points to the prominence of the word "I" in those songs. He rejects the charge that the view of selfhood being expressed there is influenced by the strong individualism of "white pietism." Rather, he argues, "the 'I' of black slave religion" was born of "the struggle to be both a person and a member of community." This in turn, Cone observes, was an expression of the slave's recognition that in spite of persistent denials of his personhood by those who claimed to "own" the slave, the singer of the slave spirituals knew that "he alone was accountable to God, because somewhere in the depth of the soul's search for meaning, he met the divine."[5]

Cone's description here provides a striking contrast to Sartrean individualism. As Sartre peers into the depth of his own selfhood, he sees only radical will. When the slaves looked into those depths, they saw the face of the Living God in whose likeness they had been created. They also heard, of course, God's call to community. But—to repeat Cone's point—they also knew that each individual self is accountable to the Lord for how to respond to that call.

Cone was certainly right to highlight the unique dimensions of the slave community's awareness of the "I" of human selfhood. And he was also wise to distinguish the theology at work in the slave songs from the more persistent individualism that often has characterized white evangelical pietism. But at the heart of each Christian expression—white and black—is the desire to preserve the *coram Deo* reality of the individual self. In the white evangelical movement, we have often preserved this reality at the cost of ignoring God's desire that we commit ourselves to a community of disciples whom God wants to equip for active service in the world. In this regard there is something important to learn from Sartre's "plagiarism": the standing *apart from* our roles and relationships is meant to make us aware of the responsibility we have in our commitments *to* those roles and relationships. Our difference with Sartre, though, makes all the difference in the world, which is why we also need to learn from the slave tradition. Our commitment does not arise out of the "nothingness" of our radical freedom. It is a response to what we have seen and heard in the presence of the Living God.

# 13

............................................................................

# On Being a "Public Intellectual"

............................................................................

T HE IDEA FOR THIS CHAPTER CAME TO ME RATHER LATE IN THE writing of this book. The stimulus was a request that I received from a student who wanted to do a phone interview with me. For a theology course at her divinity school, she was writing a paper on my career as a "public intellectual" and wanted to have some background beyond the extensive reading she had done.

My first reaction to the request was a sense of awkwardness. This was not the first time that someone referred to me using the "public intellectual" label, but up to this point I had not ever had to decide whether actually to own the label. And I had to admit that I had some ambivalence about doing so.

The positive part of the ambivalence had to do with the fact that when people have applied the label to me—often when introducing me as a visiting speaker or lecturer—they obviously meant it as a commendation. This is an intellectual, they were saying, who has had some influence beyond the academy. And it would be silly for me to deny that, having been quoted and interviewed often in the popular media.

Where was the negative part of the ambivalence coming from, then? As I thought about that question, I found myself rehearsing a conversation that I once had with a scholar who was very intentional about being a public intellectual. He taught at a major university, and, he confessed, his colleagues were very suspicious of his visible public role. Their attitude toward him was not so hostile that they could challenge his tenured status. And each year he would devote some time to publishing a scholarly work in a peer-reviewed journal in his academic field—so he in fact kept his faculty credentials in excellent shape. "But," he said to me, "I do the purely academic stuff to keep my colleagues from punishing me for my more public intellectual activities. And they still see that public side of my life as a real dumbing down of good scholarship!"

While I admired him for his public intellectual contributions, I also realized that I feel more vulnerable than he expressed feeling about the attitudes of academic colleagues. And as I thought about it, at least two factors figured into this sense of vulnerability. One was my journey into the academy from a decidedly anti-intellectual evangelical environment. I wrote about that in *Called to the Life of the Mind*, and I will not rehearse the details here. Suffice it to say that having made my way into the academy over serious objections from family and friends, the thought that my academic colleagues would see me as "dumbing down" serious scholarship was a disturbing one.

The other factor had to do with my decision to go into full-time academic administration, first as Fuller's provost, then as president. Several of my old friends expressed disappointment at the time that I was "leaving scholarship for fund-raising and things like that." While I did not see the decision in those terms, I felt the sting of the negative comments—yet another fear of being seen as "dumbing down."

Unlike the scholar who supplemented his public intellectual activities with just enough peer-reviewed research to keep his academic detractors at bay, I genuinely wanted to maintain scholarly engagement. After I had been in the presidency for a few years, while also publishing some essays in academic journals, another president asked me how I was able to keep up the scholarly side of my career to the degree that I had. "I haven't read a serious book in my academic field for five years," he said. "I just don't have the time. I don't know how you manage it!" What I wanted to say was that if he really had not read a serious academic book for five years, then I could not give him any helpful advice on the subject. Reading serious scholarship for me was simply a measure to maintain intellectual health.

Being Fuller's president put me at a distinct advantage in that regard. The trustee leadership of the seminary maintained a sense of the "scholar president." My three predecessors in the role (Harold John Ockenga, Edward Carnell, and David Hubbard) clearly modeled this. Each year when the trustees conducted their job performance review with me, they would ask me if I was keeping up on some scholarly projects.

Again, I did manage to keep up with some scholarly contributions. But I also kept up with the activities associated with the "public intellectual" role.

### Focusing on "Public"

The "public" part of being a public intellectual has been, for me, itself a matter of scholarly focus. Increasingly in my career I became interested in the *study* of public life. This was an expansion on my earliest interests. The first two books I wrote were explicitly concerned with politics: *Political Evangelism* (1973) and *Politics and the Biblical Drama* (1976). But then my focus began to broaden—an expansion that had much to do with a phone call that I received from a crusty Englishman, Mark Gibbs.

Our family spent the 1975–76 academic year in Princeton, where I had a postdoctoral National Endowment for the Humanities fellowship in sociology at the university. Early in the fall of '75, I received a call out of the blue from Mark Gibbs, a stranger to me at the time. It was an odd conversation, with him addressing me in a rather curt, lecturing manner. It went something like this: "You don't know me, but I know about you. You probably don't realize exactly what you are doing, but your writings about the need for evangelical Christians to be actively involved in politics in service to Christ are really all about the ministry of the laity in the world." Then he told me—not asked me, but told me—that I would be speaking at a conference in Dallas on the subject. To prepare for that conference, he said, I had to read Hendrik Kraemer's *Theology of the Laity*. And Mark would soon be coming to Princeton to tell me more.

Well, that was the beginning. He did come to Princeton, and I did speak at Dallas University at "The Laity: A New Direction." I was initiated there into a group of people, mostly mainline Protestants and Catholics, who met regularly at various places around the country to strategize about promoting the cause of the laity.

Most important, though, was that Mark became a dear friend. A rather strange friend, to be sure. He was never very warm—until near the end, which I will describe soon. He was always school-marmish with me: "You *will* do this. . . . You *will* read this." The relationship shaped me in significant ways. Reading Kraemer on the laity was certainly a major theological event for me. And I became part of a movement—comprised in a special way by people whom Mark Gibbs had enlisted—that gave direction to a lot of what I have done theologically.

I came to see Mark as an itinerant Franciscan-type lay friar (by affiliation he was an Anglican), whose mission in life was driven by a passionate commitment to upgrading the status of the laity in the theological understanding of the church. He was an ecumenist of a special sort, and he saw me as a key link to evangelicalism. While he often derided my Dutch Calvinism, he was genuinely interested in bringing my kind of Kuyperianism into the mix. His overall strategy seemed to be to bring various strands—Vatican II's "Apostolate of the Laity" theology, the best of Lutheran teaching about vocation, the theological instincts that gave shape to so many vocation-specific laity groups in evangelicalism (Christian Nurses Fellowship, Christian Legal Society, Fellowship of Christian Athletes, etc.), Anglican insights about the meaning of baptism—into a rich interaction that could provide a broad-based movement to promote the cause of the laity as God's people in the world.

The gatherings around the country were interesting. A group of us, maybe ten or twelve, would show up in some retreat center and report on what was happening in the cause of the laity. We would often read something in preparation for theological discussion. Mark always acted kind of crotchety at these events, but we all had become very affectionate toward him. Once we were at a Catholic center where another group was having a silent weekend during which their only mode of communication was to use Tinker Toys to express themselves. He was horrified. Another time, one of the denominational leaders in our group suggested an exercise where we would begin our time together answering two questions: Where would I rather be than at this meeting? And what is my worst worry about our project? People got into it, but when it was Mark's turn he answered the questions this way: "Where would I rather be? It is none of your damn business! What is my worst worry? That we will have to do more of this nonsense!"

When I moved to Fuller in 1985, Mark was upset with me. He felt strongly that my teaching at Calvin College was in essence an important exercise in the education of the laity for broad patterns of ministry. For me to move to a seminary was, for him, my running the risk of joining the enemy. We had good arguments about this.

A few months before he died, Mark came to visit me in Pasadena. I had not seen him for a while, and I was shocked at how frail he was. We spent several hours together in my office, and then at lunch. While he was very weak, he was still his schoolmarmish self—until he was ready to leave. Then he thanked me for my friendship and told me this was probably the last time we would see each other. "There is no need to be emotional about it," he said. But then he began to cry. "I have told you it was a mistake to come here to Fuller," he said. "But it does not have to be. You can promote the cause here, and it can have a big impact. Promise me you will stay faithful." I promised, and I moved to give him a hug, but before I could embrace him he turned and left.

My third book, *Called to Holy Worldliness*, was published in 1980 in a series that Mark had edited. My interest in politics was not completely absent, but I paid considerable attention to broader areas of Christian service—the larger world of business, entertainment, education, and family life—where Christians actually spend their weekday lives. I was addressing a broader "public," including, but more than, the political.

This focus of mine fit nicely with a scholarly concern that was emerging in the broader academy. Theologians in particular began exploring a subject matter that has come to be labeled "public theology." This was an expansion of what had been associated with such fields as "Christian social ethics," "political theology," and "church and society." This expanded theological focus had a parallel in—and has been to some degree influenced by—discussions in the broader American academic community in recent decades. Already in the 1970s the well-known sociologist Peter Berger coauthored a book with the theologian Richard Neuhaus, in which they complain that too much attention was being given by social scientists and social commentators to the relationship of individuals to the political order. If we are to avoid the twin evils of individualism on the one hand and statism on the other, they argue, we must pay attention to the ways we can strengthen a whole variety of associational patterns ("mediating structures")—neighborhood organizations, youth clubs, service groups, churches, and families themselves—that can provide a buffer zone between the state and the individual, thus providing crucial resources for character formation.[1] Since then this focus has blossomed into some robust discussions of "civil society." In attending to the scope of "public" life, scholars have been exploring the importance of those contexts for human association that extend beyond the realm of kinship but are not yet—or at least they ought *not* to be—swallowed up by the "political." And many of us have been especially interested in how the Christian community can effectively address this broader public agenda. My "Gibbsian" interests in the theology of the laity have connected nicely with this scholarly agenda.

## On "Saying Something Theological"

When the ethicist James Gustafson was invited to deliver the 1981 Ryerson Lectures at the University of Chicago, he gave his presentation the title "Saying Something Theological." To explain his choice of a title, he recounted a bar conversation he had with a biologist colleague at the end of a long day of work at a conference exploring issues in human genetics. After a few drinks, the scientist confessed to Gustafson that the nature of his religious upbringing, the tenets of which he had long abandoned, made him uneasy about being in the presence of theologians. The time they were now spending together, the scientist said, was the longest he had experienced in his adult life with someone committed to the theological enterprise. Then, toward the end of their conversation, Gustafson reported, "with great sentiment he put his left arm around my shoulder and said, 'Gustafson, say something theological!'" While Gustafson was caught off guard, he told his Ryerson audience that he at least "had the presence of mind to say, 'God.'"[2]

If someone were to conduct a poll of the persons attending a plenary session of a biennial gathering of the Association of Theological Schools, it is quite likely that there would be clear consensus that Gustafson's response was a proper one. Theology, we would all agree, has something to do with the deity—with thinking about God and what belief in the reality of the divine means for contemporary life. Beyond that, however, differences would quickly surface about how to move on theologically from that basic starting point.

This willingness to come together, in spite of our differences, is motivated by a shared conviction that our individual institutions are strengthened by agreed-upon standards for accreditation facilitated by active support for processes of peer review. And in our willingness to participate in the activities and programs of the Association of Theological Schools, we are giving expression to our conviction that while we have much in common with other kinds of educational institutions in the broader academy, it is important to focus together specifically on the opportunities, challenges, and norms for evaluation that have to do specifically with something called *theological* education.

## "As We Saw It"

There are many good reasons, then, for studying the ways in which church members should be engaging in public life, as well as studying how educational institutions can best foster that kind of public engagement. But what about the usual meaning of "public intellectual"—namely, that of using one's role in the intellectual community as a platform for directly *speaking to* the issues of public life? I started doing quite a bit of that in the early 1970s, not long after I began my full-time teaching career at Calvin College, and especially in my involvement with the *Reformed Journal*.

The *RJ*—"a magazine of Reformed comment and opinion"— was a labor of love on the part of the William B. Eerdmans Publishing Company. I started reading it when I was at the University of Chicago, and it became my lifeline to Calvinist orthodoxy in a time when it would have been easy for me to move in other directions. In the broader evangelical world at the time, it was one of those rare periodicals in which writers would criticize liberal theology while also condemning racism and militarism.

When I joined the Calvin College faculty, I quickly connected with the *RJ* leadership, who were at both Eerdmans and Calvin. After a few years I became one of the editors.

The magazine never had more than a few thousand subscribers—certainly not enough to have made it without the support (financial and editorial) of the Eerdmans company. We always said, though, that "our influence is greater than our numbers would suggest"—although I grew somewhat cynical about that line when I met the head of a very small seminary that I had never heard of who said the same thing about his school. What was clear, however, was that among the few thousand people who did read the magazine, there was a cadre of readers who were intensely loyal and who will to this day express deep regret that the magazine ceased to exist in the late 1980s.

A key benefit of my involvement with the magazine was the personal relationships. What we called our "editorial meetings" were long evenings when we typically met in the basement study of the home of Henry Stob (the revered ethicist at Calvin Seminary). Nick Wolterstorff and George Marsden were among the other editors, and we always ranged widely in our discussions, leaving it up to the two Eerdmans editors, Marlin Van Elderen and Jon Pott, to do the hard work of putting an actual issue together. One time, for example, someone had submitted an article alleging that the Super Bowl was an idolatrous "civil religion" rite, glorifying patriotism, militarism, consumerism, and male chauvinism. This was a rather common line for religious elites to take in those days, and we had a lengthy discussion about whether to run the piece. At the end of our long deliberations, we decided to run the article, even though we all had misgivings about doing so. As we left the meeting together, Marlin remarked that he thought the author of the article was probably right about a few things—but, he added, "I still hope Dallas gets creamed!"

A more specific benefit for me was submitting to the discipline of writing pieces of about nine hundred words in length. We had a special section at the front of the magazine—reader surveys always ranked this as the most-read part of each issue—called "As We See It." This section featured brief commentaries about all sorts of "public" topics: public policy, sports, TV shows, and so forth. I wrote at least seventy-five of these over the course of a decade or so, and the experience was a formative factor for me in articulating thoughts about a broad span of public topics.

## The "Luck" Factor

The widely influential British philosopher Bertrand Russell once remarked that he was very much aware, when he began his scholarly career, of not being the brightest or the best of his generation in the academy. What made him more successful than the others, he said, was that he got all the lucky breaks.

I'm not in Russell's league in terms of prominence (or intelligence!), but like him I am surprised—given that so many of the folks I started out with, in studies and in teaching, had much more talent than I possess—that I have come to have access to a fairly large "public." Like Russell, I have to chalk up much of it to the breaks that have come my way.

A case in point: Two years after joining the Calvin College faculty, I read a paper at the annual Wheaton College Philosophy Conference, on the subject of obeying divine commands. It was well received, and in the hope of refining it for publication I sent it to the great Princeton University ethicist Paul Ramsey, asking for his critique. I had no previous contact with Ramsey and fully expected that I would not hear from him. But he quickly got back to me, saying that he liked the paper very much and had sent it on to Richard Neuhaus, with the recommendation that it appear in *Worldview*, the journal Richard was editing at the time. Paul was a member of that journal's editorial board. Very soon after hearing from Ramsey, Richard called to tell me he would like to publish my piece. It appeared in *Worldview*, and I even received seventy-five dollars as a payment for it. From that experience I got to know Ramsey fairly well, and he included me in a couple of conferences that he sponsored. I also became a regular participant in Richard Neuhaus's frequent consultations on such topics as civil religion, multinationals, liberation theology, and Jewish-Christian relations. More importantly, Richard enlisted me as an active drafter and participant in the "Hartford Appeal" project that he convened with Peter Berger, through which I got to work with Avery Dulles, Alexander Schmemann, George Forell, George Lindbeck, William Sloane Coffin, and others.

That was in the early 1970s, when evangelicals were typically not yet welcomed into broader faith-based discussions. I never doubted that Richard's friendship with me was genuine, but it was also clear that his reaching out to me was part of a larger strategy. He was forming new alliances, and he saw evangelicalism as an important part of the picture, well before others in the mainstream would come to decide (usually grudgingly) that the evangelicals deserved a place at the intellectual table. He, along with Peter Berger, took me on for a while as a kind of protégé—one of a younger generation of evangelicals whom they saw as important to their emerging coalition.

The Hartford project received much publicity, and since I was (along with Lewis Smedes, whom I encouraged Neuhaus and Berger to invite) a novelty, as an evangelical associated now with a group of well-known religious experts, I was interviewed by and quoted in *Newsweek* and the *New York Times* in stories about the Hartford document. This in turn put me on the list of folks that journalists kept for occasional calls about newsworthy topics. That sequence of events certainly counts for me as a series of fortunate happenings.

But as lucky breaks go, this next one is difficult to top. Sometime in the mid-1970s the Christian Reformed Church, the denomination to which I then belonged, was invited to send an "observer" to a North American consultation on ecumenical issues, sponsored

by the World Council of Churches. It was held at a Catholic retreat center in the Midwest and was attended by forty or so mainline theologians and denominational leaders. I was very much a
stranger in that crowd. I knew none of the other folks present,
except by reputation, and I was only politely acknowledged as a
participant. Then very suddenly things changed. During the first
plenary session a staff person from the retreat center came in and
interrupted the proceedings: "Is there a Dr. Richard Mouw here?"
she asked. "The religion editor of *Time* magazine would like you
to call him. He says it is urgent." Every eye followed me as I left
the room, and I made some new friends after that at the gathering.

Here is the background: The *Time* magazine religion editor was
Richard Ostling, who was an elder at his local Christian Reformed
congregation in New Jersey. The church was searching for a new
pastor, and two of the leading candidates being considered were
recent graduates of Calvin Seminary. The search committee was
meeting that evening, and Dick wanted to ask me if I had any
perspective on the candidates. He had called my office at Calvin
College, and the secretary had given him the retreat center phone
number where I could be reached. No one at the consultation asked
me about the nature of the phone call from *Time* after I rejoined
the meetings—nor did I volunteer the information!

## Discovering Some "Smart Ones"

As I have described my breaks, they clearly occurred within a larger
context in which evangelicals were marginalized in mainstream
public life. I have already discussed a new evangelical activism
that was beginning to show its face publicly during these years in
the early 1970s. But an important part of the picture I have just
been describing was a presumption in the mainstream of a lack
of intellectual fiber in the evangelical movement.

This presumption was expressed to me in a rather blunt manner
by the dean of a major secular university, who called during this

same period to invite me to serve on a panel at a conference his program was sponsoring. He had seen me quoted as a member of the Hartford group and decided that I might fit into the conference he was planning. I had to turn him down because of a prior commitment. He expressed disappointment, saying that he really wanted to have me as an evangelical on the panel. And then this: "I don't know how to ask this in any other way," he said, "but are there any other smart ones that you can recommend?" I tried to maintain a polite tone in offering several names.

Things have obviously changed dramatically since then. I served for several years as a member of Harvard Divinity School's Visiting Committee and was actively involved in the beginning stages of planning the establishment of their Alonzo L. McDonald Family Professor of Evangelical Theological Studies. The evangelical professor who was appointed to that chair is, as I am writing this, the dean of the Divinity School. Evangelical scholars have prominent roles in the broader academy: in philosophy and history, for example, but also in other disciplines. In 2012 I gave a plenary address to a group called the Society of Vineyard Scholars—and came away greatly impressed by the high level of scholarly achievement in the Pentecostal movement. I regularly speak on the campuses of evangelical liberal arts colleges, as well as at events of organizations ministering to university students—and I always learn more than I contribute. The evangelical academy these days has much intellectual vitality. "Smart ones" indeed!

### Still a "Scandal"?

In 1995 my friend Mark Noll published *The Scandal of the Evangelical Mind*, in which he argues that there still was not much intellectual fiber in the evangelical community. He was pointing to an important reality. Of course, Noll himself was and is a highly visible intellectual player in the evangelical community, and the fact that his book was praised by hundreds of evangelical scholars suggested that there was more fiber than Noll was admitting to. But taken as an overall point about evangelicalism, Noll had it exactly right. The movement was, and still is, lacking in adequate intellectual strength.

A friend of mine, a non-Christian academic, once told me that he had been familiarizing himself with Fuller Seminary's mission and was impressed with the quality of what we were doing. "The level of academic discourse here at Fuller is as good as it gets anywhere in the scholarly world. I wish my secular colleagues—many of whom are 'cultured despisers' of evangelicalism—could spend some time here."

But then he expressed a worry. "You have a problem, Mouw," he said. "Right now Fuller manages to maintain the highest level of scholarship with a strong connection with grassroots evangelicalism. But that can't last. Either you are going to start dumbing things down or you are going to move to the 'ivory tower' thing!"

In candor I have to admit that my secularist friend may have been a little too optimistic in his reading of the present relationship between the evangelical academy and popular evangelicalism. There is a "mind" within the evangelical movement, but there is a serious gap between what the mind says and how the rest of the body often acts. In our public life, especially in recent years, we evangelicals have consistently embarrassed ourselves by mindless behavior. My friend was offering important advice, however. To the degree that there is some mutual support between the evangelical academy and the grass roots, we need to work hard to keep the mutuality strong. If the creative tension cannot be maintained, the results will be tragic. The two components of evangelicalism need each other. Neither can sustain a healthy evangelical character without the other.

In 1656 John Reeve, the self-styled prophet of the British sect known as the Muggletonians, ridiculed the notion, quite popular in his day, that Christ would soon return to earth to establish a literal millennial kingdom over which he would reign as king.

Reeve insisted that it is highly unlikely that Jesus would want to return to earth to establish any sort of political regime. After all, he observed, Jesus had already suffered much during the last time that he lived on earth—why would he want to come back as a politician and suffer again? Isn't one round of intense divine misery enough? In recent years, in light of the ways a new evangelical activism has invaded the public arena, I have been tempted to add my own spin to Reeve's line of argument. Even if Jesus did not suffer enough during his first earthly tour of duty, I ask myself, isn't it likely that he has by now had his fill of "Christian politics"? Hasn't at least his capacity for suffering in the public arena finally reached its limit? And even if he still has an interest in such matters, doesn't he wish the evangelicals would stop embarrassing him in the public square?

In my better moments, however, I am grateful for the way the evangelical movement has begun to operate with a broader vision of Christ's kingdom. And I pray for many new evangelical public intellectuals who will be able to translate the best of sound scholarship for those who are seeking to serve the Lord in the complexities of public discipleship.

# 14

Interfaith Engagements

My first sustained interfaith dialogue was with Mary Jane, when we were both in eighth grade in a Watervliet, New York, public school. I had a mild crush on Mary Jane, a very smart Italian Catholic. Our romance—insofar as it was carried on outside of school activities—consisted of long bike rides interspersed with theological arguments about the role of Mary, the mother of Jesus. Mary Jane was a Fatima enthusiast, and she talked a lot about how the Blessed Virgin had appeared in 1917 to three shepherd children in the countryside on the outskirts of the Portuguese town where they lived, delivering to them some important prophecies that would soon come to pass. My crush on Mary Jane lasted only a few months, but it was enough to produce a personal religious crisis while it lasted. Part of it was worrying about the state of Mary Jane's soul, given the big differences we discussed. But I was also distressed by the thought that as an adult I would fall in love with Mary Jane, or someone with her kind of faith.

That never happened. Nor have the Blessed Virgin's Fatima prophecies come to fruition yet. But what did happen in the early 1960s was the Second Vatican Council. Looking back to my year in eighth grade, I now believe that Mary Jane was a genuine Christian. I hope her life has been sustained by a continuing faith in Mary's Son. And I'm grateful for the way she prepared me for later dialogues with other Catholics.

I have had an active role in my adult life in two official dialogues with Catholics: one was cosponsored by the Archdiocese of Los Angeles and Fuller Seminary—I helped get it started in the late 1980s, and it is still going strong—and the other was the North American Reformed-Catholic Dialogue, which I cochaired for several years with a Catholic bishop. I also was an original signer of the 1994 Evangelicals and Catholics Together document.

## "Intra" and "Inter"

My active engagements with Catholics—beginning with the bike ride discussions with Mary Jane—have clearly been "intra" and not "inter" dialogues; they have been dialogues within the context of shared Christian faith. Generally, my dialogue involvements with representatives of nonevangelical (including non-Christian) religious communities have actually been a mix of intra and inter. The ones that I have taken on seriously, particularly with Jews and Muslims, have a unifying theme that crosses the intra-versus-inter boundary. The unity has to do with my sticking close to "Abrahamic" identities.[1] More specifically, I have focused on dialogue with groups whose relationships with evangelicals are marked by the wounds of disruption. Here is the series of major disruptions: Christianity departed from Judaism in the conviction that Jesus was the heaven-sent Messiah. Six centuries later Islam presented itself as the corrective alternative to both Judaism and Christianity. The sixteenth-century Reformation saw Protestants break with

Catholicism. During the nineteenth century, a variety of new religious movements—Mormonism, Christian Science, and Jehovah's Witnesses are the obvious cases—departed from the historic Christian mainstream. In the early twentieth century, evangelicals left—or were forced out of—mainline liberal Protestantism. Later, at midcentury, the "new evangelicalism" distinguished itself from the fundamentalism that had nurtured most of its leadership. Needless to say, I have not pursued dialogue with all these groups. A good part of that has to do with time and energy. But much of it has also been the availability of willing dialogue partners.

Rick Warren gave me a helpful biblical reference in this regard. He told me that when his wife, Kay, would visit African villages on a mission to assist in counteracting the AIDS epidemic, the first contact she would seek out in the village leadership was the local shaman, or witch doctor. If that person was willing to work with her, she could expect some success from the shared efforts. If that person opposed the project, it presented serious obstacles. This was a way of following, Rick said, the commission of Jesus to "the seventy" in Luke 10:5–6. When his disciples entered a village, the Savior instructed them immediately to visit a home with the message, "Peace to this house." If they found that "someone who promotes peace is there" (NIV), then they were to stay. If not, they were to move on. I have been fortunate to have formed friendships along the way with many "promoters of peace" representing other faith traditions. This has been especially true with a number of Catholic theologians, a few liberal Protestant leaders, several rabbis who have become close friends, and some warm friends in the Mormon community. My relations with Muslims have been infrequent, and fundamentalist theologians have not typically been open to serious dialogue with me.

I have written quite a bit about the dialogues in which I have been involved—including a short book, actually, on the Mormon exchanges[2]—and I will not repeat the details here. While I cannot completely skip over some of the substantive issues at stake in each of the dialogues, my focus here will be on some general lessons learned.

## Focusing on Questions

At a number of points in previous chapters, I have mentioned specific authors who have influenced me significantly along the way. My main reason for doing so, in addition to recalling those influences myself as I have been writing this, is to acknowledge explicitly that many of the ideas I have set forth throughout my career owe much to stimulating thoughts from other—and more profound—thinkers.

On the subject of interreligious engagement, I do want to pay particular attention to the influence of a book that I read rather early in my intellectual journey. The book, and especially one paragraph in the book, has profoundly shaped my thinking on this subject—and indeed on several other related subjects that have occupied my attention over the years.

In seminary I took an elective course on the theology of religions. The professor organized the subject matter with reference to three general schools of thought regarding "world religions." One was the "all religions are legitimate paths to the divine" approach that has often showed up among liberal scholars. Having read and discussed writings from that perspective, we then looked at the other end of the spectrum: the Barthian-type critique of "religion as such." Christianity on this view is not to be thought of as one religion among many. Insofar as our faith is seen as a "religion," it falls far short of honoring the transforming Word of God who has broken into our human condition in a way that judges our highest "religious" aspirations, calling us to repentance and service.

I wrestled with those two options, but I was eager to find an alternative. And I found it in what I still see as a wonderful book by Stephen Neill, a Scottish missionary to India who had helped to form the Church of South India, in which he subsequently served as a bishop. In the book *Christian Faith and Other Faiths: The Christian Dialogue with Other Religions*, Neill criticizes the "comparative method" approach to the study of religions for the way it treats "all religions as commensurables," with their particularities being undergirded by more basic commonalities. We cannot simply lay different religious formulations about the divine side by side, Neill says, while ignoring the fact that in doing so we are, in each case, isolating the specific conception from other ideas with which it is interconnected. To do so is to detach a specific idea of God or the world "from the living experiences" of those who hold to it, thus ignoring "the living fabric of the religion from which the idea has been somewhat violently dissevered."[3]

The proper alternative, argued Neill, is to enter into the perspective of the person representing another faith, trying as much as possible to place ourselves "within" the framework of the other belief system, in order to probe the deep questions that are being asked within that framework. To do this is to make genuine communication possible. This, in turn, means not succumbing to the much-too-common temptation to win rhetorical victories and thus cut off the potential for interesting conversations.

I found Neill's overall case compelling, but I was especially taken by the way he applied it specifically to the Christian engagement with Hinduism, in the concluding paragraph of his chapter on Hindu thought. I have returned to this passage many times and have quoted it frequently in lectures and publications.

> The Christian must not be surprised if, between now and the end of this century, the work of Christian witness in India becomes more difficult than it has been for a century. The Christian must be prepared to face the possibility that the greater part of our work must be from within Hinduism, in putting questions to the Hindu and helping the Hindu understand himself better. All the time the Christian will be attempting to help the Hindu to see the radical unsatisfactoryness of all the answers that have been given to his

questions and so to point him to the one in whom those questions can receive their all sufficient answer, the Lord Jesus Christ.[4]

After following that "from within" approach for a couple of decades, with continuing gratitude for its insights, I would certainly want to add some clarifications of my own. For one thing, while I, like Neill, want to help Hindus and others better understand themselves, I also believe that in our Christian engagements with them, we ourselves are given an opportunity to gain in self-understanding. And I would also tone down the claim that "all" of Hinduism's answers to the basic issues of life are characterized by "radical unsatisfactoryness." Instead I want to argue that the answers of other religions *ultimately* fall short of providing satisfying solutions to the human condition.

## The "Bracketing" Project

One of the patterns that has guided me in interfaith dialogue is the "bracketing" of interests in evangelism and apologetics as we engage in conversations with people of other faith communities. I have taken my lead on this from Herman Bavinck, who criticizes, in his solidly orthodox *Reformed Dogmatics*, the ways that "in the past the [Christian] study of religions was pursued exclusively in the interest of dogmatics and apologetics." This exclusive focus led to the common assessment that "the founders of [non-Christian] religions, like Mohommed, were simply considered imposters, enemies of God, accomplices of the devil." This way of seeing things is no longer tenable, Bavinck argues, now that those religions "have become more precisely known"—by our drawing new lessons about the past from "both history and psychology." And then Bavinck offers this theological verdict: "Also among pagans, says Scripture, there is a revelation of God, an illumination by the Logos, a working of God's Spirit."[5] It is interesting that in this brief comment Bavinck is suggesting a rather robust

character to the kind of "revealing" that takes place apart from
what we think of as "special revelation." For one thing, his formulation here has a distinct trinitarian structure: in addition to
a "revelation" from God there is the "illumination" of the Logos
and the "working of God's Spirit." This suggests a more dynamic
character to God's "natural" dealings with other religions than
the more static patterns often suggested by the idea of a "general
revelation." A case in point is the bluntness of the Westminster
Confession on the subject: "Although the light of nature, and the
works of creation and providence, do so far manifest the goodness, wisdom, and power of God, as to leave men inexcusable;
yet are they not sufficient to give that knowledge of God, and of
his will which is necessary unto salvation."[6] Bavinck's dynamic
portrayal of God's interaction with other religions clearly implies
that individual religious perspectives may each benefit in different
ways from the active interest that the divine Trinity takes in their
particularities. How Buddhism and Hinduism are each impacted
by the illuminating work of the Logos and the active "working" of
the Spirit may differ significantly from how those same dynamic
influences are at work in Islam or Confucianism. And in the case
of Islam, we must also take into account the ways in which Muslims have from the very beginning been in close interaction with
the content of biblical revelation.

My bracketing strategy takes seriously Bavinck's insistence that
we should no longer view non-Christian religions "exclusively in
the interest of dogmatics and apologetics." This means, as I read
him, that we have to temporarily set aside questions about who
is saved or not, or whether the overall perspective of a specific
religion points to the reality of the God of the Scriptures. When
the main question is whether we have good reasons to believe that,
say, a fully committed Buddhist—someone whose understanding
of reality is spelled out in consistently Buddhist terms—can go
to heaven, then many of us will have to answer in the negative. In
this context it is appropriate for evangelicals to say that Buddhism

is a "false religion," in the sense that a person who wants to enter into a saving relationship with the one true God will not achieve that goal by following the Buddhist path. But this is not the same as saying that there is no truth in Buddhism. If we can bracket the question of whether Buddhists qua Buddhists can be saved, then we are free to evaluate this or that particular Buddhist teaching or practice in terms of whether it illuminates reality, and we may well find many good and true elements in the Buddhist worldview. Indeed, we might even find things in the Buddhist understanding of spiritual reality that can enrich our own Christian understanding of religious truth—even by calling our attention to spiritual matters that we have not thought about clearly.

Is there some theological risk in promoting this kind of bracketing? Yes, definitely. And I worry about the risks. I will explain in more detail in my final chapter my personal worries about this and other theologically dangerous paths that I have walked. But it would be wrong, I am convinced, not to take the risks—particularly in engaging in dialogue with other religious perspectives.

### A Learning Posture

It is a little easier to "bracket" the salvific questions when we move away from explicitly theological matters. We can engage, for example, Sigmund Freud's arguments in his *Civilization and Its Discontents* or Simone de Beauvoir's *The Second Sex* without concentrating on whether either of them is going to heaven. What is important for all of these kinds of cases, though, is the willingness to learn, and even to admit that we have misunderstood these perspectives in the past. Truthfulness is a key biblical ideal, and it is a sin to bear false witness against our neighbors, whether they are Muslims, Viennese psychoanalysts, or Parisian existentialists. In his "Dialogue Decalogue," often cited by folks engaged in interfaith discussions, Leonard Swidler strongly emphasizes the need for empathy. The ability to see things from the point of

view of the persons we are engaging is crucial for better understanding. Here is how Swidler puts it: "Each participant needs to
describe her/himself. For example, only a Muslim can describe
what it really means to be an authentic member of the Muslim
community. At the same time, when one's partner in dialogue
attempts to describe back to them what they have understood of
their partner's self-description, then such a description must be
recognizable to the described party."[7]

Empathy is experiencing the feelings and concerns of others
as if they were your own. We engage the ideas of someone like
Freud by attempting to grasp the feelings and concerns that give
rise to his ideas about the human self. To be sure, attempting to
understand the views of a self-professed atheist from the "inside,"
as it were, can be a special challenge for a Christian. But it is an
important challenge. Indeed, it may be that we Christians have
special advantages in nurturing the necessary kind of empathy.
The humble awareness of our own sin can lead us, as Simone Weil
put it bluntly, "to contemplate our stupidity."[8] We know we are
finite creatures. God is God, and we are not, which means that we
fall far short of omniscience. And the cognitive defects that stem
from finitude are even more greatly exaggerated because of our
sinful rebelliousness. This means that what might at first glance
appear to be our radical disagreement with a certain point of view
might, upon humble reflection, require a confession of sin. I can
hold to conservative views about sexuality while also confessing
that we traditional Christians have been inexcusably cruel toward
persons who experience, for example, same-sex attraction. Or,
while I find Wicca to be a rather bizarre religious perspective, I
also have to remind myself about the witch burnings of the past.
But there is more to consider than repentance regarding our own
misdeeds and misunderstandings, as important as those matters
are. A spirit of genuine learning must enter into the picture. Often
there is truth to be culled from a serious reflection upon distorted
truths. And, as John Calvin rightly insisted in the case of Seneca,

there are straightforwardly positive truths to be found outside the boundaries of the Christian community. The Spirit of God is at work, promoting the cause of truth, in the larger world.

## Mormonism: Inter or Intra?

Earlier in this chapter I distinguished between intrafaith and interfaith dialogues. In most cases it is quite easy to know which label applies to a given dialogue. Talking with Catholics and liberal Protestants for me is certainly intrafaith, and dialogues with Jews and Muslims are clearly interfaith.

I have to admit, though, that deciding where Mormonism belongs is a continuing puzzle for me. There is no question that around the time our Mormon-evangelical dialogue got started at the turn of this century, I would have said "inter," and most of my Mormon friends would have agreed. But these days I struggle with the question of whether Mormons and evangelicals are branches of the same broad Christian community. I know that in even posing the question I am challenging a broad evangelical consensus. Our standard assessment of Mormonism in the second half of the twentieth century was that of the "counter-cult" movement. Mormons, like Jehovah's Witnesses and Christian Scientists, have so redefined the traditional Christian terms, according to that assessment, that they are not only non-Christian—they are, in effect, *anti*-Christian. And many Latter-day Saints would also resist the "intra" label. It has not been unusual for Mormons to insist, for reasons very different, to be sure, from those offered by evangelicals, that Mormonism is not a branch of Christianity. In each case the "inter" assessment has been shaped by a century and a half of hostility. Buddhists and Catholics can describe each other as representing different faiths without meaning thereby to insult each other. But the history of Mormon-evangelical relations was antagonistic from the outset. In his "First Vision" account, Joseph Smith reported that the Son of God had informed him regarding the traditional Christian communities "that all their creeds were an abomination in his sight."⁹ One of the standard terms employed by Mormons in describing the traditional Christian communities was "apostasy"—the abandonment of a faith that was now being restored in the establishment of Mormonism. Nor were representatives of those communities any less condemning of the views expressed by the prophet and his followers.¹⁰

But a history of mutual condemnation does not make the intra-or-inter question irrelevant. The Protestant Reformers often condemned the Catholics as members of a "false church," and the Catholics consistently responded in kind. Some of that still continues today, but in the larger picture, Catholics and Protestants these days do not perpetuate those stereotypes of each other. I repeat: I have not settled the question. A few years before I began my initial involvement in the dialogue, I was much influenced by the verdict offered by Jan Shipps in her 1987 study of Mormonism. Shipps, a Methodist scholar who was the first non-Mormon to serve as president of the Mormon History Association, proposed that Mormonism should be seen as a "new religious movement." The relationship of Mormonism to Christianity, she has argued, is much like the relationship of Christianity to Judaism. In each case there are both continuities and discontinuities.¹¹

In offering that picture, Shipps is clearly suggesting that Mormonism is a different faith than Christianity. Mormonism shares much in common with Christianity, of course, just as Christianity shares much in common with Judaism. But they are, as Shipps has made her case, different religions. This seemed to sit well with the Mormon academics who admired Shipps's work. Her placement of Mormonism outside the broad Christian household certainly provoked no outcry from her Mormon colleagues.

Again, I began my active involvement in dialogue with Mormon scholars in general agreement with Shipps's account, with her characterization of Mormonism as a "new religious movement." It allowed me to approach Mormons with respect and a genuine desire to learn from them. It gave me a framework for exploring both continuities and discontinuities, without descending into accusations about being "pseudo-Christian."

Right around the time that we began our dialogue, however, Jan Shipps published another book, *Sojourner in the Promised Land: Forty Years among the Mormons*. As her subtitle makes clear, in this volume Shipps is gathering together her thoughts about her four-decade academic "sojourn" in Mormon studies. The book contains some essays previously published in various journals, plus some essays making their first appearance. In the final section of the book, Shipps moves to a directly autobiographical mode. Of special interest for me was her chapter "Is Mormonism Christian? Reflections on a Complicated Question"—an essay originally published in *BYU Studies* but extensively reworked for this book. Throughout her career studying Mormonism, Shipps says, there has been "a clear modulation . . . in the way I have approached what Mormonism is and whether it is Christian."[12]

In reflecting back on her "new religious movement" discussion of 1987, Shipps does not retract her placement of Mormonism within this category. But in explaining it she touches on a nuance that I had missed in my reading of her earlier book. Yes, she had argued there that Mormonism was discontinuous with Christianity in much the same way that Christianity had seen itself with Judaism. But in her reflections on that thesis in her later book, she notes that "just as the early Christians believed that they had found the only proper way to be Jewish, so the early followers of the Mormon prophet believed they had found the only proper way to be Christian."[13]

The point here that I had not adequately attended to in accepting her placement of Mormonism as a new religious movement was that the analogy she draws in making that decision is itself a complicating factor. There was a time, for example, when Islam occurred as a "new religious movement," and it emerged in an environment deeply formed by Judaism and Christianity. But its relationship to those other religious movements was not the same as Christianity's to Judaism, or Mormonism's to Christianity. Muslims did not see themselves as having discovered "the only proper way" to be a Jew or a Christian. The continuity-discontinuity pattern in Islam's relationship to those other two faiths was not of the intimate sort that Mormonism bears to Christianity, or Christianity to Judaism.

Again, this is an important nuance to the use of the "new religious movement" category. Some movements are "newer" than others. Hinduism and Judaism are "faiths" that are different from Christianity, but as a Christian I see Christianity as in a very obvious way the *fulfillment* of Judaism in a way that I do not see Christianity in its relationship to Hinduism. My differences with my Jewish friends have much to do with my conviction that there is something significant within their own faith tradition that they fail to understand properly. And my Mormon friends make similar claims about my understanding of Christianity.

That does not settle the inter-versus-intra issue, however. I can say, as I want to say, that Christianity is a better way of grasping and honoring the basic claims of the Jewish faith than Judaism, and yet I can still consider my dialogue with Jewish friends to be "inter." Christianity and Judaism are, in the final analysis, different religions—much closer to each other than either is to Islam, but still different faiths. And it could be argued the same holds for Christianity and Mormonism—close to each other, to be sure, but still different religions. Jan Shipps, however, leans strongly now in the direction of an "intra" relationship. After forty years of studying Mormonism as a Methodist, she concludes that to ask whether Mormons are Christians is to pose—to use the phrase included in the title of her essay—"a complicated question." And it has become even more complicated in recent years, she observes, because of what she sees within the Mormon community as "a contemporary rhetorical shift that seems to be turning Mormon into an adjectival modifier used to signify a particular kind of

Christian."[14] In the early years, Mormons—like others who claimed a "restorationist" identity—explicitly distanced themselves from the traditional Christian denominations in order to emphasize the ways they were restoring something that had long been corrupted. But in our present context, she argues, Mormons "no longer need an *other* to set themselves apart either rhetorically or categorically."[15] Thus, claiming their place within the broad Christian tradition—to be sure, as a purer form than others who claim Christian identity—has become an acceptable posture.

In coming to her own conclusion about whether Mormons are Christians, Shipps points to the ways in which the question of who is "truly" Christian has loomed large in many splits that have taken place in Christian history. It has been quite common, she argues, for a group that separated from another group—Constantinople from Rome, Protestants from Catholicism, Methodists from Anglicanism—to raise the question of whether what they had left deserved to keep the label "Christian." Her own assessment on who has a right to claim the label, she confesses, is presently an agnostic one. The final verdict must await, she says, "the fullness of time, [when] a decision will be made in a higher court." Until that day arrives, she will live with the knowledge that she is "one who sees 'through a glass darkly,'" which means that all she can do is to "withhold judgment, counting within the definition of Christian any church, sectarian movement, liberal or conservative coalition, or new religious tradition that gathers persons together in the name of Christ and, in so doing, creates genuine community wherein women and men may—to use Methodist phraseology—take up the cross and follow him."[16]

I agree with Jan Shipps that we humans should not second-guess God about what will be revealed at the last judgment. None of that releases us, however, from serious attempts to discern the workings of the Spirit in ways that are available to us in our pre-eschaton present situation: "Dear friends, do not believe every spirit, but test the spirits to see whether they are from God"

(1 John 4:1 NIV). In our past relations with Mormons, though, I am convinced that we evangelicals have not always gone about this testing-the-spirits in a manner that honors another important biblical mandate: "Always be prepared to give an answer to everyone who asks you to give the reason for the hope that you have," the apostle Peter instructs believers. Then he immediately adds: "But do this with gentleness and respect" (1 Pet. 3:15 NIV). We have often fallen short on the "gentleness and respect" part of it.

Gentle respect for people with whom we disagree is key to productive efforts at dialogue. One reason we evangelicals have had difficulties in this kind of engagement has to do with the way that our approaches to other perspectives—and this has certainly been the case with our approach to Mormonism—have been dominated by soteriological and apologetic concerns. We have seen people of other faiths as souls whose eternal destinies are imperiled, and we have also wanted to disprove key elements in their worldview. To be sure, there is much merit in caring about salvation and doctrinal truth. But having these issues dominate our approaches to others can also lead to dangers. The most basic one is also spiritual in nature: the real possibility that we will bear false witness against our non-Christian neighbors. In evangelization contexts we rightly want to get people to see the inadequacy of their present religious commitments. But this can lead us to portray those commitments in the worst possible light, so that Christian belief and practice can clearly be seen as the better way. It is easy in such contexts to emphasize the negative aspects of the other perspective, or even to distort the positive elements of that perspective, so that things are portrayed as worse than they really are.

The challenge is to seriously engage other religious perspectives while being very careful not to say anything in our theology of religions that would deny what is at the core of our own deepest convictions. Certainly one criterion for the adequacy of an evangelical theology of religions is whether our formulations comport well with our attempts to bring the gospel to those who have not yet accepted Christ. Nonetheless, it is a helpful exercise to attempt, temporarily at least—and especially because of our overemphasis in the other direction in the past—to bracket our overt interests in evangelism and apologetics as we think about some broader topics in this area.

## "God's Offspring"

In a lecture I once gave to the Fuller community, I explained my approach to witnessing to people of other faiths, appealing to the Acts 17 account of the apostle Paul, when he was invited to explain Christianity to a group of Stoic and Epicurean thinkers on Mars Hill in Athens. Paul's internal reaction to the religious marketplace on display there was a negative one: "he was greatly distressed to see that the city was full of idols" (v. 16; all quotations from this passage are from the NIV). But when he actually addressed his pagan audience, he began with a gentle observation: "People of Athens! I see that in every way you are very religious" (v. 22). And then, pointing out that they had constructed one altar inscribed "to an unknown god," he tells them that "you are ignorant of the very thing you worship—and this is what I am going to proclaim to you" (v. 23), at which point he quotes their own poets: "For in him we live and move and have our being," and "We are his offspring" (v. 28).

My colleague Peter Wagner, well known for his "church growth" strategies, did not like my looking to that text for positive guidance for bringing the gospel to unbelievers. Paul got very few converts out of that encounter, Wagner said. We should read the Acts 17 story, then, as a warning about how *not* to go about evangelism. Wagner was not questioning the Bible's authority in telling us about what happened on Mars Hill. What we are given in Acts 17, he was insisting, is an authoritative account of a failed church growth strategy.

Wagner's response was clever, but completely unconvincing. The results of Paul's encounter, as reported in the text, fit my Calvinist perspective nicely. "When they heard about the resurrection of the dead, some of them sneered" (v. 32). No surprise in the fact that many of Paul's hearers had hearts of rebellion and were not open to the truth of the gospel. "But others said, 'We want to hear you again on this subject.' . . . Some of the people became followers of Paul and believed" (vv. 32–34). No surprise there either: by sovereign grace God draws some people to himself.

Paul's Mars Hill approach is actually a profound one theologically. The four elements that I find illuminating for a more general approach to presenting the gospel are these: Like Paul we should be "greatly distressed" by the widespread reality of idolatrous worship. But, second, like him also, when we approach folks caught up in unbelief, we should be open to discovering genuine spiritual impulses at work, albeit in distorted forms: "I see that in every way you are very religious." John Calvin's doctrines of the *semen religionis* and the *sensus divinitatis* are based on empirical evidence. Third, contextualization is an important project. Paul appealed to their own poets, showing that he understood key elements of their culture. And fourth, the apostle pointed them to Jesus.

For my purposes in this book, I want to stress how, in this Athenian encounter, Paul features human commonness in his message. In appealing to their own writings, he emphasizes that we are all "offspring" of the God who, having "made the world and everything in it[,] is the Lord of heaven and earth" (v. 24)—the God who, having sent the Son into the world, "now . . . commands all people everywhere to repent" (v. 30).

In my dialogues with persons of other faith communities, I work hard to try to discern the legitimate spiritual yearnings and impulses at work in their quests. In doing so, I find it helpful also to work intentionally at temporarily "bracketing" the issues of apologetics and soteriology. But those issues cannot stay bracketed for long for those of us who have heard and believed the call to repent and turn to Jesus. In the conclusion to my study of common grace, I allow for the possibility that "for all I know—and for all any of us can know—much of what we now think of as common grace may in the end time be revealed to be saving grace."[17] I made some evangelicals nervous in saying that, and I can understand why. All I can say in my defense is that engaging folks of other religious persuasions has left me with a lot of mystery about how God draws people to himself. In the "for all I know" comment I just cited, I quickly go on to take refuge in Deuteronomy 29:29, a verse that has been quoted much by Calvinists in the past: "The secret things belong to the LORD our God, but the revealed things belong to us and to our children forever, to observe all the words of this law."

I take great hope from the fact there are indeed "secret things" in the mind and heart of God. Billy Graham appealed to the same hope when, in an extensive interview with a *Newsweek* reporter in August 2006, he was asked about the eternal destiny of "good Jews, Muslims, Buddhists, Hindus or secular people." The evangelist responded: "Those are decisions only the Lord will make. It would be foolish for me to speculate on who will be there and who won't. . . . I don't want to speculate about all that." At the same time, though, he expressed his firm confidence that Jesus is the only way to salvation.[18] That seems to me to be exactly the right balance between allowing for mystery and being obedient to "the revealed things [that] belong to us and to our children forever."

# 15

## Of Hymns and Dialogues

I N OCTOBER 1997 A GROUP OF CATHOLICS AND EVANGELICALS issued a joint statement with the title "The Gift of Salvation." A central focus of the document was the doctrine of justification by faith, which had—beginning with the very origins of Protestantism in the sixteenth century—long been seen as the central point of disagreement between Catholics and Protestants. The joint statement affirmed much more agreement than had been apparent in the past and emphasized the fact of their shared "unity in Christ."

The document was issued by a group called Evangelicals and Catholics Together, whose earlier declaration, "Evangelicals and Catholics Together: The Christian Mission in the Third Millennium," published in the spring of 1994, had been seen as a breakthrough in relations between Catholics and evangelicals. I was one of the signers of both the 1994 and the 1997 documents. And I considered myself to be in good evangelical company in my involvement. Some of the key leaders on the evangelical side were stalwarts: Charles Colson, Bill Bright, James Packer, and Timothy George, among others. The documents received considerable publicity, both in the secular and the religious press. The effort was touted by many in both the evangelical and the Catholic communities as a manifestation of what Timothy George labeled "an ecumenism of the trenches." People on both sides of the traditional divide had been finding each other in various local and national causes, particularly on matters of social concern, and out of that kind of cooperation theological discussions had begun to take place, and new levels of mutual understanding were reached.

Not everyone was happy with what "Evangelicals and Catholics Together" was accomplishing, however. A number of evangelical leaders, particularly those representing strong Calvinist convictions, spoke harshly of the project. One such critic was the well-known pastor and author John F. MacArthur Jr., who was particularly disturbed by the group's treatment of justification by faith. In his critique, MacArthur took the evangelical participants to be saying "that while they believe that the doctrine of justification as articulated by the Reformers is true, they are not willing to say that people must believe it in order to be saved. In other words, they believe that people are saved who do not believe the Biblical doctrine of justification."[1]

My response to this charge is "Of course!" That is precisely what I believe, and there is much solid Christian support for this response. To start with what is so obvious that I would be surprised if MacArthur would dissent, if by "believing" the doctrine we mean being able to give a clear articulation of it, then certainly the vast majority of the saved fall short. My maternal grandmother was a deeply godly woman who was a member of the choir at her Reformed congregation. She sang much about salvation— "Jesus paid it all, all to him I owe . . . ," "O for a thousand tongues to sing my great redeemer's praise . . ."—but I am quite sure she could not have answered with any degree of precision a request to explain "justification by faith." And evangelical pastors are not being theologically defective when they regularly assure parents of three-year-olds who have died that their children are in heaven—even though those boys and girls could not have explained justification at that stage in their young lives.

Of course, the evangelical critics of the joint Catholic-evangelical declaration were making a somewhat more precise point. My grandmother did not oppose the Reformation doctrine of justification by faith. Nor do the three-year-old children of evangelical parents. MacArthur and others are clearly thinking about people who sincerely and knowingly teach an alternative to our understanding of justification. By denying our version of the doctrine, the argument goes, Catholics and others are making it clear that they are not putting their trust in Jesus Christ alone, and his atoning work, for their salvation. Here too I see the MacArthur-type view as deeply misguided. And rather than getting into a detailed discussion of the doctrine of justification itself, I rely heavily on the support for my perspective by persons whom most theologians would consider to be unimpeachable adherents to evangelical orthodoxy. Since the issue at stake figures into criticisms I have regularly received regarding, for example, topics relating to our evangelical dialogue with Mormons (and I will get around to that subject soon), I have assembled examples of such supporting affirmations—each of which comes from thinkers of strict Calvinist conviction. The first of these supporters is Charles Hodge, the great theologian of the "Old Princeton" of the nineteenth century. One thinker whom Hodge regularly singled out for criticism in his three-volume *Systematic Theology* was the German theologian Friedrich Schleiermacher. When Hodge had studied in Germany in his younger years, he had seen firsthand the influence of Schleiermacher's liberal theology. Hodge was deeply disturbed by Schleiermacher's embrace of the rationalist critique of biblical authority, which had the effect, Hodge insisted, of undermining the most fundamental tenets of the historic Christian faith, including the full divinity and atoning work of Jesus Christ.

At one point, though, where Hodge is setting forth his critique of Schleiermacher—who had by this time been dead for several decades—he offers, in a footnote, a brief personal comment about the person whose theology he has been criticizing. He tells how, as a student, he had frequently attended services at Schleiermacher's church. He was taken, he says, by the fact that the hymns sung in those services "were always evangelical and spiritual in an eminent degree, filled with praise and gratitude to our Redeemer." He goes on to report that he had been told by one of Schleiermacher's colleagues that often in the evenings the theologian would call his family together, saying: "Hush, children; let us sing a hymn of praise to Christ." And then Hodge adds this tribute to Schleiermacher: "Can we doubt that he is singing those praises now? To whomever Christ is God, St. John assures us, Christ is a Saviour."[2]

My second supporter, also from the nineteenth century, is Herman Bavinck. In his systematic writings, Bavinck frequently criticized Roman Catholic theology, not in the least because of what he saw as the Catholic emphasis on salvation by good works. But here is a comment he offers at one point about that element of Catholic thought: "We must remind ourselves that the Catholic righteousness by good works is vastly preferable to a protestant righteousness by good doctrine. At least righteousness by good works benefits one's neighbor, whereas righteousness by good doctrine only produces lovelessness and pride. Furthermore, we must not blind ourselves to the tremendous faith, genuine repentance, complete surrender and the fervent love for God and neighbor evident in the lives and work of many Catholic Christians."[3]

My third example is from a personal conversation with the late Cornelius Van Til, longtime professor of apologetics at Westminster Seminary. I visited him once in his Philadelphia home, shortly after I graduated from college, and asked him some questions about his stern rejection of Karl Barth's theology. While others in the evangelical world were welcoming many of Barth's contributions as a clear step back toward traditional orthodoxy, Van Til— as I have already mentioned—was insisting that Barth's theology was nothing more than "the new modernism" in disguise.[4]

In posing a question to Van Til about this, I began with these words: "As someone who does not see Karl Barth as a real Christian, what—" Van Til cut me off sharply right there. In an excited voice he said, "No! No! I have never said Barth is not a Christian. Never! What I have said is that his *theology* is not genuinely Christian. If all that a person knew about the gospel is what they learned from his theology, they could not come to Christ!"

Van Til was saying something here that is simple and straightforward: a person can have what we see as a highly defective theology, and yet we can still acknowledge that the person's heart has been transformed by the power of the gospel of Jesus Christ. Barth, from Van Til's perspective, was setting forth a theological system that fell far short of biblical fidelity. But that did not mean he was not a genuine Christian. Hodge was making the same point about Schleiermacher: bad theology, he said, but we can tell from the hymns that he sang that he longed to be with his Savior in heaven. And Catholicism in Bavinck's portrayal: Righteousness by good works? Not a doctrinal formulation that a good Calvinist can live with. But in spite of that, some folks who believe that kind of thing clearly exhibit a "complete surrender and . . . fervent love for God."

## The Role of Hymn Singing

One reason I am especially fond of Hodge's expression of appreciation for Schleiermacher's love of the evangelical hymns is that I am convinced that often the hymns people love to sing are a better indication of their spiritual state than the theological formulations they set forth. David Hubbard was fond of saying that hymns contain "compacted theology" set forth in poetic form. His favorite example was this line: "His oath, His covenant, His blood, / Support me in the whelming flood." "There are several centuries of theology packed into those lines," he would say. Our favorite hymns are often helpful indicators, in compacted form, of the actual theology that we embrace.

In the light of that, here is an experience that has influenced the way I see the faith of many of my Mormon friends: I had been invited to speak to a meeting of Mormon professors at a Latter-day Saints (LDS) Institute of Religion adjacent to a large public university in Utah. The institute served a large Mormon student population at that university with regular courses meant to supplement the university curriculum—primarily in religious history and what Mormons refer to as "ancient scriptures." My assigned topic was to explain what I understand to be the essential tenets of Calvinism and how that perspective enters into my assessment of Mormon thought.

I entered the seminar room just as they were beginning their weekly session. The leader announced a number—193—from the LDS hymnal, and a pianist began to play. They knew the words well. This hymn was familiar to me from my evangelical childhood, but I had not heard it sung for years. It was moving for me to sing it again with these LDS academics.

> I stand all amazed at the love Jesus offers me,
> Confused at the grace that so fully he proffers me.
> I tremble to know that for me he was crucified,
> That for me, a sinner, he suffered, he bled and died.
>
> (Chorus)
> Oh, it is wonderful that he should care for me
> Enough to die for me!
> Oh, it is wonderful, wonderful to me!
>
> I marvel that he would descend from his throne divine
> To rescue a soul so rebellious and proud as mine,
> That he should extend his great love unto such as I,
> Sufficient to own, to redeem, and to justify.
>
> I think of his hands pierced and bleeding to pay the debt!
> Such mercy, such love and devotion can I forget?
> No, no, I will praise and adore at the mercy seat,
> Until at the glorified throne I kneel at his feet.[5]

As we sang this together, I noticed that none of the Mormon scholars opened the book. They sang with gusto, obviously knowing the words by heart. And I saw one scholar's eyes clearly tear up as he was singing the final verse. That was the first of two hymn-and-tears events that day. Two hours later I spoke at a Mormon worship event on campus, attended by about two thousand people, mostly students but also LDS leaders from Salt Lake City who were on the platform with me. I spoke on 1 Peter 3:15–18, emphasizing the need to "be ready always to give an answer to every man that asketh you a reason of the hope that is in you," where that hope must be grounded in the assurance that "Christ also hath once suffered for sins, the just for the unjust, that he might bring us to God" (KJV).

Just before I spoke, the large LDS student choir sang, and the director announced that, having read about my fondness for the music of George Beverly Shea, they were dedicating their song to me. They began with a rousing version of "Give Me Jesus"—"Give me Jesus, give me Jesus / You can have all this world, / But give me Jesus"—and then transitioned into Bev Shea's classic "I'd Rather Have Jesus." As they sang the final refrain, "I'd rather have Jesus / Than anything this world affords today," I saw tears streaming down the cheeks of a young woman in the front row of the choir. What do the tears of Mormons mean when they are singing about their relationship with Jesus as the most important thing in their lives, and when they are longing for the day when, because he has paid the debt of their sin and guilt, they will kneel in worship before the heavenly mercy seat?

Most evangelicals who know anything about Mormonism will tell you that Mormons believe they are saved, in good part at least, by the merits of their own good works and that, furthermore, being "saved" means being on a path toward becoming gods. And that is surely what many Mormons in the past have affirmed, and many still do. But there are other strands in present-day Mormon thought and practice. Not long after the speaking event that I just described, I received a phone call from a Mormon scholar who wanted to discuss the Epistle to the Romans. He was teaching the Pauline Epistles to Mormon undergraduates, and he wanted to test his interpretation of Romans with me. "I think I am making Paul sound like a Calvinist, and I want to know if you think that's right."

It was right. It is clear from Romans, he said, that God's law is given to us to show us how far short we fall of what God wants us to be. Our efforts to live in obedience to the law do nothing to merit salvation. Our only hope is the grace of God that is available to us because of the atoning work of Jesus Christ on Calvary. We are justified by a faith that comes to us as a gift of divine grace. Good works come into the story only as our response of gratitude for God's having done for us what we could not do for ourselves.

I assured him that what he was saying was not only compatible with my Calvinism; it was the correct way to read what Paul is setting forth in Romans. He was pleased. Then I asked him how his Mormon students respond to this perspective. "At first they are kind of taken aback," he said. "Last week after class several of them came up to me and asked whether it really is OK to believe what I had told them was the view of Romans. I said, 'Absolutely,' and they responded by telling me how relieved they were. 'That fits our experience with the Savior,' they said. 'It's great to know that it fits with being a good Mormon!'"

Before we hung up, I asked him whether he felt vulnerable as a Mormon scholar who was teaching these things. "Just the opposite," he said. "I am being encouraged to do what I am doing." He told me that just recently he had met with high-level LDS church authorities in Salt Lake City, informing them of his interpretation of Paul, and they assured him that he was doing exactly what they wanted him to be doing. "Whatever else we teach them," they said, "it has got to be consistent with what the apostle Paul says in Romans!"

Well, what about the "whatever else we teach them"? I have
many disagreements with those other things. Here is how one
of the Mormon scholars in our dialogue put it in the context of
a heated discussion of some of that "whatever else": The views
that we evangelicals don't like in Mormonism are really there,
he said. But it is important for us to see them as components
of only one line of a doctrinal symphony—perhaps the soprano
or alto lines in a great piece of music. And sometimes, he said,
Mormons fail to call attention to other important lines in the
symphony, therefore not clearly pointing to the fact that we are all
in desperate need of a Savior. We are all, he said, "beggars" who
need to be rescued from our helpless sinful condition. I find all of
that—these theological formulations, the hymns Mormons sing,
the tears they shed—spiritually reassuring. This is yet another
case where genuine piety trumps defective theology.

## A Theology That Sustains Piety

During the 1960s and '70s there was considerable discussion among
Anglo-American philosophers about St. Anselm's version of the
ontological argument for God's existence. If, Anselm argued, we
grant the definition that God is "that being than which nothing
greater can be conceived,"[6] then it is impossible to imagine God
as nonexistent. This argument had been pretty much dismissed
since Kant had argued that it mistakenly treats "existence" as a
"property" that something or someone possesses alongside other
properties, such as shape, size, and the like. The Kantian criticism
was itself called into question by some twentieth-century philosophers, with the result that new assessments of the argument were
featured in the philosophical journals.

One philosopher who joined the back-and-forth was Norman
Malcolm, a devout Christian and a longtime professor at Cornell
University. In an essay on the subject, he offers his own case for
seeing the ontological argument as having some philosophical

merit. What I found memorable about Malcolm's essay was not
the technical points he makes but a fascinating comment toward
the end of his discussion about what he sees as the real merits of
Anselm's argument. In the final analysis, Malcolm observes, the
argument will make sense only to people who are coming to it
with some spiritual questions. To appreciate the definition of God
being discussed, he says, one has to have a proper understanding
"of the phenomena of human life that give rise to it." Then he
offers this explanation:

> There is the phenomenon of feeling guilt for something that one
> has done or thought or felt or for a disposition one has. One
> wants to be free of this guilt. But sometimes the guilt is felt to
> be so great that one is sure that nothing one can do oneself, nor
> any forgiveness by another human being, would remove it. One
> feels a guilt that is beyond all measure, a guilt "a greater than
> which cannot be conceived." Paradoxically, it would seem, one
> nevertheless has an intense desire to have this incomparable guilt
> removed. One requires a forgiveness that is beyond all measure,
> a forgiveness "a greater than which cannot be conceived." Out
> of such a storm of the soul, I am suggesting, there arises the
> conception of a forgiving mercy that is limitless, beyond all mea-
> sure. This is one important feature of the Jewish and Christian
> conception of God.[7]

I find Malcolm's observations about the importance of an
understanding "of the phenomena of human life that give rise
to" the conception of a "being than which nothing greater can be
conceived" to be profoundly provocative. Why is it so important
for us to be discussing together the attributes associated with the
"being" of God? As a philosopher, I am not turned off by charges
that explorations of Anselm's subject matter are "abstract." But
in this case, Malcolm is helping us to see that underlying what
may strike many people as a debate about "mere abstractions"
are matters of profound existential importance.

What Malcolm is saying is that the question of whether there is a being "a greater than which cannot be conceived" has deep spiritual significance if one is asking what kind of being would be required to remove an "incomparable guilt." More simply put, the question is, what would it take to save a person like me?

The nineteenth-century Princeton theologian Geerhardus Vos preached a marvelous sermon, "Seeking and Saving the Lost," based on Jesus's declaration in Luke 19:10 that "the Son of man came to seek and to save that which was lost."[8] Vos observes that to understand "the inherent logic of the structure of the gospel" is to be clear about the fact that to dilute the meaning of the word "lost" we also must dilute the meaning of what it means "to save." His point that a reduced understanding of our sinful condition inevitably leads to a reduced Savior is extremely important. And the corollary is also true: an incomparable burden of guilt requires an incomparably sufficient Savior. It is precisely this question that I have found to be an excellent starting point for a productive theological discussion with Mormons. Rather than citing the formulations given by my Mormon friends, which are often taken as misleading by evangelical critics of our dialogues ("They are just telling you what they think you want to hear from them!"), I can offer an example from a context where it is clearly a Mormon speaking to fellow Mormons. Here is the late Glenn L. Pearson, a longtime faculty member at Brigham Young University, on the proper spirit for entering into God's presence, writing in an LDS study book published for church members in the early 1960s: "There has to be down payment of a broken heart and a contrite spirit. Who has a broken heart and contrite spirit? One who is stripped of pride and selfishness. One who has come down in the depths of humility and prostrated himself before the Lord in mighty prayer and supplication. He has realized the awful guilt of his sins and has pled for the blood of Christ to be a covering to shield himself from the face of a just God."[9]

It is precisely statements of this sort by Mormons that have motivated me to keep the theological conversations with them going. Indeed, the comment here by Pearson embodies the spiritual concerns that have made me into a Calvinist. I have found no other theological system that best explains for me, not just in my mind but in the deep places of my soul, what it means to have found a Savior who can relieve the burden of my own "awful guilt." I am happy to talk theology—and to sing hymns—with anyone who is willing to make that subject the starting point for a serious theological dialogue.

# 16

## Concerns about the Journey

A ND NOW, AS PROMISED, BACK TO THOSE EDINBURGH CAL-
vinists whom I discussed briefly in the early pages of this
book. They were solid in their commitment to Reformed doctrine,
I noted, but they wanted to bring their Calvinist convictions into
the larger cultural arena in a way that promoted, in the words of
the historian whom I quoted, "genteel manners, religious moderation and tolerance, and high esteem for scientific and literary
accomplishments."[1]

My own intellectual-cultural quest, begun about two centuries
later than theirs, is pretty close to what they wanted to cultivate.
I am a Calvinist who has tried to promote "convicted civility," a
moderate tone in dialoguing with people whom we evangelical
types disagree with on serious matters, and a posture of learning
from what I see as the scholarly and cultural gifts distributed by
God to the larger human community. I think I have been right in
the way I have engaged in that overall quest. And generally speaking, I am convinced that I have pursued the quest with the proper
theological perspective. But, as I said in those early pages, I do

have some qualms about the net effect of all this. Those Edinburgh Calvinists meant well in pursuing their laudable goals, but in the long run their efforts had some regrettable consequences. I worry about the same for my own quest.

## Ground "Levels"

In my childhood we evangelicals sang a lot about the importance of "pressing on the upward way" toward "Canaan's tableland":

> My heart has no desire to stay
> Where doubts arise and fears dismay;
> Though some may dwell where these abound,
> My prayer, my aim, is higher ground.[2]

I can still sing those words without mental reservations. I don't want to be shaped by doubts and fears, nor do I want simply to "dwell where these abound." When I reflect upon the basics of Reformed orthodoxy, I sense that my feet are firmly planted on the higher ground of God's truth. I have not been content, however, simply to stand on that higher ground in a way that keeps me from engaging that territory "where doubts arise and fears dismay." While I don't want simply to "dwell" in that territory, I do want to explore it. In that sense, my own intellectual quest has been a constant traveling back and forth between the higher ground of firm Christian conviction and the common ground of an engaged civility.

It is important, however, not to create too big a distance between the "higher" and the "common" grounds. The basic point here is one that I learned early on from Cornelius Van Til. There is some irony, of course, in the way I want to apply his point here. Van Til, as I reported in this book's early pages, severely criticized his former student Edward John Carnell for Carnell's insistence on looking for common ground between believer and unbeliever in both evangelism and apologetics. I eventually became a Carnellian on this issue, but not without retaining an important emphasis in Van Til's thought—one that actually, as I see it, lessens the impact of Van Til's criticisms of Carnell.

In a little pamphlet that Van Til wrote to illustrate his approach to apologetics, he engages in a lengthy monologue addressed to a non-Christian intellectual. In explaining to his imaginary conversation partner why the idea of epistemic "neutrality" is not feasible, he tells the non-Christian that his refusal to accept God's existence is in fact a denial that "the world belongs to Him, and that you are His creature, and as such are to own up to that fact by honoring Him whether you eat or drink or do anything else. God says that you live, as it were, on His estate. And His estate has large ownership signs placed everywhere, so that he who goes by even at seventy miles an hour cannot but read them. Every fact in this world, the God of the Bible claims, has His stamp indelibly engraved upon it."[3]

What Van Til is in effect arguing here is that the believer and the unbeliever, when they engage each other's worldviews, are in fact occupying a common ground—God's real estate, on which are posted many clear signs of ownership. To be sure, Van Til's point here is ontological in nature: in reality both parties stand on ground created by the very God about whose existence they are arguing. What Van Til refuses to accept in Carnell's approach is his epistemic application of that ontology: Carnell considers it legitimate to get the unbeliever to acknowledge what some of the real estate ownership signs point to—a shared moral sense, transcendent norms for cognitive assent to the truth of something, and the like. But the real estate issue underlying the positions of both Van Til and Carnell is extremely important. The God-owned real estate that Van Til describes to his fictional unbeliever provides, for Carnell, a basis for positive engagement with the unbeliever. Carnell wants to keep discussing the real estate signs at the very point where Van Til means to be signaling that any further conversation, unless the Holy Spirit changes the heart-direction of his conversation partner, is fruitless.

I find the complex philosophical-theological issues that are at stake here to be endlessly fascinating. I will not pursue the complexities of those issues here, however. I simply want to make one point about common ground, a point that is directly related to one that I have consistently made regarding conviction and civility. Typically when people push me for clarifications on my views on the subject, they see me as insisting on maintaining a "proper tension" between conviction and civility (the phrase enclosed in quotation marks was used by a questioner in an audience I addressed while working on this chapter).

The truth is that civility is not something that stands over against biblically based convictions in a kind of "tension" relationship. To put it bluntly: the obligation to be civil *is itself* a matter of biblical conviction. This is very clear, for example, in 1 Peter 3:15, a verse I cited in the previous chapter: "Always be prepared to give an answer to everyone who asks you to give the reason for the hope that you have." That is a mandate to nurture strong convictions about the content of the gospel. The next part of the verse, though, is also an apostolic mandate: "But do this with gentleness and respect" (NIV). The fact that civility—the cultivation of a gentle and respectful spirit in representing the cause of the gospel—is something that pleases the God of the Scriptures is itself a conviction on which the Bible calls us to stand firm.

A direct parallel can be drawn to the relationship between the "higher" and the "common" grounds. This can be seen in an insightful observation made by Willie Jennings in his book on the negative impact of colonialism on theology. "Christianity, wherever it went in the modern colonies, inverted its sense of hospitality," he writes. "It claimed to be the host, the owner of the spaces it entered . . . and yielded a form of religious life that thwarts its deepest instincts of intimacy."[4]

In referring to "the spaces," Jennings may be thinking in part of very physical spaces, but he clearly implies a broader sense. While I am not convinced that all missionaries bought uncritically into the mentality associated with cultural imperialism, there is no question that much too frequently the missionary movement was deeply shaped by a Western contextualization of the Christian message. When that has been the case, we have often, when entering into non-Western cultural settings, seen ourselves as—to use Jennings's apt term—"the host" of our conversations with others. Thus we have failed to accept the hospitality of those to whom we have been sent.

I confess that when I first came upon Jennings's reference to an "inverted . . . sense of hospitality," I was taken aback. I had been much influenced by Christine Pohl's excellent book on hospitality and found her "making room" imagery particularly helpful in thinking about *intellectual* hospitality.[5] To host is to create space for others, attending to their needs for lodging, sustenance, and human relationships. In our intellectual encounters with others, we also "make room" for ideas and questions we would not otherwise engage.

I still think Pohl has the idea of hospitality exactly right. What Jennings is adding to the topic, though, is the importance of our cultivating the willingness not only to grant hospitality but also to *accept* it. Engagement with people of other perspectives should not be permeated by inviting them into our agenda; we need to take their questions, ideas, and concerns seriously. In one sense, genuine dialogue with others means entering into their intellectual-spiritual space. But in an even deeper sense—and this is Van Til's insight—we meet them on real estate that in fact belongs to God. Or to switch to Jennings's formulation, we can allow ourselves to be hosted by them because we know that in reality we are each being hosted by God. They, like us, are surrounded by the "ownership signs" that Van Til describes. And it may be that God has invited us to a conversation that he is hosting in order for us to learn from the non-Christian new ways of reading those signs that enhance our own understanding of the owner's purposes in the world.

## Why the Quest?

I have just outlined the overall perspective that has informed my desire to stand on common ground with people with whom I have deep disagreements. I am quite satisfied with the rationale I have offered. But there are still deeper questions, rather personal ones, that I need to raise about my quest. Why do I care so much about commonness? What is it that has informed my quest in the various aspects and stages? It is one thing to explain, as I did at one point in my discussion in these pages, that in interfaith matters I have chosen to focus on "Abrahamic" groups. But there is a deeper issue, one about *personal motivation*. Why have I gotten into this at all? And how has my interest in inter- and intrafaith commonalities fit into the larger quest for commonness—a shared human nature, cross-cultural realities, and underlying agreements with secular thinkers? I have many academic colleagues who have had sterling careers in which they dealt with important Christian topics and concerns but who have not pushed commonness in the way I have.

I don't want to engage in psycho-autobiography here, but I can't address this issue honestly without touching very briefly on a bit of personal history. I am grateful for what I see as basically a happy upbringing, but those childhood years were not without some elements of painful conflict. When family arguments got too passionate, I felt an obligation to work at smoothing things over—the same for divisive disagreements in our extended family relations. As a pastor's son, I took a deep interest in congregational and local ecclesial disputes—and experienced on occasion a kind of wrenching helplessness when I knew that there was nothing I could do to ease the conflicts. I want to make it clear that the conflicts I am describing are within the bounds of what just about any child

will see up close. Nor should I absolve myself of responsibility
for the pain that I have brought into other people's lives because
of my own rebellious spirit. I am simply noting that because of
what I see as certain traits that I *brought* to many of my childhood experiences, I had a strong tendency in my early years to
see the inability to intervene successfully in conflict situations as
a serious personal failure. And I see that same tendency at play
in my adult years. I have made a point of intervening when, for
example, I have experienced—in studying religious movements
such as Mormonism—conflicts between "us" and "them" that I
become convinced are subject to some degree of resolution. Again,
I see that as *a* factor—certainly not the only one, but one matter
that has figured into my reflections on the subject of personal
motivation in the quest for commonness.

## Uniquely Calvinist Challenges

Another obvious factor that has contributed to my quest for commonness is primarily theological in nature. I am a Calvinist, and
we Calvinists have our own special theological forces at work in
emphasizing a lack of commonness with other human beings. The
one that first comes to mind is the classic Calvinist insistence that
the human race is divided into two categories: the elect and the
non-elect. To be sure, other evangelicals—as well as other groups
adhering to historic Christian teachings—posit a fundamental
duality in this regard. But the common division between, say, the
"saved" and the "lost" does not necessarily promote the rigidity
that may appear to be endemic to Calvinism. A Wesleyan can
preach, without any theological confusion about the doctrinal
boundaries of Wesleyanism, that Christians should nurture "a
heart for the lost." Unsaved people can be viewed, from that perspective, as having lost their way, as experiencing predicaments that
are of their own making. For a Calvinist to advocate the nurturing
of "a heart for the reprobate" does not have the same spiritual or

theological feel to it. If one's eternal destiny is decided by God's eternal decrees rather than our own free choices—and this is a standard expression of a Calvinist-type logic—then why should we have a "heart" for those for whom God himself has no "heart"?

I don't accept that logic, and I can illustrate why by offering what I take to be a deeply disturbing application of that way of thinking to a specific case, set forth by David Engelsma in a book devoted to responding to my book on common grace. Engelsma represents the perspective of the Protestant Reformed Church, founded by Herman Hoeksema in 1925, after he was expelled from the Christian Reformed Church for his outspoken criticisms of the position on common grace that the denomination had officially adopted in 1924.

In the course of criticizing me for basing my theology more on feelings than on Reformed orthodoxy, Engelsma confesses that while on occasion he is himself inclined to agonize over a particular case of suffering in the life of a non-Christian, he realizes the need to hold that tendency in check by reminding himself of his Calvinist convictions. He then offers an example of a temptation that he had to overcome personally in this regard. Reading William Shirer's book *The Rise and Fall of the Third Reich*, he reports, he came upon an incident where a group of Jews were lined up along a pit filled with bodies of their fellow Jews who had been machine-gunned by the Nazis. He continues with this story:

> In the new batch of Jews lined up at the edge of the pit is a little Jewish boy, about ten years old. As the Nazis wait, cold, callous, even enjoying what they are about to do, cigarettes dangling out of their mouths, the little boy, not comprehending, but fearful, clings to his father. Looking down on his son's anxious face, the helpless father tries to comfort his child. In a moment father and son will go down into the huge grave, atop a mass of dead bodies, to be shot.

I am deeply grateful for what Engelsma says next. "Yes," he confesses, such an incident "breaks our hearts." Unfortunately, he quickly adds, it is important to recognize that "the suffering of the reprobate wicked outside of Jesus Christ does not break the heart of God," for "God acts through these despicable murderers and evildoers to punish the ungodly in righteousness."[6]

Again, I firmly reject this way of viewing things, as did Abraham Kuyper, who refused to take Calvinism in this direction. He insisted instead that we must cultivate an appreciation for the cultural contributions of the unredeemed, as well as nurturing a compassion for them in their sufferings, because of the doctrine of common grace, which teaches us that God himself has this attitude of favor toward those whom he has not elected. When we Calvinists find ourselves experiencing a positive bond with those who are outside Christ's saving power, Kuyper argued, we must choose between two options: "either surrender our confession of the deadly character of sin, or hold on to that confession with all our might, but then also confess along with it that there is a common grace at work that in many cases restrains the full, deadly effect of sin."[7]

The Nazi example cited above is one that I have shared on a number of occasions, but I have typically refrained from mentioning the name of the author who used this example. This time I have named him in the text: David Engelsma. I have not wanted to link him to the way he uses the story because I find his theological verdict so disturbing. I decisively reject the notion that in gunning down the Jewish father and son, the Nazi soldiers, whom Engelsma rightly describes as "despicable murderers," were being used by God to bring his wrath to bear on "the ungodly in righteousness." I believe—and with deep conviction—that God grieved over what happened to the Jews at the hands of the Nazis.

One reason for my reluctance to name David Engelsma in this connection is that I would rather focus on the example than on the person who sets it forth. When I cite his assessment of the story of the Nazis and the Jews, people in my part of the theological world typically react in horror. I consider that reaction to be theologically appropriate, and I cite the case precisely because it serves to bolster my own endorsement of the theology of common grace.

Having said that, I also have to say that I like David Engelsma personally and intellectually. Our face-to-face dialogues have always been respectful, and his rather stern criticisms of my version of Calvinism have helped me to clarify my own position. I wish he had a different theological assessment of the story he tells, but it is the only case that has come up in my rather lengthy exchanges with him where I find what he says as not only theologically wrong but also morally offensive. Having said many morally offensive things in my own life, however, I do not take this one disagreeable case as a barrier to my learning from him.

Engelsma is one of the key present-day spokespersons for the theological perspective of Herman Hoeksema, who—as I mentioned earlier—was dismissed from the ministry of the Christian Reformed Church for his consistent and vocal rejection of the theology of common grace. I find myself in strong opposition to many points in Hoeksema's theology, but I continue to read and study his works. He was a brilliant—and in his own way extremely creative—theologian. I see it as a tragedy in his life that, having left the Christian Reformed Church, he spent the rest of his career at the margins of North American theology, where his important scholarship has been largely ignored.

## Two Kuyperian "Pulls"

Hoeksema and Engelsma represent what we can think of as, roughly, one half of Abraham Kuyper's overall theological perspective. Kuyper insisted on both a clear doctrine of the antithesis—the radical opposition between the cause of righteousness and the patterns represented by the forces of unrighteousness—and the reality of common grace. In his own life Kuyper held the two together in a fairly integrated manner. But the next generation of those influenced by his thought tended to divide between those who succumbed to the "pull" of one or the other of these theological themes. Hoeksema and Engelsma have been so intent upon affirming the antithesis consistently that they simply deny the common grace teaching. Cornelius Van Til did not go that far, but he formulated his understanding of common grace in such a way that his theology was dominated by antithesis themes. A prime example of pulling in the opposite direction is the thought of Quirinus Breen, who served as a Christian Reformed minister during the years when common grace was a much-debated topic in Dutch Calvinist circles. He eventually left the denomination because he came to see the antithesis idea as evidence of an unfortunate "contradiction" in Calvin's thought.[8] Having in his own mind disposed, then, of any obligation to follow carefully Calvin's thought in its theological details, Breen proceeded to work—in a long and distinguished scholarly career, most of it spent at the University of Oregon—with very fluid theological categories. For example, in his own attempts to define who is to be included in the believing community, he wrote that he strongly preferred an account that is "as inclusive as the generosity of divine charity could make it." These inclusive impulses led Breen to encourage the church to think of the likes of the Beat poet Lawrence Ferlinghetti and the artist Pablo Picasso as "the church's sons," as prophetic voices who serve the Christian community faithfully as they "devote themselves to knowing the truth about man and his actual attitudes to himself, to other men, to nature, [and] to the mysterious forces beyond man's control."[9]

I will be blunt here in confessing that I find Breen's views to be theologically distressing. One reason for my distress is that I see the same tendency at work in my own thought. To be sure, I have held that tendency in check better than he did. But I still have had to hold it in check—in a way that I have not had to work at getting carried away with the doctrine of the antithesis. With the antithesis I have had to keep reminding myself to give it its theological due.

In my mind, seeing the direction in which Breen took the common grace teaching lends considerable credence to the views of Herman Hoeksema and others who, in the Christian Reformed disputes over common grace in the early part of the twentieth century, insisted that the espousal of any notion of common grace was in itself a denial of the basic tenets of Reformed theology. I must quickly add, however, that I do not agree with them that the idea of common grace *as such* is destructive to Reformed orthodoxy. I am convinced that the risks are worth taking, as long as we are careful to use the idea with discernment.

One among the lineup of grand teachers in the history of Calvin College was the philosopher William Harry Jellema. Jellema was clearly on the common grace side of things. He famously argued, for example, that Socrates would be in heaven. This made him one of the examples often cited by Cornelius Van Til in his discussion of the dangers of placing too much emphasis on common grace. As someone personally familiar with the antagonisms between Van Til and Jellema, from my conversations with each of them, I was delighted by a story that John R. Muether tells in his biography of Van Til. Toward the end of his life, Van Til returned to Grand Rapids and visited Jellema, who was close to death. On this occasion Van Til thanked his former teacher, who had first taught him philosophy, for what he had learned from him. Jellema responded: "Yes, but Kees, it was you who at times kept us from going too far."[10] I am painfully aware of the danger in my own theological life of "going too far" in the quest for commonness. I can endorse Jellema's expression of appreciation for the way that Van Til's thoroughgoing antitheticalism has reminded others of us about the dangers of forgetting the pervasive effects of our shared depravity.

I have been blessed in recent years with a number of PhD students at Fuller who have worked with me on some highly creative projects in neo-Calvinist thought. They too remind me frequently of the "going too far" danger. One of them made a poignant comment to me just before he went off to join the faculty of another seminary. He told me how much he agreed with my views about convicted civility. His own journey had been from an evangelical world where strong convictions were in abundance, and he had come to see the need to hold on to these, but with a healthy measure of civility. There is a problem, though, he said, in emphasizing this to a younger generation. Many of us have had to move beyond a harsh acceptance of strong convictions to a gentler spirit of civility. But many of the younger evangelicals today need to move in the opposite direction. They don't have to work as hard at being civil people, but they do need to be guided in the direction of strong convictions. They aren't very literate biblically. Nor do they have the theological memories of those past struggles that gave birth to the strong convictions in the evangelical community.

That perspective captured the kind of worries I have been describing here. Indeed, it intensifies those worries a bit, since if I have to be on guard on the civility side of things, given my own long involvement in the strong convictedness of evangelicalism, then my own preachments about civility could easily be encouraging serious theological decline.

I offered some of those civility preachments recently at a large conference, and my presentation seemed to be well received. But at another session, a well-known speaker gave a passionate address in defense of a rigorous evangelical orthodoxy. As the audience responded with an extended ovation, the person sitting next to me—another of the speakers—leaned over and said, "Well, that was certainly a take-no-prisoners approach! I wish he showed some evidence that he had learned the lessons about civility from you!" I nodded in agreement.

A little later, in the quiet of my hotel room, however, recalling my doctoral student's observation, I decided that the speech I had just heard served an important purpose at that conference. It was a youngish crowd, and they had heard, not only my call for civility, but also a straightforward message about strong biblically based convictions. I did have some disagreements with the theology of the "take-no-prisoners" address, but they were minor ones. I decided that it would not be a bad thing if the listeners left the conference having absorbed the strong convictions. That result would give me—and especially the scholars I was helping to train—the task of helping them move from strong convictions to a spirit of convicted civility. I chastened myself: if I recognized the need for help from the Van Tils and Hoeksemas and Engelsmas in my own journey, why would I be resentful of voices like theirs who are still around, speaking to the same audiences that I have the privilege to address?

I use "privilege" here advisably. I have been given wonderful opportunities for a half century to represent the cause of an evangelicalism that engages others "with gentleness and respect." I have sensed a genuine call to do this, and I have been privileged to work at the project in diverse—and for me, exciting—settings, learning many good things in the process.

This does not lay all my worries to rest. All any of us can do, though, is to move ahead with what we believe God wants us to do, in the confidence that his sovereign purposes will come to pass.

I once received memorable counsel in this regard from an older Christian Reformed minister. He told me about a church split that he lived through in his youth in the Netherlands. Both sides were orthodox Calvinists, but his family had aligned with the less rigid group. "Our side was right about the issues," he said, "although it also set some theological forces in play that went in a bad direction."

I was in my forties at the time and was beginning to worry about the possible consequences of my own alignments, as I have been describing my qualms in these pages. I confessed my qualms to him. "Ja, Ja," he replied (with his pleasant Dutch accent). "It's good to think about that, and even to worry a little. But we need to do what God is calling us to do with the sensitivities and opportunities he gives us right now. Doing so has always led to some good things, but also sometimes to some bad things. When the bad things happen, the Lord will raise up some new folks who will then know how to set things back on course. For now, we just have to be faithful and keep at what needs to be done in the present!"

## Our Mysterious Selves

For me, the path of faithfulness described by that pastor has been relatively easy. I have been afforded much privilege along the way. In taking advantage of that privilege, I have tried to be consistent in honoring those who fought battles that have cleared the path for my own present privileges.

A prominent case in this regard is Edward Carnell, one of my predecessors in the Fuller presidency. When Carnell was installed as president of Fuller Seminary in 1955, he delivered an inaugural address that caused considerable controversy—so much so that the faculty and trustees refused to allow the publication of the text of his speech. Carnell's "heresy" was his call for an evangelicalism that encouraged a more loving spirit toward people with whom we disagree. A healthy seminary, he argued, must nurture a spirit of theological humility, avoiding the arrogance "of thinking that sheer possession of truth is an index to the virtue of the person." A true Christian humility, he said, does not mean that we should be insensitive to the divine mandate to avoid theological error. But our critical assessments must have a "provisional" character. To fail to respect this requirement is to be "guilty of disregarding the divine order."[11] Only God himself, "free from insecurity that sin breeds, can pass final judgment on the hearts of men without vindictiveness."[12] David Allan Hubbard, my immediate predecessor in the Fuller presidency, took a bold initiative in correcting the serious error of Carnell's colleagues by publishing Carnell's address. During my presidency we included that address in a volume of important Fuller historical documents. And on many occasions I gave tributes to Carnell's courage in campus events. Carnell's courage was no easy thing to sustain. The nasty treatment regarding his inaugural address was one of several times when he was dealt with in a mean-spirited manner by his fellow evangelicals. Eventually he sank into a deep depression and died alone in a hotel room after swallowing an overdose of sleeping pills. The tragedy of Carnell's last years gives special meaning to this wonderful passage from his inaugural address, one from which I have drawn much inspiration:

> Whoever meditates on the mystery of his own life will quickly realize why only God, the searcher of the secrets of the heart, can pass final judgment. We cannot judge what we have no access to. The self is a swirling conflict of fears, impulses, sentiments, interests, allergies, and foibles. It is a metaphysical given for which there is no easy rational explanation. Now, if we cannot unveil the mystery of our own motives and affections, how much less can we unveil the mystery in others?[13]

Carnell's quest for common ground required what was for him—and for some other evangelicals who have attempted to travel a similar path to common ground in the past—much painful rejection. These days some of us can pursue the journey with fewer obstacles. This does not mean, though, that the quest is without its dangers—which is why it must always be carried on under the illumination of the Word that "is a lamp for my feet, a light on my path" (Ps. 119:105 NIV).

# Notes

### Chapter 1  Calvinists in an Edinburgh Pub

1. Richard B. Sher, *Church and University in the Scottish Enlightenment: The Moderate Literati of Edinburgh* (Princeton: Princeton University Press, 1985).
2. Ibid., 60–61.
3. Ibid., 40.
4. Ibid., 57.
5. Ibid.
6. Martin E. Marty, *By Way of Response* (Nashville: Abingdon, 1981), 81.

### Chapter 2  A Tale of Two Authors

1. Letter by Matthew Arnold to Ralph Waldo Emerson, June 19, 1864, in Cecil Y. Lang, ed., *The Letters of Matthew Arnold*, vol. 2, *1860–1865* (Charlottesville: University Press of Virginia, 1996), 343, quoted in Nicholas Murray, *A Life of Matthew Arnold* (New York: St. Martin's Press, 1997), 44, 205.
2. Martin Buber, *Between Man and Man*, trans. Ronald Gregor Smith (Boston: Beacon Press, 1955), 22–23.
3. Cornelius Van Til, *Common Grace* (Phillipsburg, NJ: P&R, 1954).
4. Cornelius Van Til, *The Defense of the Faith* (Phillipsburg, NJ: P&R, 1955), 321.
5. Edward John Carnell, "How Every Christian Can Defend His Faith," *Moody Monthly*, January 1950, 313. Van Til cites this article in *Defense*, 321.
6. Van Til, *Defense*, 320–21.
7. Van Til, *Common Grace*, 24–25.
8. John Calvin, *Institutes of the Christian Religion*, ed. John T. McNeill, trans. Ford Lewis Battles (Philadelphia: Westminster, 1960), 2.2.15 (p. 274).
9. Ibid., 2.3.14 (p. 273).
10. Ibid., 2.3.13 (p. 273).
11. Ibid., 2.3.4 (p. 294).

12. Ibid., 2.2.12 (p. 270).

13. William Bouwsma, *John Calvin: A Sixteenth-Century Portrait* (New York: Oxford University Press, 1988), 230–31.

14. Abraham Kuyper, "Common Grace," in *Abraham Kuyper: A Centennial Reader*, ed. James D. Bratt (Grand Rapids: Eerdmans, 1998), 181.

15. Abraham Kuyper, *Common Grace: Temptation–Babel*, trans. Nelson D. Kloosterman and Ed M. van der Maas (Grand Rapids: Christian's Library Press, 2014), 115–16.

16. Thomas G. Weinandy, OFM Cap, *Does God Suffer?* (Notre Dame, IN: University of Notre Dame Press, 2000), 32–34.

17. David Cannadine, *The Undivided Past: Humanity beyond Our Differences* (New York: Knopf, 2013).

## Chapter 3  A Many-Faceted "Imaging"

1. P. F. Strawson, *Individuals: An Essay in Descriptive Metaphysics* (London: Methuen, 1959), 115.

2. Ibid., 116.

3. Ibid., 102.

4. Ibid., 116.

5. Karl Barth, *Church Dogmatics* III/1 (Edinburgh: T&T Clark, 1958), 183–95.

6. This view is spelled out and defended by David A. J. Clines, "The Image of God in Man," *Tyndale Bulletin* 19 (1968): 53–103.

7. I discuss these matters in greater detail in my book *Politics and the Biblical Drama* (Grand Rapids: Eerdmans, 1976), 22–29.

8. Harry Kuitert, *Signals from the Bible*, trans. Lewis Smedes (Grand Rapids: Eerdmans, 1972), 32.

9. G. C. Berkouwer, *Man: The Image of God* (Grand Rapids: Eerdmans, 1962), 199.

10. Ibid., 203.

11. Ibid., 199.

12. Oscar Cullmann, "Immortality of the Soul or Resurrection of the Dead? The Witness of the New Testament," in *Immortality*, ed. Terence Penelhum (Belmont: Wadsworth, 1973).

13. Ibid., 60–63.

14. Ibid., 69.

15. Ibid., 81.

16. Robert McAfee Brown, "Soul (Body)," in *A Handbook of Christian Theology*, ed. Arthur Cohen and Marvin Halverson (New York: Meridian Books, 1958), 354–55.

17. Berkouwer, *Man*, 269–78.

18. Cullmann, "Immortality," 79.

19. Ibid., 83.

20. Ibid.

21. This perspective is developed at length by Nancey Murphy, *Bodies and Souls, or Spirited Bodies?* (Cambridge: Cambridge University Press, 2006).

22. Ihab Hassan, "The Critic as Innovator: A Paracritical Strip in X Frames," *Chicago Review* 28, no. 3 (1977): 19, quoted in Richard Bernstein, *The New Constellation: The Ethical-Political Horizons of Modernity/Postmodernity* (Cambridge, MA: MIT Press, 1992), 199.

23. J. H. Elliot, "The Rediscovery of America," *New York Review of Books*, June 24, 1993, 38.

24. Herman Bavinck, *Reformed Dogmatics*, vol. 2, *God and Creation*, ed. John Bolt, trans. John Vriend (Grand Rapids: Baker Academic, 2004), 577–78.

25. Arthur F. Holmes, *Contours of a World View* (Grand Rapids: Eerdmans, 1983), 128.

26. Plato, *Meno* 81A, in *Great Dialogues of Plato*, trans. W. D. H. Rouse (New York: New American Library, 1956), 42.

## Chapter 4  More Than Calisthenics

1. Isaiah Berlin, *The Hedgehog and the Fox: An Essay on Tolstoy's View of History* (New York: Simon & Schuster, 1986).

2. Gilbert Ryle, *The Concept of Mind* (New York: Barnes & Noble, 1949), 181.

3. David Hume, *Dialogues concerning Natural Religion* (1779), part 2, https://ebooks.adelaide.edu.au/h/hume/david/h92d/contents.html.

4. Ibid.

5. Bertrand Russell, *Our Knowledge of the External World* (New York: New American Library, 1960), 59.

6. Maurice Merleau-Ponty, *Phenomenology of Perception* (New York: Humanities Press), 349.

7. Ibid., 361.

8. Joseph Butler, *Five Sermons* (New York: Liberal Arts Press, 1950), 28.

## Chapter 5  Lessons from the Philosophical "Moderns"

1. For Gewirth's elaboration of these three questions, see his introductory essay to *Political Philosophy*, ed. Alan Gewirth (New York: Macmillan, 1965), 1–30.

2. Mark Lilla, *The Stillborn God: Religion, Politics, and the Modern West* (New York: Knopf, 2007), 298.

3. Ibid., 75.

4. J. W. N. Watkins, "The Posthumous Career of Thomas Hobbes," *Review of Politics* 19 (1957): 356. I owe the Watkins comment to Willis B. Glover, "God and Thomas Hobbes," *Church History* 29, no. 3 (September 1960): 275–97.

5. J. G. A. Pocock, *Politics, Language and Time: Essays on Political Thought and History* (New York: Atheneum, 1973), 160.

6. A. P. Martinich, *Hobbes* (New York: Routledge, 2005). Of special importance in Martinich's discussion of religious topics was the access he had, not available to previous commentators on Hobbes's theology, to Noel Malcolm's edited collection *The Correspondence of Thomas Hobbes* (Oxford: Clarendon, 1994).

7. Martinich, *Hobbes*, 354; the quotation is from *The English Works of Thomas Hobbes of Malmesbury*, ed. Thomas Molesworth (London: John Bohn, 1845), 4:250–51, 342.

8. Martinich, *Hobbes*, 109.

9. Ibid., 107.

10. Ibid., 195. Martinich makes the case for Hobbes's Calvinism at much greater length in *The Two Gods of Leviathan: Thomas Hobbes on Religion and Politics* (New York: Cambridge University Press, 1992).

11. Martinich, *Two Gods*, 1.

12. Sir Robert Filmer, *Patriarcha and Other Writings* (New York: Cambridge University Press, 1991).

13. John Locke, *A Paraphrase and Notes on the Epistles of St. Paul to the Galatians, Corinthians, Romans, Ephesians*, in *The Works of John Locke, in Nine Volumes*, 12th ed. (London: Rivington, 1824), 7:3.

14. Gordon H. Clark, *A Christian View of Men and Things* (Grand Rapids: Eerdmans, 1952), 136.

15. Robert N. Bellah, Richard Madsen, William M. Sullivan, Ann Swidler, and Steven M. Tipton, *Habits of the Heart: Individualism and Commitment in American Life* (Los Angeles: University of California Press, 1985), 143.

16. Locke, *Paraphrase*, 404–5.

17. Ibid.

18. John Calvin, *Institutes of the Christian Religion*, ed. John T. McNeill, trans. Ford Lewis Battles (Philadelphia: Westminster, 1960), 4.20.4 (p. 1489).

19. Ibid., 4.20.8 (p. 1493).

20. Quentin Skinner, *The Foundations of Modern Political Thought*, vol. 2, *The Age of the Reformation* (New York: Cambridge University Press, 1979), esp. 36–47.

21. Francis Oakley, *The Conciliarist Tradition: Constitutionalism in the Catholic Church 1300–1870* (New York: Oxford University Press, 2008).

22. Samuel Rutherford, *Lex, Rex: The Law and the Prince; A Dispute for the Just Prerogative of King and People* (London: John Field, 1644), 70.

23. Jacques Maritain, *Three Reformers: Luther-Descartes-Rousseau* (New York: Charles Scribner's Sons, 1955), 4.

24. Jean-Jacques Rousseau, *The Social Contract*, trans. Willmore Kendall (Chicago: Regnery, 1954), 43.

25. Ibid., 19.

## Chapter 6  Commonalities in the Public Square

1. Carl F. H. Henry, *Confessions of a Theologian* (Waco: Word Books, 1986), 127–31.

2. John Howard Yoder, *The Politics of Jesus: Vicit Agnus Noster* (Grand Rapids: Eerdmans, 1972).

3. Hendrikus Berkhof, *Christ and the Powers*, trans. John Howard Yoder (Scottdale, PA: Herald, 1962), 58–61.

4. John Howard Yoder, *The Christian Witness to the State* (Newton, KS: Faith and Life Press, 1964), 27.

5. H. Richard Niebuhr, *Christ and Culture* (San Francisco: Harper & Row, 1951).

6. D. A. Carson, *Christ and Culture Revisited* (Grand Rapids: Eerdmans, 2008), 40–44.

7. Nation's blurb is for the cover of Craig A. Carter, *Rethinking Christ and Culture: A Post-Christendom Perspective* (Grand Rapids: Brazos, 2006).

8. See Lesslie Newbigin, "The Gospel in a Culture of False Gods," interview by Andrew Walker, 1988, http://www.shipoffools.com/1998/Newbigin.Interview.html, published in full in Andrew Walker, *Different Gospels: Christian Orthodoxy and Modern Theologies* (London: Hodder & Stoughton, 1988).

9. John J. Conley, *The Suspicion of Virtue: Women Philosophers in Neoclassical France* (Ithaca, NY: Cornell University Press, 2002), 164–65.

10. Stanley Hauerwas and William Willimon, *Resident Aliens: Life in the Christian Colony* (Nashville: Abingdon, 1989), 23.

11. Lesslie Newbigin, *Foolishness to the Greeks: The Gospel and Western Culture* (Grand Rapids: Eerdmans, 1986), 100–101.

12. Stanley Hauerwas, *The Peaceable Kingdom: A Primer in Christian Ethics* (Notre Dame, IN: University of Notre Dame Press, 1983), 100; emphasis added.

13. Richard J. Mouw, *When the Kings Come Marching In: Isaiah and the New Jerusalem* (Grand Rapids: Eerdmans, 1983), 50–51.

14. Ibid., 52.

15. Stanley Hauerwas, *After Christendom? How the Church Is to Behave if Freedom, Justice, and a Christian Nation Are Bad Ideas* (Nashville: Abingdon, 1991).

16. Hauerwas and Willimon, *Resident Aliens*, 23.

17. Max L. Stackhouse, "Liberalism Dispatched vs. Liberalism Engaged," *Christian Century* 112, no. 29 (October 18, 1995): 963.

18. Ronald Thiemann, *Constructing Public Theology: The Church in a Pluralistic Culture* (Louisville: Westminster John Knox, 1991), 43.

## Chapter 7 Preaching Civility

1. Robert N. Bellah, Richard Madsen, William M. Sullivan, Ann Swidler, and Steven M. Tipton, *Habits of the Heart: Individualism and Commitment in American Life* (Los Angeles: University of California Press, 1985), 239, 281–82.

2. Ibid., 218.

3. Sheldon S. Wolin, *Politics and Vision: Continuity and Innovation in Western Political Thought* (Boston: Little, Brown, 1960), 167.

4. Ibid.

5. Ibid., 166–67.

6. Ibid., 168.

7. Ibid., 183.

8. Ibid., 181.

9. John Calvin, *Institutes of the Christian Religion* 4.20.2, quoted in Wolin, *Politics*, 182 (Wolin's own translation of Calvin).

10. Wolin, *Politics*, 175.

11. John Murray Cuddihy, *No Offense: Civil Religion and Protestant Taste* (New York: Seabury, 1978), 202; emphasis original.

12. Glenn Tinder, "Community: The Tragic Idea," *Yale Review* 65, no. 4 (Summer 1976): 551, quoted in Cuddihy, *No Offense*, 211.

13. Ronald Thiemann, *Constructing Public Theology: The Church in a Pluralistic Culture* (Louisville: Westminster John Knox, 1991), 43.

14. John Calvin, *Institutes of the Christian Religion*, ed. John T. McNeill, trans. Ford Lewis Battles (Philadelphia: Westminster, 1960), 4.20.12 (p. 214).

15. Jean-Jacques Rousseau, *Politics and the Arts: Letter to D'Alembert on the Theatre*, trans. with notes and an introduction by Allan Bloom (Ithaca, NY: Cornell University Press, 1960), 126.

16. Richard J. Bernstein, "The Meaning of Public Life," in *Religion and American Public Life: Interpretations and Explorations*, ed. Robin W. Lovin (New York: Paulist Press, 1986), 47.

17. *Gaudium et Spes* 1, Promulgated by His Holiness, Pope Paul VI, on December 7, 1965, http://www.vatican.va/archive/hist_councils/ii_vatican_council/documents /vat-ii_cons_19651207_gaudium-et-spes_en.html.

## Chapter 8 Depravity: Less Than "Total"?

1. For the full text of the "Three Points" of 1924, see Herman Hoeksema, *The Protestant Reformed Churches in America: Their Origin, Early History and Doctrine* (Grand Rapids: First Protestant Reformed Church, 1936), 84–85; Hoeksema's book also provides the texts of other relevant documents and gives the most detailed account of the events surrounding the official proceedings, as well as his interpretation of the ecclesiastical and theological issues at stake.

2. Letter from W. Heyns to J. K. Van Baalen, November 3, 1922, Heritage Hall, Calvin College; translation by Dirk Mouw.

3. John H. Yoder, "Reformed versus Anabaptist Social Strategies: An Inadequate Typology," *TSF Bulletin*, May/June 1985, 2; see also my supportive response to Yoder's case in the same issue: "Abandoning the Typology: A Reformed Assist," 7–10.

4. Richard Mouw and John H. Yoder, "Evangelical Ethics and the Anabaptist-Reformed Dialogue," *Journal of Religious Ethics* 17, no. 2 (1989): 121–37.

5. For a comprehensive account of the rather acrimonious "disputations" between the Reformed and the Anabaptists at the time of the Reformation, see Willem Balke, *Calvin and the Anabaptist Radicals*, trans. William Heynen (Grand Rapids: Eerdmans, 1981).

6. Belgic Confession, art. 36, in *The Creeds of Christendom, with a History and Critical Notes*, ed. Philip Schaff (Grand Rapids: Baker, 1996), 3:433.

7. See Roelf C. (Karlo) Janssen, "A History of Calvinist Churches in the Netherlands," http://theoluniv.ub.rug.nl/31/2/2009Janssen%20Dissertation.pdf.

8. Leonard Verduin, *Honor Your Mother: Christian Reformed Church Roots in the 1834 Separation* (Grand Rapids: CRC Publications, 1988), 21.

9. See F. Ernest Stoeffler's now-classic account of Dutch Reformed pietist thought in *The Rise of Evangelical Pietism* (Leiden: Brill, 1965), chap. 3. For an account of how the tensions between these two understandings of the church were played out in a specific dispute within Dutch Calvinist church life, see Willem van't Spijker, "Catholicity of the Church in the Secession (1834) and the Doleantie (1886)," in *Catholicity and Secession: A Dilemma?*, ed. Paul Schrotenboer (Kampen: Kok, 1992), 82–89.

10. K. Schilder, *Christ and Culture*, trans. G. van Rongen and W. Helder (Winnipeg: Premier Printing, 1977), 69–70.

11. Ibid., 55.

12. Ibid., 59.

13. Robert W. Brimlow, "Solomon's Porch: The Church as Sectarian Ghetto," in *The Church as Counterculture*, ed. Michael L. Budde and Robert W. Brimlow (Albany: State University of New York Press, 2000), 115.

14. Ibid., 123.

15. John H. Yoder, *The Politics of Jesus: Vicit Agnus Noster* (Grand Rapids: Eerdmans, 1972), 192.

16. See Emil Brunner and Karl Barth, *Natural Theology*, trans. Peter Fraenkel (London: Centenary, 1946).

17. Stanley Hauerwas and William Willimon, *Resident Aliens: Life in the Christian Colony* (Nashville: Abingdon, 1989), 25.

18. H. Richard Niebuhr, *Christ and Culture* (San Francisco: Harper & Row, 1951), 194.

19. John J. Conley, *The Suspicion of Virtue: Women Philosophers in Neoclassical France* (Ithaca, NY: Cornell University Press, 2002), 165.

20. Emil Brunner, "Nature and Grace: A Contribution to the Discussion with Karl Barth," in Brunner and Barth, *Natural Theology*, 59.

21. Barth, "NO! Answer to Emil Brunner," in Brunner and Barth, *Natural Theology*, 101.

22. Ibid., 103.

23. Ibid., 104.

24. Stephen J. Grabill, *Rediscovering the Natural Law in Reformed Theological Ethics* (Grand Rapids: Eerdmans, 2006), 96–97.

25. Ibid., 39.

26. Ibid., 43.

27. G. C. Berkouwer, *General Revelation* (Grand Rapids: Eerdmans, 2001), 154.

28. Ibid., 164.

29. Ibid., 242.

30. Ibid., 169.

31. Carol Zaleski, "Case for the Defense: Arguing for God's Existence," *Christian Century*, June 26, 2007, http://www.christiancentury.org/article/2007-06/case-defense-0.

32. Abraham Joshua Heschel, *God in Search of Man: A Philosophy of Judaism* (New York: Farrar, Straus & Giroux, 1955), 137.

33. Belgic Confession, art. 2, in Schaff, *Creeds of Christendom*, 3:384.

34. Grabill, *Rediscovering*, 50.

35. Ibid., 50–52. Grabill is referring here to my discussions in both *The God Who Commands: A Study in Divine Command Ethics* (Notre Dame, IN: University of Notre Dame Press, 1990) and *He Shines in All That's Fair: Culture and Common Grace* (Grand Rapids: Eerdmans, 2001).

36. Herman Bavinck, *Reformed Dogmatics*, vol. 1, *Prolegomena*, ed. John Bolt, trans. John Vriend (Grand Rapids: Baker Academic, 2003), 370.

37. John Calvin, *Institutes of the Christian Religion*, ed. John T. McNeill, trans. Ford Lewis Battles (Philadelphia: Westminster, 1960), 1.1.2 (p. 37).

38. Canons of the Synod of Dort, Third and Fourth Heads of Doctrine, art. 16, in Schaff, *Creeds of Christendom*, 3:591.

39. See Herman Dooyeweerd, *A New Critique of Theoretical Thought*, vol. 1, trans. David H. Freeman and William S. Young (Philadelphia: P&R, 1953), 93–99.

40. Abraham Kuyper, *Lectures on Calvinism: Six Lectures Delivered at Princeton University under Auspices of the L. P. Stone Foundation* (Grand Rapids: Eerdmans, 1931), 71–72.

41. Gordon J. Spykman, *Reformational Theology: A New Paradigm for Doing Dogmatics* (Grand Rapids: Eerdmans, 1992), 180.

42. Dooyeweerd, *New Critique*, 99n1.

43. Geertsema's observation was made during the course of a discussion time at a symposium commemorating the hundredth anniversary of the birth of Herman Dooyeweerd, sponsored by the Vereniging voor Reformatorische Wijsbegeerte, held in Hoeven, the Netherlands, August 1994.

44. Alasdair MacIntyre, *A Short History of Ethics: A History of Moral Philosophy from the Homeric Age to the Twentieth Century* (New York: Macmillan, 1966), 121–24; see also his *After Virtue: A Study in Moral Theory*, 2nd ed. (Notre Dame, IN: University of Notre Dame Press, 1984), 52–53.

45. See Louis Berkhof, *Systematic Theology* (Grand Rapids: Eerdmans, 1941), 211–14.

46. Max L. Stackhouse, *Covenant and Communities: Faith, Family, and Economic Life* (Louisville: Westminster John Knox, 1997), 150.

47. Ibid., 144.

## Chapter 9  Our "Direction-Setting"

1. Elizabeth Clark George, "Life with Father, Part 1," in *Gordon Clark: Personal Recollections*, ed. John W. Robbins (Jefferson, MD: Trinity Foundation, 1989), 22–23.

2. Herman Bavinck, *The Philosophy of Revelation* (London: Longmans Green, 1909), 215.

3. Herman Bavinck, *Reformed Dogmatics*, vol. 1, *Prolegomena*, ed. John Bolt, trans. John Vriend (Grand Rapids: Baker Academic, 2003), 268; emphasis added.

4. The published version of this lecture appeared as Nicholas Wolterstorff, "The AACS in the CRC," *Reformed Journal* 24, no. 10 (December 1974): 9–16.

5. George Marsden, "Reformed and American," in *Reformed Theology in America*, ed. David F. Wells (Grand Rapids: Baker, 1997), 3. Marsden rightly notes that these designations are "ideal types." As they actually function, he says, "all three groups typically embody the traits dominant among the other two."

6. See, for example, Nicholas Wolterstorff, *Until Justice and Peace Embrace* (Grand Rapids: Eerdmans, 1983), 4.

7. Abraham Kuyper, "Sphere Sovereignty," in *Abraham Kuyper: A Centennial Reader*, ed. James D. Bratt (Grand Rapids: Eerdmans, 1998), 488.

8. Journal of John Wesley, May 24, 1738, *Christian Classics Ethereal Library*, http://www.ccel.org/ccel/wesley/journal.vi.ii.xvi.html.

9. F. Ernest Stoeffler, epilogue in *Continental Pietism and Early American Christianity* (Grand Rapids: Eerdmans, 1976), 271.

10. Ibid., 270–71.

11. See Ockenga's introduction to Carl F. H. Henry, *The Uneasy Conscience of Modern Fundamentalism* (Grand Rapids: Eerdmans, 1947), xx–xxii.

## Chapter 10  Paying Attention to Context

1. Ludwig Wittgenstein, *Philosophical Investigations*, 2nd ed. (New York: MacMillan Company, 1958), 82e.

2. Ibid., 118e.

3. Ludwig Wittgenstein, *Lectures and Conversations: On Aesthetics, Psychology, and Religious Belief*, ed. Cyrill Barrett (Berkeley: University of California Press, 1967), 2.

4. R. M. Hare, *Freedom and Reason* (London: Oxford University Press, 1963), 204; emphasis added.

5. Stephen Edelston Toulmin, *An Examination of Reason in Ethics* (Cambridge: Cambridge University Press, 1958).

6. Kurt Baier, *Moral Point of View: A Rational Basis of Ethics* (Ithaca, NY: Cornell University Press, 1958).

7. Hare, *Freedom and Reason*, 194.

8. Alasdair MacIntyre and D. R. Bell, "The Idea of a Social Science," *Proceedings of the Aristotelian Society, Supplementary Volumes* 41 (1967): 95–132, http://www.jstor.org/stable/4106718.

9. Peter Winch, "Understanding a Primitive Society," *American Philosophical Quarterly* 1, no. 4 (October 1964): 307–24, http://www.jstor.org/stable/20009143.

10. Bryan R. Wilson, ed., *Rationality* (Evanston, IL: Harper & Row, 1970); Martin Hollis and Steven Lukes, eds., *Rationality and Relativism* (Cambridge, MA: MIT Press, 1982).

11. Michael M. J. Fischer and George E. Marcus, *Anthropology as Cultural Critique: An Experimental Moment in the Human Sciences* (Chicago: University of Chicago Press, 1986), 137.

12. James L. Peacock, *The Anthropological Lens: Harsh Light, Soft Focus* (New York: Cambridge University Press, 1986), 144.

13. Barbara Frankel, "Two Extremes on the Social Science Commitment Continuum," in *Metatheory in Social Science: Pluralisms and Subjectivities*, ed. Donald W. Fiske and Richard A. Schweder (Chicago: University of Chicago Press, 1986), 360.

14. W. T. Stace, "Ethical Relativism: A Critique," par. 21, http://faculty.mc3.edu/barmstro/stacerelativism.html.

15. Ibid.

16. Kenneth Gergen, *The Saturated Self: Dilemmas of Identity in Contemporary Life* (New York: Basic Books, 1991), 256.

17. Jacques Derrida, letter in "'L'Affaire Derrida': Another Exchange," *New York Review of Books*, March 25, 1993, 65.

18. Jeffrey Stout, *Ethics after Babel: The Languages of Morals and Their Discontents* (Boston: Beacon, 1988), 3.

19. Ibid., xi.

20. Ibid., 74.

21. Later published as John Courtney Murray, SJ, *The Problem of God: Yesterday and Today* (New Haven: Yale University Press, 1965).

22. Ibid., 120.

23. On Diederich's thought, see Dunbar Moodie, *The Rise of Afrikanerdom: Power, Apartheid, and the Afrikaner Civil Religion* (Berkeley: University of California Press, 1975), 156–59.

24. Allan Aubrey Boesak, *Farewell to Innocence: A Socio-Ethical Study on Black Theology and Power* (Maryknoll, NY: Orbis, 1977), 12; emphasis original.

25. Albert Borgmann, *Crossing the Postmodern Divide* (Chicago: University of Chicago Press, 1992), 6.

## Chapter 11 Reformed and Evangelical

1. My use of "thick" and "thin" here follows the pattern employed by many commentators in recent years. The imagery was made popular by Clifford Geertz,

who borrowed the terms from Gilbert Ryle. See Clifford Geertz, "Thick Description: Toward an Interpretive Theory of Culture," in *The Interpretation of Cultures* (New York: Basic Books, 1973), 3–30; and Gilbert Ryle, "The Thinking of Thoughts: What Is *Le Penseur* Doing?" in *Collected Papers* (London: Hutchinson, 1971), 2:480–96.

2. Alister McGrath, "Evangelical Anglicanism: A Contradiction in Terms?," in *Evangelical Anglicans: Their Role and Influence in the Church Today*, ed. R. T. France and A. E. McGrath (London: SPCK, 1993), 14.

3. C. H. Spurgeon, "A Defense of Calvinism," Spurgeon Archive, http://spurgeon .org/calvinis.php.

### Chapter 12 When Truth Is Distorted

1. S. U. Zuidema, *Sartre* (Philadelphia: P&R, 1960), 56, http://www.reformational publishingproject.com/pdf_books/Scanned_Books_PDF/SatreZuidema.pdf.

2. John Courtney Murray, SJ, *The Problem of God: Yesterday and Today* (New Haven: Yale University Press, 1965), 120.

3. H. Richard Niebuhr, *Christ and Culture* (San Francisco: Harper & Row, 1951), 194.

4. See my *The God Who Commands: A Study in Divine Command Ethics* (Notre Dame, IN: University of Notre Dame Press, 1990), 54.

5. James H. Cone, *The Spirituals and the Blues: An Interpretation* (New York: Seabury Press, 1972), 67–68.

### Chapter 13 On Being a "Public Intellectual"

1. Peter L. Berger and Richard John Neuhaus, *To Empower People: The Role of Mediating Structures in Public Policy* (Washington, DC: American Enterprise Institute for Public Policy Research, 1977).

2. James M. Gustafson, *Moral Discernment in the Christian Life: Essays in Theological Ethics* (Louisville: Westminster John Knox, 2007), 86.

### Chapter 14 Interfaith Engagements

1. I know the objections, by the way, of those who consider "Abrahamic" to be inapplicable for grouping Islam together with Judaism and Christianity—see, e.g., the case made by Alain Besançon, "What Kind of Religion Is Islam?," *Commentary*, May 1, 2004, https://www.commentarymagazine.com/articles/what-kind-of-religion -is-islam/.

2. Richard J. Mouw, *Talking with Mormons: An Invitation to Evangelicals* (Grand Rapids: Eerdmans, 2012).

3. Stephen Neill, *Christian Faith and Other Faiths: The Christian Dialogue with Other Religions* (New York: Oxford University Press, 1961), 3.

4. Ibid., 98.

5. Herman Bavinck, *Reformed Dogmatics*, vol. 1, *Prolegomena*, ed. John Bolt, trans. John Vriend (Grand Rapids: Baker Academic, 2003), 318.

6. Westminster Confession of Faith 1.1, http://www.creeds.net/Westminster/c01 .htm.

7. Leonard Swidler, "Dialogue Principles" (originally titled "Dialogue Decalogue"), Dialogue Institute, http://institute.jesdialogue.org/resources/tools/decalogue/.

8. Simone Weil, "Reflections on the Right Use of School Studies with a View to the Love of God," in *Waiting for God*, trans. Emma Crauford (New York: Harper, 2009), http://www.hagiasophiaclassical.com/wp/wp-content/uploads/2012/10/Right -Use-of-School-Studies-Simone-Weil.pdf.

9. Joseph Smith Jr., *History of the Church of Jesus Christ of Latter-day Saints*, ed. B. H. Roberts (Salt Lake City: Church of Jesus Christ of Latter-day Saints, 1950), 1:18–19.

10. J. Spencer Fluhman provides abundant examples of early anti-Mormon rhetoric in chaps. 1 and 2 of his *"A Peculiar People": Anti-Mormonism and the Making of Religion in Nineteenth-Century America* (Chapel Hill: University of North Carolina Press, 2012).

11. Jan Shipps, *Mormonism: The Story of a New Religious Tradition* (Urbana: University of Illinois Press, 1987), 148–49.

12. Jan Shipps, *Sojourner in the Promised Land: Forty Years among the Mormons* (Urbana: University of Illinois Press, 2000), 329.

13. Ibid., 337–38.

14. Ibid., 345.

15. Ibid., 347.

16. Ibid., 356.

17. Richard J. Mouw, *He Shines in All That's Fair: Culture and Common Grace* (Grand Rapids: Eerdmans, 2001), 100.

18. Jon Meacham, "Pilgrim's Progress," *Newsweek*, August 13, 2006, http://www .newsweek.com/pilgrims-progress-109171.

## Chapter 15  Of Hymns and Dialogues

1. John MacArthur Jr., *Ashamed of the Gospel: When the Church Becomes Like the World* (Wheaton: Crossway, 1993), 250.

2. Charles Hodge, *Systematic Theology* (Peabody, MA: Hendrickson, 2003), 2:440n1.

3. Herman Bavinck, *The Certainty of Faith*, trans. Harry der Nederlanden (St. Catherines, ON: Paideia, 1980), 37.

4. See Cornelius Van Til, *The New Modernism: An Appraisal of the Theology of Barth and Brunner* (Phillipsburg, NJ: P&R, 1947).

5. Charles H. Gabriel, "I Stand All Amazed," https://www.lds.org/music/library /hymns/i-stand-all-amazed?lang=eng.

6. Anselm of Canterbury, *Proslogion*, chap. 2, http://legacy.fordham.edu/Halsall /basis/anselm-proslogium.asp#CHAPTER%20II.

7. Norman Malcolm's contribution to a symposium on "Contemporary Views of the Ontological Argument," in *The Ontological Argument: From St. Anselm to Contemporary Philosophers*, ed. Alvin Plantinga (Garden City, NY: Anchor Books, 1965), 158.

8. Geerhardus Vos, *Grace and Glory: Sermons Preached in the Chapel of Princeton Theological Seminary* (Edinburgh: Banner of Truth Trust, 1994), 56.

9. Glenn L. Pearson, *Know Your Religion* (Salt Lake City: Bookcraft, 1961), 169.

## Chapter 16  Concerns about the Journey

1. Richard B. Sher, *Church and University in the Scottish Enlightenment: The Moderate Literati of Edinburgh* (Princeton: Princeton University Press, 1985), 57.

2. Johnson Oatman Jr., "Higher Ground."

3. Cornelius Van Til, "Why I Believe in God," Center for Reformed Theology and Apologetics, 1996, http://www.reformed.org/apologetics/index.html?mainframe=/apologetics/why_I_believe_cvt.html.

4. W. J. Jennings, *The Christian Imagination: Theology and the Origins of Race* (New Haven: Yale University Press, 2010), 8.

5. Christine D. Pohl, *Making Room: Recovering Hospitality as a Christian Tradition* (Grand Rapids: Eerdmans, 1999).

6. David J. Englesma, *Common Grace Revisited: A Response to Richard J. Mouw's "He Shines in All That's Fair"* (Jenison, MI: Reformed Free Publishing Association, 2003), 47–48.

7. Abraham Kuyper, *Common Grace: Temptation–Babel*, trans. Nelson D. Kloosterman and Ed M. van der Maas (Grand Rapids: Christian's Library Press, 2014), 115–16.

8. Quirinus Breen, *Christianity and Humanism: Studies in the History of Ideas* (Grand Rapids: Eerdmans, l968), 255.

9. Ibid., 257.

10. John R. Muether, *Cornelius Van Til: Reformed Apologist and Churchman* (Phillipsburg, NJ: P&R, 2008), 213.

11. Edward John Carnell, "The Glory of a Theological Seminary," in *Fuller Voices: Then and Now*, ed. Russell P. Spittler (Pasadena, CA: Fuller Seminary Press, 2004), 27.

12. Ibid., 28.

13. Ibid.

# Index

237